ELIJAH
and the
RABBIS

D1603894

ELIJAH
and the
RABBIS

Story and Theology

Kristen H.
LINDBECK

COLUMBIA UNIVERSITY PRESS | NEW YORK

Columbia University Press

Publishers Since 1893

New York Chichester, West Sussex

Copyright © 2010 Columbia University Press

Library of Congress Cataloging-in-Publication Data

Lindbeck, Kristen H.

Elijah and the rabbis : story and theology / Kristen H. Lindbeck.

p. cm.

Includes bibliographical references and index.

ISBN 978-0-231-13080-6 (cloth: alk. paper) —ISBN 978-0-231-13081-3 (pbk.: alk. paper)

1. Elijah (Biblical prophet)—In rabbinical literature. 2. Talmud—Criticism, interpretation, etc. I. Title.

BM496.9.E4L56   2010

296.1'2506—dc22   2009051476

Casebound editions of Columbia University Press books are printed on permanent and durable acid-free paper.

Printed in the United States of America

c 10 9 8 7 6 5 4 3 2 1

p 10 9 8 7 6 5 4 3 2 1

For my parents,
Vi and George Lindbeck

CONTENTS

PREFACE

ELIJAH IN RABBINIC TIMES AND BEYOND

Elijah has many faces. In Kings he is a zealous prophet of God, in the later prophetic book Malachi a herald of the last days. He appears several times in the New Testament. Elijah's role in Judaism, however, comes mostly from his character in rabbinic literature. Rabbinic Judaism knows Elijah as herald of the last days, as legal authority, teacher of the wise, and helper of those in crisis. During the medieval period "Elijah's cup" became part of the Passover Seder. At the Seder, throughout the world, families still open the door for Elijah as herald of the Messiah, and children look eagerly at Elijah's cup to see if he has sipped any wine. Elijah plays an esoteric role in kabbalah, and a better-known and more homely one as the hero of Jewish folk tales. In these stories Elijah often comes in the guise of a poor stranger, and if he is welcomed he brings benefits and blessings.

This book focuses on the Elijah of the Talmudic period, a time when Elijah first acquired many of his roles in later Judaism. In these centuries the legendary Elijah becomes a recognizable character, a mysterious individual quite different from the Elijah of the Bible. He is partly angelic and partly human, therefore he can connect humankind to God, serving as a supernatural mediator. He teaches wisdom and gives advice, but he can also help people directly, even with material gifts. Elijah, in part, resembles the legendary Christian saints in that he mediates God's saving power. In rabbinic Judaism, however, Elijah is rarely sent in response to prayer, and he has no role in ensuring anyone's future salvation, though Christian saints of those days were fulfilling these roles. Elijah comes unpredictably, without warning, to address the problems of this life.

A good example of Elijah as rescuer is the fascinating "antimartyrdom" of Rabbi Eleazar ben Perata (B. Avodah Zarah 17b). This story is set during the second-century Roman persecution of Judaism, but it was written down and perhaps composed many centuries afterward. The story begins when Rabbi Ḥanina ben

Teradion, soon to be a famous martyr, meets Rabbi Eleazar in prison. Rabbi Ḥanina prophesies that Rabbi Eleazar will escape death because he combined good works with his study of Torah. Encouraged by this prediction, Rabbi Eleazar later lies or blusters his way out of every charge of the Roman court, until only one Roman official remains to accuse him. When this last man stands up to condemn the rabbi, Elijah appears in the form of a Roman noble and tries to dissuade the accuser, and when the accuser does not listen, Elijah comes and tosses him "four hundred leagues." Through its absurdist humor, this story expresses a humanistic point, one rare in religious narrative, at least up until the twentieth century: it emphasizes that martyrs and survivors need not be enemies of one another. Both martyrs and survivors are heroes, each in their own way.

Elijah also serves as a source of privileged information about God. On request, Elijah reports on what God is saying or doing in the heavenly court, providing a fascinating window into rabbinic belief. Twice, for example, Elijah relays that God accepts multiple understandings of a single biblical story, supporting rabbinic belief that Scripture has many meanings. In one of these passages, Elijah says that both rabbis' ideas "are the words of the Living God" (B. Gittin 6b), making it clear that in the practice of homiletic—as opposed to legal—biblical interpretation every single rabbinic understanding is holy, "words of the Living God." Thus Elijah not only makes a theological point about the legitimacy of competing interpretations, but affirms and strengthens the role of the rabbinic Sages as interpreters of Torah.

Many Elijah stories teach rabbinic values and ethical standards. For example a man with a legal problem brings Rav Anan a gift of fish and convinces him to accept it, even though rabbis were supposed to refuse gifts from potential litigants. Impressed by this thoughtful gift, and the flattery accompanying it, Rav Anan—properly—refuses to try the man's lawsuit, but—improperly—sends him off to another rabbi with a personal message that he, Anan, is unfit to try the case. The other rabbi, on getting the message, assumes that the enterprising plaintiff is a relative of Rav Anan and therefore shows the man respect. In fact, he shows the man so much respect that his opponent is hopelessly intimidated and justice is not done. Elijah *had* been in the habit of visiting Rav Anan, but after this he stayed away. Elijah had been teaching the rabbi the mysterious Order of Elijah, so Rav Anan must fast and pray to God for the prophet's return. When Elijah returns, however, he comes in frightening form, and now Rav Anan must hide in a box to endure his presence and receive his teaching (Ketubot 105b). This story is unusual in naming a specific body of knowledge that Elijah comes to teach and, in the odd and humorous detail of the box, is also unique. The main point, however, is found in other stories: Elijah disappears in order to make the point that the ethical standards required of rabbis are higher than the standards required of others.

THE BIBLICAL ELIJAH AND THE RABBINIC ELIJAH

The rabbinic picture of Elijah is based on the biblical Elijah, but it moves beyond him. In a famous passage, the prophet Elijah journeys to the mountain of God and experiences God there, not in wind or earthquake or fire, but in the "still small voice" (1 Kings 19:11–12). Elijah is fed by ravens in the wilderness and revives the widow's son from death (1 Kings 17:4, 18–22). These are the stories that people like to recall, but the biblical Elijah was also a man of violence. He kills the prophets of Baal with his own hands after they fail to call upon their god (1 Kings 18:40) and he calls down fire from heaven three times to burn up three bands of soldiers that King Ahaziah of Israel sends to fetch him (2 Kings 1:9–12).

The Rabbis of late antiquity held that the biblical Elijah was righteous, but found him too harsh and unforgiving. The Mekhilta of Rabbi Ishmael, an early midrash from the third century, calls the biblical Elijah the prophet who "seeks the honor of the Father, but not the son" (4). Elijah honors God but not Israel, the midrash explains, because, even after hearing the still small voice of God, Elijah pours out the same stream of complaints in precisely the same words. Untouched by God's revelation, he repeats, "I have been very zealous for the LORD, the God of hosts; for the children of Israel have forsaken your covenant, thrown down your altars, and put your prophets to the sword. I, I alone, am left, and they are seeking to take my life" (1 Kings 19:14, cf. 19:10, based on NRSV and JPS). For most rabbinic midrash, God's order to Elijah to anoint Elisha as prophet in his place is a punishment. Elijah focused on God and his own troubles, rather than asking God to help the people, and was thus no longer fit to be prophet.

The biblical Elijah has another side, however, in an entirely different book. The prophet Malachi, writing after the return from the Babylonian exile in the late sixth century before the common era, says: "Lo, I will send you the prophet Elijah before the coming of the great and terrible day of the LORD. He shall turn the heart of the fathers to the children and the heart of the children to the fathers, so that, when I come, I do not strike the land with utter destruction." (Mal. 3:23–24; Christian text, 4:5–6). These two verses gained resonance after canonization because they conclude the book of Prophets in Hebrew Scriptures and end the entire Christian Old Testament. Here Elijah comes to call families to reconciliation, so that God's curse will not strike them on the day of judgment.

Why does Malachi say that God will send Elijah? Because he is available. Unlike an ordinary mortal, Elijah did not die. Instead God took him up to heaven in a whirlwind. Elijah and Elisha, his disciple, were walking and talking, and "Behold! A chariot of fire and horses of fire separated the two of them and Elijah went up to heaven in a whirlwind" (Kings 2:11). For Malachi, and for the Rabbis of Talmudic times, Elijah's ascension is the necessary but not sufficient cause of his further career. For the Rabbis, as for other people of their time, the righteous dead were very much present, but they were present only with God in the heavenly court or at their grave sites. Only Elijah was free to travel throughout the world, and between heaven and earth, appearing to people in his own form or in disguise.

Thus when the Rabbis of Talmudic times speak of Elijah as historical prophet or messianic herald, they continue and interpret biblical traditions. On the other hand, when they tell stories about Elijah as a supernatural but human figure who helps and advises rabbis of previous generations, they are expressing a new creation, a uniquely rabbinic Elijah found in Judaism to the present day. The Rabbis do not say how Elijah stepped into this role; they simply assume it. Such unstated assumptions are characteristic rabbinic texts. From the Mishnah of the early third century to the Babylonian Talmud about four hundred later, these texts testify to the rebirth of Jewish faith after the destruction of the Temple and the transformation of Judaism into essentially the religion known today. No rabbinic text, however, tells us *how* Judaism was reborn and recreated. The Mishnah, for example, gives us the basic outline of how to observe Jewish holidays without the Temple, much as they are now observed, and the Talmud expands and elaborates. Yet, aside from a few brief passages in the Mishnah describing limited changes in observance after the destruction of the Temple, the decisions and informally evolving practices behind the development are hidden from us. The same is true for the development of Elijah's character.

In one brief story in the Babylonian Talmud, however, the midrashic Elijah intersects with the legendary Elijah. Rav Yossi, interpreting Scripture, said, "Father Elijah was a hot-tempered man." In reaction, Elijah stays away for three days. When he returns, Rav Yossi asks him, "Why didn't you come?" Elijah responds, "You called me hot-tempered." The rabbi, completely unintimidated and far from contrite, tells Elijah, "It is [now] clear that you *are* hot-tempered, Sir" (B. Sanhedrin 113a–b).

The humor of this story is clear, but exactly how it would have operated in rabbinic times is less so. Is the source of comic incongruity the *textual* disjunction between rabbinic midrash on the biblical Elijah and rabbinic legends of Elijah in the present? Or did the tellers of the tale want to emphasize the *actual* disjunction they saw between how Elijah behaved in biblical times and how he behaves now? In Scripture Elijah kills people, but in the present he does not strike Rav Yossi down; he only complains to him and even allows the mortal the last word. Like many stories of Elijah in the two Talmuds, this one is accessible on some levels and mysterious on others. We, as modern readers, smile at Rav Yossi's chutzpah, but we cannot really know how the story's audience would have understood it. Does part of its original humor come from their certainty that the encounter really happened? If so, there is an element of relief that Rav Yossi was not punished as well as a strong current of wonder that, through God's mercy, Elijah is now fully beneficent, if sometimes irritable.

ELIJAH AND THE MESSIAH

The best-known legend in the Bavli (Babylonian Talmud) that derives from Elijah's role as messianic herald has a comparable element of mystery. Unlike the story of Rav Yossi, it is not funny, but it carries heavy ironic weight. After an enigmatic encounter with Elijah at Rabbi Shimon bar Yoḥai's tomb, Rabbi Joshua asks about his own salvation and asks:

"When will Messiah come?"

He said to him, "Go ask him."

"And where [is he]?"

"He sits at the gate of Rome."

"And how will I know him?"

"He sits among the poor who suffer from diseases, and all of them loosen their bandages and tie up them all at once; he loosens one and ties one at a time. He says, 'Perhaps I will be needed [at any moment] so I should not be delayed.'"

Rabbi Joshua goes immediately to Rome—his journey assumed rather than described—recognizes the Messiah among the poor, and goes up to him.

He said to him, "Peace be with you, my master and teacher."

"Peace be with you, son of Levi."

"When are you coming, Sir?"

"Today."

Afterward, Rabbi Joshua goes to Elijah (whether in Rome or back home is unsaid) and bursts out in painful accusation: "Surely he lied to me, for he told me, 'Today.'"

Elijah responds, "Today, if you will hear His voice." Elijah is not merely expanding on the Messiah's words, but quoting Psalm 95:7, "We are His people, and the flock of His pasture—today, if you [plural] will hear His voice." In other words, the Messiah will come only as soon as the Jewish people accept their role as God's flock and obey his voice. Then Elijah asks Rabbi Joshua a question:

"What did he say to you?"

"Peace be with you son of Levi."

He said to him, "He promised you and your father the world to come."

(B. Sanhedrin 98a, following Florence and Munich manuscripts)

I quote rather than paraphrase this story because the images invoked by its stark language are unforgettable. No one, having heard it, can forget the Messiah standing among the diseased beggars at the gate of Rome, suffering yet stubbornly optimistic. One is immediately struck by Joshua's angry outburst, "He lied to me!" Only a little later, the irony of the whole encounter sinks in. Elijah tells the rabbi how to recognize the Messiah by describing his behavior: He has a characteristic way of unwrapping and rewrapping his sores one by one precisely because he does not know when he will be called. So Elijah, who does not know when the Messiah will come, sends Rabbi Joshua to ask the Messiah, who does not know either.

Nor can one overlook the place where the Messiah suffers. He sits at the gate of Rome, the nation that destroyed of Jerusalem, which even for Babylonian Jews was the symbol of all that is unredeemed in the world. Nevertheless, Elijah's interpretation of the Messiah's response, "Today, if you will hear His voice," puts responsibility for redeeming the world squarely in Jewish hands. The might of Rome is not what stands between the present and the coming of the Messiah; rather, the Jewish people must repent and return to God. This may be taken as encouraging or discouraging news, but it does assert that Jewish devotion has power over destiny, even though the world, then as now, considered raw power more important than the ethics and piety of the oppressed.

Yet many things about this story remain unexplained. Rabbi Joshua's question about his personal salvation is a very rare one in rabbinic texts, particularly in comparison to the texts of Patristic Christianity in the same era. Why does it come up here? How does Joshua ben Levi's concern for his own salvation fit in with his desire to know when the Messiah will come and his quest to ask the Messiah himself?

We can partially explain these questions by examining the history of the story. No one created it from scratch, but rather some unknown author or preacher made a story based on a set of preexisting interpretations of Scripture, especially of "Today, if you will hear His voice," which was already attributed to Rabbi Joshua ben Levi. The questions that remain unanswered stem in part from how the story came into being. It was most likely composed orally in a cultural context now lost to us. Thus its written version is very likely not complete, but appears as what John Foley, a leading scholar in oral-formulaic studies today, calls a libretto: notes for performance rather than a complete product (see Foley, *The Singer of Tales in Performance*, pp. 46, 66).

THE ELIJAH STORIES AS FOLKLORE

Some of the techniques I use to study the Elijah stories come from oral-formulaic studies, a discipline that draws from both literature and folklore studies. It focuses on poetry or prose, ancient or modern, meant to be recited or read out loud and mostly created by trained specialists in cultures that value the spoken word. Rabbinic literature certainly fits this definition. In examining the roles of writing and speaking in rabbinic times, we find that the Bavli describes teaching and study, social events and legal cases, all happening without writing or reading. The Talmud advocates memorizing and reciting rather than writing and reading the Oral Torah, rabbinic teaching, as opposed to Written Torah, Scripture. In fact, the whole Talmud is presented as a series of conversations among Rabbis, and thus the whole text testifies to the basically oral culture and traditions of the Sages.

On the other hand, because the Talmud comes to us in written form, it is impossible to say that any particular story was composed or transmitted completely orally. The key point for this book is that the Elijah stories, as a whole, were once stories told by the Rabbis themselves, and thus the stories, as a whole, can tell us things about rabbinic culture. They testify to commonly held rabbinic beliefs about Elijah as well as those of particular writers or editors. Seeing the Elijah stories as derived, directly or indirectly, from oral traditions of storytelling and preaching lets one compare Elijah with other mediators between God and humanity in both Judaism and other traditions of the same era. Rabbis and non-rabbis, Jews and non-Jews, shared stories even though they did not share technical aspects of law or scriptural interpretation. Traditions of supernatural mediators, whether gods, saints, or angels, entertained and inspired the interacting oral cultures of late antiquity. Comparing Elijah stories to tales of other supernatural mediators within Judaism allows us to consider what makes Elijah like these other figures and what makes him special. Similarly, comparing Elijah to non-Jewish supernatural mediators allows us to explore what Jewish culture had in common with surrounding societies and what made it unique.

Over the course of the book, I compare Elijah to mediators that he might be expected to resemble, such as angels, Christian saints, and saintly rabbis, and find some resemblances, especially to the Sages. I also discuss two unexpected figures who have interesting parallels to Elijah: the angel of death and the Greek god Hermes. Both Elijah and the angel of death have a relative freedom of action, and a corresponding fallibility, compared to other angels. In both cases, it seems, it was important to remove God from direct responsibility for the actions of the these beings. In the case of the angel of death, God can be at least psychologically removed from directly causing every death. In the case of Elijah, God is removed from directly choosing whom to help and whom not to, which might make the divine will seem arbitrary. Elijah's resemblances to Hermes, on the other hand, lie in their shared roles. They range from guiding the dead and frequenting graveyards to providing money. These correspondences are numerous enough to suggest some competitive cultural borrowing, along the lines of "our prophet is better than your so-called god."

Form criticism is another useful technique that follows from the idea that the Elijah stories have oral roots. Form criticism of narrative involves identifying and analyzing repeated patterns in wording and plot structure to determine relationships among stories and perhaps their earlier history. In this book form criticism is used with the literary perspective of oral-formulaic studies. Oral-formulaic studies emphasizes that narrative patterns are much more than labels for various genres of story—they are essential tools for conveying meaning and generating expectations with very few words. The commonest modern examples are jokes, for example: "So and so dies and goes up to the heavenly gates and meets St. Peter . . . " This format is so common that even Jewish people will use it, sometimes substituting a more Jewishly appropriate keeper of the keys to heaven. This plot formula, in which someone dies and meets the doorkeeper at the gate of heaven, immediately tells the hearer about the story line: this will be a joke, often with religious content and often including ethnic or political satire; it will not be bawdy; and it will almost certainly revolve around whether the dead person will get into heaven.

More than jokes and anecdotes in late antiquity circulated by word of mouth. As is still true in Hasidic circles today, sacred legends were told and retold, the Elijah stories among them. Most of the longer Elijah stories can be divided into three categories by formulaic phrasing and content. Stories in the first category, represented by the "antimartyrdom" of Rabbi Eleazar ben Perata, tell of Elijah arriving in disguise to rescue Jews in danger, usually from Gentile violence. These stories always contain the phrase "he appeared to him," only used for supernatural figures appearing in disguise. Stories in the second category, or "generic group," are represented by the story of Rav Anan, whom Elijah refuses to visit because of his slight judicial faux pas. In this set of stories Elijah stops appearing to someone because of something that person did wrong or appears to one person and not to another who is less virtuous. Rav Yossi's disagreement with Elijah over whether the prophet is hot tempered is also part of this group, or perhaps a joke based on it. The next generic group is more diverse. Its opening formula always states that someone met Elijah and asked him a question, generally a question that only Elijah would be able to answer. After that, the stories take many forms, because an answered question can lead in many directions, even Rabbi Joshua's trip to Rome to meet the Messiah.

ELIJAH STORIES AS A WINDOW ON RABBINIC CULTURE AND THEOLOGY

The three generic groups of Elijah stories, taken as a whole, provide us with unique insights into rabbinic culture. While any isolated story tells us mostly about its individual composer, these groups, each with its own stable verbal formula, its shared plot motifs, and its characteristic theme or themes, provide a window into perceptions of Elijah that were widely distributed within the rabbinic subculture and, perhaps, within the wider Jewish society the Rabbis shared. We can better understand the Judaism of the time simply by considering that Elijah is a supernatural mediator who is as much or more a teacher and ethical guide than a savior. Elijah's activities reinforce rabbinic society's emphasis on learning and ethics and its relative deemphasis of earthly miracles and after-death salvation.

The generic group in which Elijah refuses to visit someone emphasizes ethical behavior and human responsibility. In these stories Elijah makes it clear, by ceasing or refusing to visit, that certain actions are unacceptable to him. Often the erring parties, as rabbis or simply pious Jews, are aware of Elijah's absence because they had a connection with him before he left, temporarily or for good. In a story in the Talmud Yerushalmi, Elijah deserts Rabbi Joshua ben Levi for a time, and on the prophet's return the rabbi defends his action, saying, "I acted according to the law." Elijah, in turn, retorts, "is this the law of the truly devout?" (Y. Terumot 46b). This question echoes throughout this whole generic group, in which Elijah silently advocates a higher ethical standard, beyond Jewish law, that is incumbent on the truly devout and righteous person.

Furthermore, the idea that the truly devout and righteous can be visited by Elijah reinforced the rabbinic sense that ethical behavior—even beyond what was required—was necessary for deep intellectual or spiritual insight. These legends encouraged such virtuous behavior. They also at times imply a certain rabbinic noblesse oblige. In a number of these stories, Elijah deserts people for not being good or helpful to their social inferiors, but he does not abandon anyone for failures in humility toward them. Thus many of the stories, while morally admirable, nevertheless advocate a hierarchical society with rabbis at its apex.

In contrast, the generic group in which Elijah appears in disguise celebrates freedom rather than emphasizing ethical responsibility and proper social relationships. These stories, more than the other two generic groups, have a potential inspiration in physical events: occasions in which help arose for a rabbi from an unexpected source, perhaps from a Gentile court official who was expected to be hostile. Rabbis apparently thought of these occasions as the intervention of Elijah in disguise—or at least they appreciated stories in which Elijah appeared as the real savior. The most common setting of these stories, during the Roman persecutions after the destruction of the Temple and the Bar Kokhba revolt, suggests that the genre arose in the first and second centuries of the common era. One cannot rule out, however, the possibility that the genre arose later and was retrojected into the legendary past. In either case, the stories in the Bavli were told and retold for generations before they reached the written form we possess.

The help that God sends through Elijah in these stories is unexpected and unpredictable in form. It thus expresses a common theme in the Bavli, that the righteous can receive unforeseen divine help. Elijah's saving appearance cannot be predicted or requested, but it is the more miraculous, and the more welcome, for that. This is not to say that awed gratitude is the dominant tone of the most characteristic stories in this generic group. Several of these stories have a playful quality, an apparent desire to amuse and astonish their readers and hearers as well as educate and inspire them.

When Elijah appears in disguise, he breaks the rules of the world, if not the rules of the Rabbis. For an oppressed and colonized people, Elijah breaks the rules of the rulers' game in which Romans (or the Persians who ruled Babylonia) always win and the Jews always lose. Elijah in disguise opens up the world, introduces unforeseen possibilities and unpredictable freedoms. He comes as a benign trickster, usually making fools of Gentile oppressors, and sometimes fooling those whom he saves as well (as when he saves Rabbi Meir from Roman soldiers by taking the form of a prostitute and embracing him). Elijah is a free agent and a force for freedom, embodying the liberating power of divine mercy for individuals within the Jewish community. The folkloric motif underlying these stories is that of Elijah as patron and trickster, and champion of Jews in a risky world ruled by Gentiles.

The treatment of this generic group in the Bavli, however, implies a society that thought Divine intervention in human troubles was rare and undependable. All but one of the Bavli's stories of rescue by Elijah in disguise are set in pre-Talmudic times, implying such miracles are more part of the glorious past than the mundane present. In the twenty-first century it may seem odd to describe a society that believes in miracles *at all* as pragmatic and human centered. Elijah's actions, however, reveal the practical tendencies of rabbinic society, which emphasized the miraculous much less than Christian societies of the same time.

The third generic group, in which a rabbi meets Elijah and asks a question, is not as clearly defined as the other two. The former two groups each have a characteristic plot structure: Elijah abandons someone who has acted wrongly, or he appears to help someone in danger or difficulty. When someone meets and questions Elijah, on the other hand, Elijah may teach or share secret knowledge on a wide variety of subjects. Some of the stories are barely narratives at all, only settings for a memorable saying; others have more developed plots of various kinds. Nevertheless, there are significant details that unify this group. Each of these stories begins with a verbal formula usually employed when one rabbi meets another rabbi who has some special knowledge. Elijah thus appears as a teacher, an immortal Sage who is friend to the Sages. Furthermore, in this generic group Elijah's words and actions are always positive. He generally comes to teach or encourage and never comes to actively punish sin or discourage human initiative.

One motif found in a number of stories in this group, enough to suggest it is the product of Babylonian rabbinic culture as a whole, is the use of Elijah to support and encourage human power and particularly rabbinic power and freedom to legislate and to interpret. Two stories in this group explicitly stress the freedom of individual Sages to interpret Scripture, one saying that mutually contradictory views are both "words of the Living God." Here, one can see Elijah as a supernatural supporter of rabbinic thinking. His appearance to instruct, like his appearance in disguise to rescue, comes unexpectedly, welcome but unpredictable.

Elijah's most important function, in these three generic groups and in the Elijah stories as a whole, is to support right relationship between individuals and God. Elijah provides a channel for communication with God, answering the rabbis who ask, "what is the Holy Blessed One doing?" and relaying the rabbis' responses back to God. When Elijah tells Rabbah bar Shila that God is not reciting the traditions of Rabbi Meir because he learned from Aḥer the apostate, Rabbah bar Shila defends Rabbi Meir. Immediately afterward, Elijah comes back to tell Rabbah that God has conceded the point and is now to reciting Meir's teaching (B. Ḥagigah 15b). It is hard to know today what to make of such far-reaching human authority. We may recognize the self-assertion of Rabbah bar Shila in his defense of Rabbi Meir, but we do not necessarily understand the story's conclusion that God responded well to it.

It helps somewhat to consider that Elijah is in many ways a more powerful version of the rabbinic Sage. Elijah has individual free choice combined with deep knowledge of God's will, with which he is usually, but not always, completely in harmony. The Rabbis of the two Talmuds had a complex image of God that could encompass God adorning a bride (Eve) or visiting the sick (Abraham). God was supremely powerful, but also mourned the destruction of Jerusalem and went into exile with His people. The Rabbis turned to traditions of the eternally living prophet Elijah and used them as raw material envisioning a supernatural mediator in line with their own spiritual aspirations and with their image of themselves. Like the Sages themselves, the Elijah of the Talmud is in some sense a partner of God, engaged in the great work that would come to be called *tikkun olam*, the repair of the world.

THE STRUCTURE OF THIS BOOK

This book has two major parts. In part 1, chapters 1 and 2, I focus on the work of previous scholars and on my own view of how to understand the role of oral culture in rabbinic stories. Chapter 1 discusses previous scholarship on Elijah and on folklore and form criticism in rabbinic literature. Chapter 2 describes the oral nature of rabbinic culture and its role in forming the character of the Elijah stories. These chapters also cover methodology: why I chose particular methods for analyzing the stories. In part 2, chapters 3 and 4, I give two different perspectives on the rabbinic Elijah. Chapter 3 studies Elijah as a supernatural mediator in relation to comparable figures and chapter 4 fully describes the generic groups of Elijah stories, analyzing examples from each one. Chapter 5 forms the conclusion: it reviews Elijah's role in the Talmud and briefly surveys the later career of Elijah in Judaism, including a few more ideas about what Elijah legends have to teach us about rabbinic culture and later Judaism as well.

Readers who bought this book to learn about Elijah may want to read the start of chapter 1 and then skip to chapter 3. In the long run, however, I hope you will return to the beginning, especially chapter 2, as the rabbinic Elijah is best understood in his cultural and literary context.

ACKNOWLEDGMENTS

Among those who have helped shaped the doctoral thesis that grew into this book, Yaakov Elman in particular has provided continuing encouragement. My friend Paula Reimers and my brother-in-law Steve Kemp both proofread chapters and helped me write more clearly. Herb Basser, whom I have gotten to know better recently, has also provided invaluable support, not to mention help translating medieval Hebrew verse! Richard Kalmin deserves special honor. He has moved from doctoral adviser to mentor, providing good advice as I revised and added to the book.

Acknowledging everyone who supported me while writing this book is almost equivalent to acknowledging every friend and family member who has accompanied me through the years that I worked on it. Friends met at Trinity University in San Antonio and at Tulane (especially Elizabeth Kosmetatou) have cheered me on, and my current colleagues at Florida Atlantic University have all encouraged my scholarship, especially Fred Greenspahn, Marcella Munson, Myriam Ruthenberg, and Marianne Sanua. Among personal friends, too many to name individually, Molly Weigel, a sister by choice for more than thirty years, has a very special place. So too does Natalie Polzer, my telephone Talmud study partner, whom I can always count on for a voice of kindness and reason.

As well as dedicating this book to them, I have the joy of including my parents in the acknowledgments for their encouragement, advice, and editing as I wrestled with a project that sometimes seemed endless. Last, I thank my husband Sid Kemp, an author himself, who supported me enthusiastically, from dissertation proposal, through finding a publisher, to final manuscript delivery.

ELIJAH
and the
RABBIS

THE STUDY OF RABBINIC NARRATIVE
Elijah, Folklore Studies, and Form Criticism

At some point, during the rabbinic period or shortly before it, people began to tell stories in which the prophet Elijah appeared to people of their own generation or generations just before their own.[1] When these stories were first told is now inaccessible to us, as it has not left a trace in any text. The New Testament speaks of Elijah, but usually seems to do so in a messianic context. Jesus, for example, is seen by some as the Elijah who will usher in the end of days.[2] Rabbinic literature, therefore, is the first to describe the legendary Elijah as helper and teacher in religious narrative set after biblical times and before the coming of the Messiah.

The "legendary Elijah" who appears to the Rabbis differs in actions and character from both the Elijah of midrash and the Elijah who will be the messianic herald. The Rabbis saw the biblical Elijah as harsh and inflexible in his struggle to enforce the worship of God.[3] In contrast, the Elijah met by the Rabbis is presented positively; he rarely even appears harsh and never kills. The Rabbis depict Elijah as messianic herald, impersonal and awesome. In contrast, the legendary Elijah has a very distinct personality (even a hot temper) and inspires remarkably little awe. In light of his distinctive character, and also his importance in later Jewish lore, I treat the legendary Elijah separately.

Many of the rabbinic stories tell of Elijah's relations with the Tannaim, rabbis of the Mishnaic era, and thus may come from the beginning of rabbinic Judaism. The first documents in which they appear, however, are all amoraic, dating at the earliest from the fourth century and often much later. There are several Elijah stories in the Yerushalmi (Jerusalem or Palestinian Talmud) and early aggadic midrashim. The Bavli, or "Babylonian Talmud," redacted a few hundred years after the other texts, contains thirty-eight references to Elijah's active role in rabbinic times.[4] These references to Elijah in the Bavli, more than half of them stories, suggest that Elijah's importance grew over time, that the redactors of the Bavli were particularly interested in him, or both. Elijah plays numerous roles in rabbinic works. He provides halakhic, ethical, or eschatological teaching, appears in disguise to rescue those in danger, informs rabbis what God is doing in the heavenly court, and occasionally gives money to poor rabbis—and this is only a partial list.

This chapter explores previous scholarship on Elijah and then looks briefly at the contributions of folklore studies and form criticism for the study of rabbinic narrative. Surprisingly few scholars writing on the legendary Elijah have focused on rabbinic narratives, clearly defining what makes them different from medieval or modern Elijah stories. Prior works do agree that rabbinic Elijah legends provide rich insights into rabbinic values and ideals, and most note that Elijah's encounters with individual rabbis provide insight into rabbinic theology. Many also emphasize the unique qualities of these legends and try to define them, more or less successfully.

Meir Friedmann wrote the earliest comprehensive collection of Elijah traditions in his introduction to his edition of *Tanna Devei Eliahu*, published in 1902. This aggadic work, "Teacher of the House of Elijah" was probably written, or at least completed, after the Bavli, yet may contain earlier material.[5] Friedmann cites Elijah traditions without historical distinctions, covering rabbinic legends, medieval folktales, and the kabbalistic stories, and rating the probable factual truth behind them.[6] Some of the stories, Friedmann writes, are descriptions of dreams; others are written to inspire faith; whereas others are merely fabricated to impress. A few, in contrast, are stories that record the experience of extraordinary individuals who had actual—albeit purely spiritual—encounters with Elijah.[7] Friedmann is innovative for his time in recognizing the religiously serious nature of many rabbinic Elijah stories. From today's perspective, however, Friedmann errs in trying to rate the stories according to their historicity. As now understood, the stories of the rabbinic era are not based on individual experience or historical records. Fraenkel sees them as artistic constructions created for "the educational and conceptual requirements of the authors." Hasan-Rokem characterizes them as a kind of ancient ethnography, privileging "everyday life over named historical persons and events with specific dates."[8] Furthermore, the unanswerable question of what really happened distracts from the historically more interesting question of what a particular story meant to the people of its time, a question one can answer to some extent.[9]

Samuel M. Segal, writing in the thirties, is the first author to collect only rabbinic Elijah traditions.[10] In his introduction, he tries to cover *all* rabbinic references to Elijah, from 200 to about 800 CE, attempting to synthesize the message of legends occurring in the "rabbinic present" with the meaning of midrashic and eschatological passages. Not surprisingly, Segal fails to find any dominant characteristics for the legendary Elijah, writing, "The Elijah of legend runs the whole gamut of functions. He is all things to all men." Segal does, however, make some useful observations, especially on how some of the miraculous Elijah legends resemble folk legends of the Christian saints.[11]

The next substantial work on Elijah is Aharon Wiener's *The Prophet Elijah in the Development of Judaism: A Depth-Psychological Study.* Wiener's book remains the most comprehensive survey of Elijah traditions, from the Bible through early modern times. In his chapter on the rabbinic Elijah, Wiener emphasizes the prophet's close relationship to the Sages, supporting, rescuing, and reproving them. Elijah, he writes, became "the patron of the individual relationship between man and his fellow-man and between man and God."[12] And, indeed, the stories bear out the idea that Elijah supports the individual's relationship with other people and with God. As we will see, Elijah (when not in disguise) appears only to individuals, not groups, he supports justice between people, and he tells individuals God's words or will. Wiener also notes the remarkable way in which Elijah's human fallibility coexists with his angelic power, as we will discuss more thoroughly in chapter 3.

Wiener, however, is working from a "depth psychological" perspective that draws on modern thinkers, especially Jung. As such, he is less convincing in his view that Elijah stories express individual spiritual experience as opposed to supporting community values.[13] As we will see, this holds true for some Elijah stories, but not others; Weiner's lack of focus on individual stories makes him miss exceptions and nuances within the tradition. In the end, he describes his own spiritual and psychological worldview as much as he describes the Rabbis and their picture of Elijah. While Wiener fails to do full justice to the rabbinic Elijah in his cultural context, he has valuable observations about Elijah's relationship with the individual.

Yonah Fraenkel, author of numerous studies on aggadah, is of course much more attentive than Wiener to the form of individual stories. He is interested in Elijah stories as examples of wider rabbinic thought and quotes them to illustrate his argument that rabbinic spirituality emphasizes responsibility for making one's own ethical and spiritual choices.[14] Within this framework, Fraenkel emphasizes that Elijah, despite his supernatural role, compels no one, but only teaches and advises. In addition, Elijah, despite his knowledge of heaven and earth, does not impair human freedom by assuring people that they will have eternal life. Thus Elijah preserves a "religious life built on ignorance of future reward and punishment," which Fraenkel believes necessary for true human self-determination.[15] As we will see, Elijah does not merely refrain from impinging on human free will, but often positively supports and encourages human freedom. On the other hand, some stories assume human free will, but focus on Elijah himself as free agent, recording his actions in response to people's actions or questions.

Among all the discussions of the rabbinic Elijah, Pinchas Peli's short essay, "Elijah in the Beit Midrash of the Sages," provides the most useful material, in part because he focuses on distinctive material in the Bavli and in part because he has unique insights into the texts. Peli first notes that the Elijah stories of the Babylonian Talmud are different in kind from later accounts of Elijah. He points out that encounters with Elijah in the Bavli are unexpected, rather than being the reward for specific spiritual striving or a period of prayer and abstinence, as we find in the mystical tradition of the Middle Ages.[16] Like Fraenkel, Peli wisely refrains from any effort to pass judgment on the stories' historicity, observing that their aim "is literary and rhetorical rather than . . . providing a personal testimony to mystical experience."[17] Peli is unique in seeing the role of humor in the Elijah stories; he points out that some of the Bavli's Elijah legends were almost certainly meant to be funny. Humor is sometimes tricky to identify across cultures and centuries,[18] but Pinchas Peli's treatment of the topic makes it clear that anyone reading the ancient Elijah legends must pay close attention to the wit and outright humor of the stories, which often feature rhetorical exaggeration.[19]

Peli's analysis of narrative is insightful. In one story, Elijah points out the infinity of midrashic truth, in another he conveys a tragically ironic critique of rabbinic hubris, while in a third Peli shows how Elijah reveals the deep mercy of God in a context that had emphasized God as judge.[20] However, his analysis is so specific to the individual stories that he finds it difficult to generalize effectively. Because Peli does not look at the form of stories, he does not see that Elijah legends joined by parallels in linguistic formulae and content often reflect similar themes or meanings, whereas Elijah legends from unrelated groups often have much less in common. Taken as a whole, the Bavli's Elijah legends convey a number of varied perspectives, some unique to the Elijah stories and some not. Thus one must proceed cautiously in any attempt to find any one message or quality common to *all* the Elijah stories, even though each group of formally similar stories often does tend to express a particular viewpoint.

In sum, although all the existing works on the rabbinic Elijah are useful in one way or another, none of them gives a full picture. These previous works on Elijah, with their strengths and weaknesses, open a door to a new way to approach the Elijah stories. We will start by focusing on the Elijah legends of one period and culture—in our case the rabbinic legends, especially those of the Bavli. Then, when we turn to later tales of Elijah, we can determine how, or even whether, they resemble earlier ones. Furthermore, we will separate Elijah legends from the other kinds of Elijah traditions, specifically the midrashic and messianic, except for a brief discussion of how they influence Elijah's later role in ritual. In studying the legends, this work adopts the best of previous approaches: analyzing and classifying characteristic themes and plot structures and also paying close attention to the nuances of individual stories. Finally, in order to minimize anachronism, we will analyze Elijah stories in context. Practically speaking, this means looking at the stories first in light of one another, in light of narratives from the same texts, and in light of other sources from the same era.

This work starts from the Babylonian Talmud, which has a workable number of Elijah legends, and then compares them to the smaller number of Elijah legends found in other rabbinic sources before considering later traditions. Inspired by previous scholars, we will focus on the spiritual insight conveyed by many of the Elijah stories as well as their social function. Any reconstruction of rabbinic beliefs about God and humanity is hypothetical and leads unavoidably to some degree of anachronism, but to neglect this reconstruction is to neglect that which makes many of the Elijah stories deeply compelling, both to those who chose to preserve them and to us today.

METHODOLOGY: FOLKLORE STUDIES AND FORM CRITICISM

In light of the rich variety of the Elijah stories, I have found that only multiple methodological approaches can do them full justice. This chapter discusses folklore studies and form criticism in the study of rabbinic literature, legendary narrative in particular. Chapter 2 discusses the origins of rabbinic narrative in oral transmission and describes the contribution of oral-formulaic studies to rabbinic scholarship.

A single theoretical foundation underlies all these methods of study: they consider the narrative in the two Talmuds as orally derived literature. In his methodological essay, "Word Power, Performance and Tradition," John Miles Foley uses the term *oral-derived* to refer to "works of verbal art," which, "although drawing on deep roots in the oral tradition, were written out by the very word-smiths responsible for their present form."[21] My choice of the phrase *orally derived literature* is inspired by Foley's use of *oral-derived*, but orally derived literature describes a wider range of possibilities. I use it to refer to stories whose precise relationship to oral performance cannot be known, but that bear clear markers of oral style. Some stories might be condensed paraphrases of oral performance; others might be original compositions using verbal formulae and plot structures characteristic of oral narrative; but all have some relationship to an oral milieu.

Rabbinic Elijah stories' relationship to oral forms can be seen in their use of certain fixed patterns of plot structure. Furthermore, the language of these stories, and of most rabbinic narrative, has many other characteristics of oral transmission, which we will describe in chapter 2. In their orally influenced style, rabbinic narratives resemble other ancient works that may be regarded for various reasons as orally derived texts. Because the Elijah stories contain these orally derived forms, one can apply the ideas and techniques of folklore studies, the discipline that examines narrative of all kinds (as well as songs, prayers, riddles, and so on) passed on by word of mouth.

Folklore Studies

Because of the key role played by folklore studies in this book, it will help to give a brief overview of the discipline here. Folklore studies today are interdisciplinary, drawing from and synthesizing different fields of study. Scholars of present-day folklore use techniques and categories derived from psychology, sociology, anthropology, and comparative literature. Those who study the records of folklore in ancient written works use some of the same techniques, but also draw from form-critical and historical studies.[22]

Nevertheless, folklore studies is not a mainstream discipline in the modern academy and has only begun to play a significant role in studies of rabbinic literature written in English in the last twenty-five years. Part of the reason for this delay is that contemporary folklore studies falls between the disciplinary cracks of an increasingly specialized scholarly world. Another reason, however, lies in the history of the discipline itself, which has only in recent generations freed itself from the romantic and antiquarian biases of its nineteenth-century roots.[23]

When the term *folklore* was first coined in the mid-nineteenth century, it referred to the ancient customs and oral traditions of the usually illiterate—and certainly nonliterary—rural folk of Europe, whose traditions were being diluted or destroyed by early modern urbanization and state-sponsored education. Early folklorists who studied these traditions developed a bias toward the "antique" that led to an anonymous and timeless definition of folk tradition: a story or song could only be "traditional" after its original creator was forgotten.[24]

This definition of folklore persisted into the second half of the twentieth century, and it is still the common usage of the word *folklore*. Most people would readily agree that fairy tales such as "Jack and the Beanstalk" are folklore but would be uncertain whether a joke they themselves told was folklore as well. Athough the phrase *urban legend* is fairly well known, most people are not consciously aware that these stories share stylistic features and social functions with the legends and cautionary tales of the past.[25]

Today many students of contemporary folklore understand folklore as a process, rather than a collection of linguistic artifacts. Poets, storytellers, and people who tell jokes all perform oral folklore in the context of a community of listeners, or "folk group," that influences the artistic process by their expectations and their response to the teller. A folk group may consist of an entire society or a small subculture. "Teenagers in Detroit," for example, "constitute a folk group with its own sociolinguistic identity, [and] its own social context."[26] This contemporary school of folklore studies is most interested in the social meaning of a performance to a group of listeners. Not surprisingly, when such folklorists approach ancient written texts, they tend to analyze them for clues to social context.[27]

In analyzing ancient rabbinic works, folklorists such as Ben-Amos look for ancient Jewish society's occasions for performance, such as public sermons, eulogies, and storytelling at weddings, combing the written text for clues about actual performers and audiences.[28] In addition, Ben-Amos and others of this school frequently look for the sociological and psychological meanings inherent in the text, working with the approach often called ethnopoetics.[29] Yassif describes the way in which this approach regards folk stories as "serving . . . as mirrors which clearly and precisely reflect [society's] anxieties and aspirations."[30] The present work, too, will often speak of the possible social and religious meanings of particular stories and of classes of story.

Oral-formulaic studies, as discussed in chapter 2, is more interested in the style and artistic expression of oral and orally derived works, often focusing on ancient or medieval texts. Nevertheless, folklore studies and oral-formulaic studies have many important points of contact. First of all, both disciplines are increasingly conscious of the importance of the group in which folklore is performed. Both pay "attention to verbal art as a situated, experienced event in traditional context," which is to say that both believe a story or poem is best understood as an event shared between performer and audience on customary occasions.[31]

Furthermore, practitioners of both folklore and oral-formulaic studies agree that "patterned repetition" is the aspect of folklore that translates best to written form. As Susan Niditch writes, "This repetition takes many forms as symbols, words, syntax, elements of content, structures and thoughts recur in profound economy of expression and density of emphasis."[32] Such repetition is the best indicator of oral tradition in written works, and analysis of this repetition is the most concrete and reproducible element of the methodology of both folklore and oral-formulaic studies. One can objectively, often statistically, note how words, stylistic features, and plot structures recur among stories in the Talmud and thus support an understanding of the Talmud as orally derived literature. Furthermore, one can learn much about the social, religious, and intellectual context of rabbinic texts by analyzing patterned repetition and considering why and how certain themes, motifs, and forms occur and recur.

Folklore Studies, Biblical Studies, and Rabbinics

Jewish folklorists came to understand before many others that folklore need not be an exclusively popular or entirely oral phenomenon.[33] In 1937 Louis Ginzberg wrote that "we must recognize the important fact that the material used by the learned is frequently derived from the people."[34] In the next generation, Raphael Patai lucidly describes how "Jewish folklore is characterized, in each epoch, by a continuous process of lifting out considerable bodies of folklore from the stream of oral tradition and freezing them in written form." This fixing in writing, he adds, does not destroy folklore, but rather helps to keep it alive, as written stories can easily reenter the stream of oral transmission.[35]

Ginzberg and Patai basically accepted the traditional view that folklore must by definition be common to a society at large. In part this is because it is genuinely hard to evaluate folklore's contribution to rabbinic sources. Even today, many scholars of rabbinics choose to bypass questions of oral transmission altogether and instead take a purely historical and textual approach to their sources.[36] Others, of whom Fraenkel is the best known, admit that oral folklore may provide raw material for rabbinic narrative, but assert that the stories themselves are too sophisticated and profound to be anything except the literary creations of skilled individual authors.[37] The very nature of rabbinic literature makes the relationship between folklore and rabbinic narrative complicated and subtle. The Babylonian Talmud in particular is a complex and sometimes self-contradictory document. Anonymously redacted over generations, it contains an enormous range of material, from passages of unparalleled intellectual virtuosity and spiritual wisdom to expressions of homely truths and parochial prejudices.

Many recent scholars of Jewish folklore have become interested in how one can know whether a textual narrative is folklore or derived from oral tradition. In his entry on folklore in the *Anchor Bible Dictionary*, Ben-Amos presents a performance-oriented approach to the Hebrew Bible, emphasizing its "allusions to, and representations of, ideas and performances of folklore forms." However, "the OT in itself is not folklore," not even "as a literary representation of oral forms." Furthermore, the Hebrew Bible reflects only the traditions that supported the outlook of those segments of Israel's religious elite who recorded them. Nevertheless, Ben-Amos concedes that considerable knowledge of ancient folklore may be gleaned from biblical texts.[38]

I had the opportunity to ask Dan Ben-Amos whether rabbinic stories might sometimes be closer to oral tradition than biblical narrative because they exist in less highly edited contexts, and he agreed that this seemed likely. Yet, as Ben-Amos says about folk motifs in the Bible, all the folklore in rabbinic texts is there because it validated the position of some Sages—or, I would add, because it appealed to them as inspiring, witty, or in some other way. Wherever Talmudic legends came from originally, it makes the most sense to say that they were the Rabbis' own folklore and that, if they entered rabbinic oral tradition from popular circles, they became rabbinic folklore without ceasing to be popular as well.

Ben-Amos, while conceding that rabbinic narratives might reflect the actual folkloric forms of their period, stresses that writing inevitably alters crucial features of orally performed narrative.[39] Eli Yassif, in contrast, argues that the Talmud contains some almost unedited transcriptions of oral narrative, most noticeably in cycles of stories. These story cycles are collections of stories loosely related by topic or other criteria and strung together without connecting passages and apparently without literary reworking.[40] Even if the editing of story cycles may be more artful than Yassif holds, the story cycle itself, in which stories are juxtaposed without connecting remarks, seems related to the Talmud's origins as orally derived literature.

One finds another example of this phenomenon—stories unconnected by any narrative bridge or framework—in the prose histories in medieval Ireland. The earliest of medieval Irish histories (anonymously redacted like rabbinic texts) record one story after another, without transitions. In contrast, the later Irish histories have named individual authors who use narrative bridges to join traditional narratives together into literary works resembling prose epic.[41] A cycle of midrashic narratives from the Bavli about the cruelly inhospitable people of Sodom from the Bavli provides a good example of how story cycles may be minimally edited for content. Two tales about Sodom's toll bridge, one with an anonymous poor traveler and the other with Abraham's slave Eliezer, contain many parallel motifs and considerable word-for-word repetition. Yassif points out that in a case like this it would have been easy, and rhetorically smoother, to combine the two closely parallel stories, yet the editor did not. Here, Yassif argues, the editor of the cycle arranges oral sources in writing "without even the changes which he might have been expected to make."[42] Conversely, one might just as well hypothesize that the stories were edited to *increase* the parallelism between them, as we cannot know the facts of their composition.[43] However, the text's juxtaposition of nearly identical stories still provides evidence for an editorial practice that included all stories on a topic without combining them. No one author could be expected to compose two such closely parallel narratives, although a storyteller might tell them both, and the redactors chose to include both, perhaps even increasing their similarity by adding parallel language.

Actually, Ben-Amos and Yassif both make important points. Ben-Amos, as a performance-oriented folklorist, emphasizes that the rhetorical features of oral narrative were inevitably shortened, changed, or eliminated when the redactors of a rabbinic text reduced a story to writing. This is plausible, as written versions of oral narrative often behave this way in the present.[44] Yassif, more textually oriented, is most convincing in his argument that the basic content of oral narrative is often reproduced substantially unchanged in the Talmud, and this too is plausible, for reasons already given.

Several key points emerge from this brief overview of folklore studies and rabbinics. First, scholars have long seen that oral and written versions of rabbinic stories coexisted and mutually influenced one another: originally written stories can become oral as well as vice versa. However, any story in rabbinic sources will have undergone at least some changes merely in being written down. Thus one cannot distinguish between more-or-less transcribed folklore and tales written in an oral style.

Second, all the folklore in rabbinic texts is there because it appealed to the Sages who transmitted it and redacted the texts. Though stories in the Talmud are folklore, they are not necessarily popular folklore. Rather than being common to all of Jewish society, they may have derived from the Sages' unique oral traditions. Even the most seemingly popular narrative in rabbinic texts appears in a version relevant to the Rabbis and *may* have been significantly reworked for political, legal, or aesthetic reasons, either orally or in writing. Nevertheless, "story cycles," and perhaps other legends in the Bavli, are minimally edited and thus are probably closer to oral versions than narratives contained in more highly edited passages or works. Finally, some (though certainly not all) of the stories in the Talmud have an aesthetic and conceptual sophistication usually associated with literature and reflect the conscious artistry of oral performers, writers in a traditional style, or both.

Form and Genre Criticism of Rabbinic Narrative

Most of the Elijah stories fall into one or more overlapping groups defined by characteristic narrative forms and/or verbal patterns. Because one can divide the stories by such criteria, one can use form criticism to analyze them. Genre criticism is essentially a kind of form criticism, as it too groups stories by analyzing recurring plots and themes.[45] We will discuss genre criticism in this section as well. Sometimes form and genre criticism are merely descriptive; however, especially when analyzing narrative, form and genre criticism can help one discover the meanings implicit in different forms, as we will discuss in more detail in chapter 2.

Form criticism, as its name implies, starts with the description of recurring forms, verbal formulae as well as structures of narrative, quotation, or numbered lists. Because of its recognition that ancient texts were often built of oral raw materials, form criticism, like folklore studies, understands ancient texts as orally derived literature. A number of scholars have put form criticism to good use in the study of rabbinic literature.[46] The authors who have most influenced this book are those writing on narrative: Eli Yassif, Jacob Neusner in *Judaism and Story*, Catherine Hezser, and especially Dan Ben-Amos.[47] Not all these scholars call their approaches form criticism, but they all identify and analyze recurring forms.

Form-critical studies of narrative are most useful for analyzing Elijah's activities in the time of the Sages because all but three of the thirty-eight references to Elijah's "present" speech and actions in the Bavli are found in stories. This work chooses a broad definition of "story," following Kalmin. He defines story as including all "statements found within a narrative framework"—framed by a description of a place or of an encounter—in addition to narratives with full plots.[48] This work also includes in the broad category of story the five references to Elijah's teaching a rabbi that are not stories in the usual sense, but that assume Elijah's interaction with a particular person at a particular moment.[49] Elijah is never constantly in contact with anyone. Thus, when he speaks to someone, it implies the event of his appearance.

In grouping these five "Elijah said" passages with stories, I am guided by the practice of Hellenistic rhetoric. The Hellenistic contemporaries of the Rabbis put the pithy statements of a well-known figure, stories leading up to an epigram, and brief legends into a single formal category, that of the *chreia*. In ancient textbooks of rhetoric, the *chreia* is defined as the concise account of a saying or action attributed to a prominent person, usually a philosopher or leader. Approximately fifteen of the Elijah stories fall into this category, containing a saying or a brief account of action. Chreia served as building blocks for rhetorical exercises in Hellenistic schools, and some scholars posit a connection between the practice of the rhetorical schools and that of the rabbinic houses of study.[50] Perhaps the latter borrowed the method of collecting sayings and stories of their own leaders from the practice of surrounding cultures.

Like almost all rabbinic narratives, Elijah stories can be easily separated from the surrounding legal discussions. The beginning of each story is clearly marked by the appearance of the protagonist or by the description of a particular scene or action.[51] This shows us that the redactors did in fact separate them (and other stories) from non-narrative discourse. Eli Yassif's work on story cycles, already discussed, suggests that the editors of the Talmud also recognized that groups of stories existed. Several of these little "anthologies" of stories have recurring plot motifs accompanied by specific verbal patterns. This organizing principle, which Yassif calls "generic" (ז'אנרי), includes rather specific subjects as well as particular forms. Basic theme, subject, and overall form all play a role in genre as Yassif describes it.[52]

Anyone with a moderate knowledge of rabbinic literature can call to mind sets of independently appearing stories that seem to belong to a single generic group as Yassif defines it. We find, for example, a set of stories on "Last Words and Deathbed Scenes in Rabbinic Literature," the title of an article by Anthony Saldarini.[53] Thus one can argue that such groups of stories form native categories within rabbinic literature and the Talmud in particular, even though they are not part of a named category. About half the Elijah stories in the Bavli fit into three formal groups mentioned in the preface, groups that Yassif would probably describe as generic patterns.

The rest of the Elijah stories, however, do not fit into generic groups. Some are too concise and too embedded in the surrounding discussion to be part of a narrative genre as Yassif describes it; others are best described as part of wider formal categories of story. Two Elijah stories, for example, are best seen as exempla, stories whose main purpose is to present an example of praiseworthy moral and religious behavior and its reward.[54] To develop a wider view of narrative form, I also bring in the work of Neusner, Hezser and Ben-Amos.

In *Judaism and Story* Neusner describes two formal categories of narrative found among the Elijah stories: the narrative setting for a saying and the moral precedent. The "narrative setting for a saying" is a brief story with little or no narrative development. I have found "narrative settings" among the Elijah stories, mostly stories in which a rabbi meets Elijah, asks him a question, and receives a saying as an answer. In many instances, while the plot (such as it is) is irrelevant to the saying, it matters that Elijah provides the teaching. Elijah, for example, affirms the sages' authority to interpret Scripture in two very brief stories. The second of Neusner's categories is the type of moral or legal precedent in which a rabbi teaches by his behavior.[55] Among the Elijah stories, there are seven such moral or legal precedent stories in which Elijah teaches by his actions. Six of these are part of the group in which he stays away from someone who does not behave rightly.

We find close equivalents to two of Neusner's formal categories in Hezser's work, suggesting their general validity. Hezser's definition of a pronouncement story corresponds closely to Neusner's "narrative setting for a saying," and her "legal example story" is equivalent to Neusner's "precedent."[56] These two scholars arrive at essentially the same categories, which strongly suggests that the categories were objectively present in their material. Both these categories describe what are essentially chreia, brief accounts of a saying or action endowed with authority by an important or worthy person.

We also find another of Hezser's forms among the Elijah stories in the Bavli, the "anecdote."[57] She writes: "Anecdotes tend to feature authority figures like queens, Roman officials, patriarchs, exilarchs, and court members, and persons in conflict with them, or 'historical' personalities like Shimon b. Shetach" as well as folkloristic motifs.[58] Several Elijah stories feature important authority figures other than the prophet, others have folkloric motifs such as miraculous rescue. The story of Naḥum Ish Gamzu bringing tribute to the Roman emperor has all three.

Thus, Hezser's definition of anecdote shows us that some Elijah stories fall into a wider category in which historical figures and folktale motifs combine to create religious meaning.

In contrast to Hezser, Ben-Amos explores more specific distinctions between groups of longer stories. His dissertation, *Narrative Forms in the Haggadah*, is a structural analysis of longer aggadic—nonlegal—stories that has much in common with form criticism.[59] Ben-Amos, like Yassif, works to categorize various genres among the longer stories of the Talmud, but his generic categories are wider than Yassif's. Ben-Amos considers content in broad sense, but focuses more on structure. While Yassif's methods only serve to categorize about half of the stories, Ben-Amos's categories can distinguish more widely distributed patterns among larger groups of Elijah stories. In fact, almost all the longer stories fit into his preexisting categories. Ben-Amos defines genre as "a general framework that limits the possible pattern of the plot." These structures provide a set of formal frameworks to use as a starting point for the literary analysis of individual stories.[60] One of his categories, the legend, provides particularly useful tools for analyzing a number of longer Elijah stories.

Ben-Amos does not use folklore studies' usual definition of legend as a story about a known person or place. Furthermore, he intentionally sidesteps the ongoing debate over whether legends are believed to be true within the culture that tells them. Instead, he uses the term to describe a particular genre set apart by its structure rather than its protagonist or social role. For Ben-Amos, a legend describes the temporary abolition of the boundary between the everyday world and supernatural reality. "The supernatural" is broadly defined as the existing realm of God, angels, and miracles, on the one hand, and demons and curses, on the other, whereas "the natural" simply designates the day-to-day course of events not specifically affected by the supernatural. This contact between natural and supernatural is seen as within the range of possible events, and yet special enough to be remembered and retold.[61]

For Ben-Amos, legends have three narrative elements, intrusion, mediation, and outcome. Intrusion and outcome are always present, whereas mediation is sometimes absent. Three of Ben-Amos's four categories of legend appear among the Elijah stories:

1. Supernatural intrudes into natural reality through a mediator.
2. Natural intrudes into supernatural reality through a mediator.
3. Supernatural intrudes into natural reality through its agent.

The first two categories usually begin with a situation of lack or of ongoing crisis, such as a drought.[62] Generally the mediator between the natural and supernatural realities is a human being who prays to God for a miracle. Although the intrusion may be either positive or negative, the mediation and the outcome are nearly always positive: needed rainfalls, a sick person cured, or a curse removed. On the relatively few occasions in which Elijah plays a role as a mediator, he fits the second category in which a spiritual being appears as mediator to make possible human intervention in the supernatural reality, for example, by leading Rabbah bar Abbuha to the heavenly garden of Eden to pick leaves from the trees and acquire wealth.[63]

In the third of these categories, in which the supernatural intrudes into everyday reality through its agent, the plot often hinges on the resolution of an acute crisis, as opposed to a lack or ongoing crisis, as in the first two categories. The lack of mediation itself has a narrative function because it results from an emergency situation requiring immediate rescue.[64] A number of Elijah's appearances fall into this category, most characteristically those in which he comes in disguise to rescue rabbis from the danger of Gentile violence. Elijah also appears without disguise to catch Rav Kahana when the rabbi throws himself from a roof to avoid committing adultery (B. Kiddushin 40a). Ben-Amos's definition of legend fits the majority of the longer Elijah stories; this work will adopt it, with slight modifications.

Form Criticism in This Work

Speaking broadly, this book uses form and genre criticism in three ways. First, form criticism is a tool for conveniently categorizing any one of the thirty-nine references to Elijah in the Bavli. As we will see, some of these forms also appear in other rabbinic texts and later Elijah legends, and a few new forms emerge. Second, form criticism is necessary as a first step in analyzing groups of stories in comparison to one another. It allows one to make generalizations about how various formal groups expressed different aspects of Jewish thought and why some forms may have been chosen over others. The more specific the form, the more useful it is for this purpose. For example, the generic group of stories in which Elijah appears in disguise to rescue someone, taken as a whole, says more about shared rabbinic views of the prophet than the more diverse group of pronouncement stories in which Elijah teaches something. Third, form criticism is indispensable for doing literary analyses of individual stories, because it allows one to see how shared formal conventions serve as a framework for conceptual and rhetorical creativity.

Elijah stories in the Bavli fall into six general form-critical categories. One unique story, in Sanhedrin 63b–64a, is unimportant for understanding Elijah's overall character: it is built around a verse of Scripture and unlike any of the others in form and theme. The second category constitutes two moral exempla, and the third seven legal or moral precedent stories. Fourth, there are eight pronouncement stories, fifth, three stories that may be called extended pronouncement stories, and sixth, thirteen legends, as Ben-Amos defines them. Two additional stories share the characteristics of a pronouncement story and a legend. Other rabbinic texts contain precedent stories, pronouncement stories, and a few legends. As we will discuss in chapter 5, later Elijah stories, both written and oral, generally fall into Ben-Amos's category of legend, and interesting hybrids of exemplum and legend appear as well.

The second category, the exemplum, is a story in which an action inspired by a particular ethical or religious value constitutes the fulcrum of the plot. One of two characteristic kinds of exemplum shows how a famous rabbi's dedication to Torah study raised him from poverty and obscurity. The other kind shows how righteous action gives apparently lowly people various rewards: wealth, the power of effective prayer, or assurance of eternal life.[65] As it happens, in the Bavli one Elijah story fits each one of these two forms of exemplum. Elijah makes a cameo appearance in one of the stories about Rabbi Akiva's rise to learning and fame, and Elijah is the one who informs a certain rabbi that some apparently disreputable characters are indeed "sons of the world to come."[66] Later Elijah stories, as we will see, often echo the second form of rabbinic exemplum, showing how the apparently lowly are particularly blessed. Others constitute a new form in which a specific moral action such as generosity or faith brings Elijah to reward the human protagonist, who may be pious and is usually poor.

Another common category of story, the legal or moral precedent story, is better represented in the Bavli, with seven stories involving Elijah. They are stories in which Elijah's behavior conveys a halakhic or ethical lesson, and all but one are brief, without a developed plot. In the first of them, Elijah's behavior is alluded to as indirect proof of a legal principle. The other six instances, two of which were mentioned in the preface, fit into the generic group in which Elijah abandons someone in direct response to his behavior (B. Nedarim 50a, B. Ta'anit 22a). We will study these stories in more detail in the context of their generic group.

The fourth category, the pronouncement story, includes eight very brief stories with little or no dialogue and no mention of physical or temporal setting. They provide a narrative framework, often no more than Elijah's appearance, for a saying, sometimes a proverb. As I have noted, I include in this category even passages that state "Elijah said something to Rabbi So-and-so" because they imply a special appearance of Elijah.[67] In contrast, the fifth category, the extended pronouncement story, has three stories with dialogue that contributes to the meaning of the saying rather than merely framing it. In Bavli Berakhot, for example, Rabbi Yossi meets Elijah in the ruins of Jerusalem. His dialogue with the prophet weaves legal precedents and theological material about what God calls out in the ruins and what God says when he hears Israel pray in synagogues and houses of study. In these stories, dialogue is far more prominent than action, and they end with a pronouncement rather than a specific result or failure to achieve that result. These stories have tension and resolution, but not in the same way as legends, whose tension is resolved by a change in the material circumstances of the human protagonist.[68]

The sixth category, that of legend, has thirteen stories. They correspond closely to Ben-Amos's definition of legend, which means they are set at a particular time and often in a particular place, in contrast to pronouncement stories. In nine of the thirteen stories Elijah's speech or actions are the pivotal supernatural intervention that resolves the tension of the plot, whereas in the remaining four Elijah is not the main supernatural actor, but provides information that helps the plot along.[69] In legends there is a distinct beginning, and usually a distinct middle and end. The beginning lays out an initial privation, problem, or crisis. The middle recounts the intervention of the supernatural realm into the natural or vice versa. The end describes a concrete change in the initial situation, a change always implied by the intervention.

Two Elijah stories are on the border between pronouncement stories and legends. In one, a pronouncement story featuring Elijah provides the explanation and conclusion to a legend whose actual events occurred in a previous generation. The other, discussed in more detail in chapter 3, describes a successful human intervention into the supernatural realm. Elijah gives a human being, Rabbah bar Shila, opportunity to voice his defense of Rabbi Meir and God responds positively to that defense.[70] Two more stories differ slightly from Ben-Amos's legend form but still fit into the general category of legend as used here. In them the intervention of the human into the supernatural realm, although initially promising success, is not allowed to remain in place by God because, if it were allowed to do so, humans would change the current order of the universe. In Ketubot 77b Rabbi Joshua ben

Levi steals the knife of the angel of death, but he is not allowed to keep it, and in Bava Meẓia 85b Rabbi Judah the Prince tries to force the coming of the Messiah, but, as we know, fails.

At this stage of describing the present work's form-critical methodology, I recall a saying popularized by the scientist and philosopher Gregory Bateson, "the map is not the territory."[71] Even the best set of formal distinctions will never be a perfect fit for the stories they seek to define. More general categories will fit more easily, with fewer exceptions, but, like floppy, oversized clothing, will be less successful in delineating the contours of the text underneath. More specific formal categories will inevitably give rise to exceptions and borderline cases.

The six general categories here described—the legend, the pronouncement story, and so on—fit all the stories. Nevertheless, they are not as helpful as the generic categories used by Yassif for discussing the interaction between style and traditional forms in particular stories. These "generic" groupings are more specific than the formal categories and overlap with them. They are useful because they highlight specific themes, detailed plot structures, and verbal formulae. In fact, this kind of analysis shows us that two generic groups are used only for Elijah stories in the Bavli, highlighting the prophet's unique character. These three generic groups, which together include twenty-one stories in the Bavli (and one in the Yerushalmi) were mentioned in the preface and are discussed in detail in chapter 4, so I will only name them here.

The first generic group contains the six precedent stories in which Elijah stays away from a particular person because of some failing on his part. The second group consists of the six instances of Elijah appearing in disguise—in all but one instance to rescue a deserving Rabbi. His appearance is always marked with the same phrase, "appeared to him as" (אדמי ליה כ-), which the Bavli uses only to describe the appearance of a supernatural being either beneficent or malignant. The third generic group is somewhat broader and probably includes two genres in Yassif's sense. It is made up of the ten instances in which Elijah appears in order to teach special or secret information.[72] All of these stories contain the root שכח, to "find" or "meet," and seven out of ten of them start with the phrase "Rabbi So-and-so found Elijah," and continue with the rabbi asking Elijah a question, a question Elijah always answers, often in surprising ways.

As we have discussed, dividing stories by formal and generic category allows one to consider the meaning of groups of stories, and the generic groups themselves shed light on commonly held beliefs about Elijah because they are not the creation of any one storyteller or author. Generic categories and their motifs also suggest other lines of inquiry. What does Elijah's appearance in disguise have in common with the appearance of other supernatural figures in disguise, appearances expressed with the same formula used for Elijah? Form-critical and generic categories are also invaluable for doing oral-formulaic and other literary analyses because they describe the verbal tropes and conventions that stories use as building blocks. Knowing these conventions is especially important when one comes across a story that plays with them, even using them in ways contrary to their characteristic meaning in other stories. The brief story of Rabbi Yossi and Elijah in the preface, in which the rabbi criticizes Elijah for losing his temper, is a good example.

ELIJAH, FOLKLORE STUDIES, AND FORM CRITICISM

The unique qualities of the Elijah stories and their spiritual dimension have impressed many students of rabbinic literature. No study thus far, however, has succeeded in giving a complete, yet nuanced, view of Elijah's several related roles in rabbinic times. This work takes a new approach in defining form-critical and generic groups of Elijah stories, leading to better observations on widely shared rabbinic beliefs about the prophet. More general form-critical categories of story that appear in the Elijah material, such as pronouncement stories and legends, help one see how Elijah is related to other important figures, such as rabbinic teachers or other supernatural mediators. The chapter on Elijah in medieval and later times will also use form criticism as tool for comparing categories of later stories with rabbinic categories, allowing for meaningful general observations about changes in the tradition.

Form criticism alone, however, does not provide much positive guidance for analyzing the literary style of orally derived material. Chapter 2 will address this issue, showing how oral-formulaic studies can elucidate the relationship between formal recitation and writing in rabbinic society and help us understand the artistry of the Talmud's orally derived texts.

ORAL-FORMULAIC STUDIES
AND THE CULTURE OF THE BAVLI

The first chapter has laid out why the Elijah stories are worth studying. This chapter continues to discuss how best to study them. The first section makes clear that the prevalence of oral teaching and learning in the world of the Rabbis is important for understanding legendary narrative in the Babylonian Talmud. The second section, "Why Folklore Studies Are Useful in Interpreting Rabbinic Narrative," describes how folklore and oral-formulaic studies help us interpret individual stories within their wider cultural context. The third section summarizes how the book's methodology combines comparative approaches with form-critical, oral-formulaic, and literary analyses.

THE ORAL-TRADITIONAL CONTEXT OF THE BABYLONIAN TALMUD

The boundaries between oral performance and written literature are more complex and flexible than they might seem. This is particularly true for societies such as that of rabbinic Judaism, which are literate, but in which important traditions circulate primarily orally, and artistically polished composition is done with no or little use of writing. As Ruth Finnegan writes in reference to contemporary cultures:

> There are, of course, ways in which oral literature clearly does differ from written literature—chiefly, I consider, in the matter of its being *performed*—but to speak as if there is a definite break between them is an exaggeration and a misleading one. The two terms are, I would argue, relative ones, and to assign a given piece unequivocally to either one category or the other—as if they were self contained or mutually exclusive boxes—can distort the nature of the evidence.[1]

Finnegan provides numerous examples of the overlap between oral and written work, such as the use of notes in oral performance. She reminds us, for example, how highly literate African and African American preachers use preaching as an oral art form, employing traditional performance techniques to present their interpretations of the biblical text[2]—as the ancient Rabbis once did as well.

Understanding Talmudic stories in an oral-traditional context requires one to consider several issues. One needs some understanding of ancient literary culture in general, which was significantly more oral than our own, and rabbinic culture, which was even more orally oriented than elite Greco-Roman culture. Finally, one needs to understand how the transmission of aggadic, nonlegal narrative differed from the transmission of halakhah—legal traditions and discussions. Both were largely oral, but aggadic narrative was often transmitted more like ordinary, unmemorized folklore. First, however, we will turn to the question of how to understand the Rabbis' relationship to popular, informally transmitted folklore.

Who Are the Folk?

The title of this section quotes a short essay by Alan Dundes in which he stylishly demonstrates that everyone is part of one or more folk groups: social groupings in which people relate face to face and share stories and jokes. Schools, professions, even religious orders have their own oral traditions.[3] University legends circulate about the famous professors of the past and present, just as legends once circulated about the Sages. My father, a professor emeritus, has noted how some absent-minded professor stories told at his institution have migrated from a late colleague to himself, since both of them attract the theme of absentmindedness. Similarly, certain figures in rabbinic circles attracted certain types of legends. Elisha ben Abuya, called Aḥer, "Other," attracted stories of apostasy, whereas Rabbi Joshua ben Levi attracted stories of piety, goodness, and visitation by Elijah.

Given that the answer to "who are the folk?" is clearly "everybody who ever lived, including the Sages of the Talmud," we move on to the question of how rabbinic folklore relates to popular folklore. Today, many see belief in marvels as a hallmark of popular religion: do the miracles in rabbinic stories come from "folk" sources? In this respect, late antiquity was very different from our own day. Popular stories—we might call them ancient urban legends—are reported in elite histories as facts rather than rumors. Josephus, for example, cites a cow giving birth to a lamb in the Temple court as one of the portents predicting the destruction of Jerusalem.[4] We also find that all levels of all societies believed that a powerful person, whether a rabbi or a Roman emperor, might possess supernatural powers. Roman historians recount miraculous healings performed by Emperor Vespasian (the destroyer of Jerusalem, of all people) at an Egyptian shrine.[5]

Rabbinic culture may in fact have been closer to that of ordinary Jews than Greco-Roman elite culture was to that of their uneducated compatriots. Jewish society in Babylonia, although highly stratified, lacked the vast gulfs between urban and rural, slave and free, that were part of the Gentile Hellenistic world. Though they had earlier separated themselves from uneducated Jews by dress and practice, the Rabbis gained religious leadership of most of Babylonian Jewish society by the early post-Talmudic period. They did so through persuasion, not physical policing, because they rarely had power to employ the latter, at least on purely religious issues. That their persuasion eventually worked suggests that their perspectives and interests were in relative harmony with those of ordinary Jews. Furthermore, the Rabbis' work made them part of the society around them, rather than a monastic class: they were landowners, brewers, merchants, and civil judges.[6] Given their connections with all of Jewish society, it comes as no surprise that the Rabbis told some of the same popular legends as other Jews and made them their own.

Some stories or plot motifs in the Bavli may have come from non-Jewish to Jewish folklore, then from popular performance to rabbinic performance, and finally been reduced to written form. We find a possible example of this process in a Talmudic discussion of whether the dead are aware of the lives of the living (B. Berakhot 18b). In order to support the view that they are, the passage cites two stories of rabbis communicating with the dead and then a tale that seems popular in origin. No rabbis or "disciples of the Sages" appear; the hero is only "a certain pious man" (ההוא חסידא). This virtuous man is driven to the graveyard because his wife yells at him for generosity to a beggar, but the theme of charity plays a small role, for the dominant issue becomes how the spirits' knowledge helps him have a good harvest, an issue common to any peasant society. Most strikingly, the man in the story loses his ghostly source of knowledge when his wife convinces him to tell her about it. This plot motif, in which a wife nags her husband to reveal a secret he should not, is common in both European and Middle Eastern folktales.[7] Nevertheless, this legend, apparently popular in theme and content, is used side by side with legends that are clearly rabbinic by the editors of the Talmud to support a point—that souls can remain conscious in the grave—they thought important and arguably true.[8] Like Greco-Roman elites, the Rabbis considered popular stories to be useful sources of knowledge.

We also find informally transmitted narratives that probably originated with the Rabbis. They have forms and themes typical of oral folk narratives and often appear in several versions, suggesting oral transmission, but their subject matter is particularly relevant to rabbinic circles. Stories concerning the relationships between rabbis are likely candidates for this category, for example, the one where Elijah reconciles Rabbi Judah the Patriarch and Rabbi Ḥiyya by appearing in the form of the latter and curing Rabbi Judah's thirteen-year-old toothache.[9] Of course, a legend like this might also have appealed to ordinary Jews, and been told by them, just as many legends of the marketplace or the nonrabbinic synagogue appealed to the Rabbis. As Werner H. Kelber points out, different kinds of verbal performance can and do appear in more than one social setting, making uncritical searches for single life situations (*Sitz im Leben*) problematic.[10]

Thus the Rabbis participated in the traditions of Jewish folklore and had a folkloric tradition of their own. But what effect did oral performance have on their written work? And what relationship did their folkloric traditions have to the narratives in the Talmud? These related questions can be addressed in two ways. First of all, one can analyze the plots, motifs, and formulae of stories, highlighting the oral-traditional features of rabbinic narrative in order to show the stylistic influence that oral performance had on these orally derived written texts. In the present work, this approach appears in the first chapter's treatment of form criticism and in this chapter's discussion of folklore and oral-formulaic studies. Second, one can look for clues about the relationship between oral and written expression in the lives of the Rabbis in order to make informed guesses on how much orally derived content and style characterize rabbinic works.[11] This is the approach of the next sections of this chapter.

The Relationship Between Literacy and Orality in Greco-Roman Antiquity

All literature of late antiquity, if not orally composed, was often influenced by oral forms such as the rhetor's speech, the preacher's sermon, or the storyteller's tale. The shared oral environment meant that the same stories might circulate among various popular and elite settings. In our day the wealthy may enjoy the same television programs as the poor; in ancient Rome those who were rich might hire popular professional storytellers to perform at private gatherings.[12] Furthermore, whether ancient texts were transcribed from oral performance or derived from written models, they often employ techniques associated with orally derived literature such as parallelism and punning. Thus these obvious stylistic markers cannot tell one how directly a text may have been derived from oral sources. There are, however, more ways of telling whether a text is best interpreted as an orally derived text. As we have seen, some of these signs are internal, based on structure and use of language and kinds of variation among parallel stories or sources. Other signs are social. There are now numerous studies of how speech and writing interacted in other ancient Mediterranean societies that can aid our reconstruction of the oral-traditional context of rabbinic works.

Many writers stress the oral influence on even the most sophisticated written text in antiquity, observing that acts of speaking and writing were used and understood differently than they are today. As Walter J. Ong puts it, "In antiquity the most literate cultures remained committed to the spoken word to a degree which appears to our . . . sensibilities somewhat incredible or even perverse."[13] Even in late antiquity, when writing was used more in the conduct of daily life, the written word often continued to have a different and less controlling role than in our own day. The predominantly oral environment of late antiquity meant that the act of putting traditions into writing did not eliminate their continuing circulation in authoritative oral form.[14]

Furthermore, even the acts of writing and reading had more in common with oral performance than they do today. The normal mode of formal written composition was dictation, but even solitary writers spoke as they wrote, whether they were composing or copying text. In addition, as is widely known, almost every reader read aloud. In fact, it would have been difficult to read at more than speaking speed because of the way manuscripts were written. Words were usually run together, often abbreviated, and there were no sentence or paragraph markers. In short, the visual appearance of a book gave no clue to its structure on either the general or detailed level. Instead of visual cues, ancient writers used oral/aural markers to structure the manuscript. Parallelism, change in pattern of expression, and formulae all played a role in making the text understandable to those who read it aloud and heard it read.[15] Given all of this, it comes as no surprise that throughout antiquity and into the Middle Ages many readers had only the literacy to sound out a text and learn it by heart, the way many musicians use a musical score.

One might sum up the difference between late antique Greek and Latin literature and our own by saying that although the former was not usually "oral traditional" it was oral in the sense that it was written to be spoken—often performed—and heard, rather than to be read silently. Thus, even Ruth Finnegan's basic distinction between spoken and written literature—that the former is performed while the latter is not—fails to do justice to the complexity of the "oral-literary" world of Western late antiquity. When applied to rabbinics, these studies of Greco-Roman antiquity discourage us from uncritically applying the modern dichotomy between oral and written communication. However, as shown in the following section, rabbinic circles were more orally oriented than those of Greek- and Latin-speaking literati, and their literature is likely to be more orally derived than classical texts.

Literacy and Orality in Rabbinic Society

In Greek and Latin literature, speaking played a significant supporting role to writing, but rabbinic literature stems from an environment in which writing played a supporting role to speaking. Much of my doctoral thesis's description of the Talmud as orally derived literature parallels work of Yaakov Elman and Martin Jaffee that became available to me after I started my research. My own picture of the Bavli as an orally derived document was confirmed by the work of these two scholars who themselves studied different rabbinic texts, thus providing a replication of results that one rarely finds in the humanities. As Martin Jaffee writes, the transition from Second Temple versions of Judaism to rabbinic culture in the second and third centuries of the Common Era saw an eclipse of scribal authority. The culture of textual experts ended, to be replaced by the Sages' "orally mediated textual tradition," embodied by the individual rabbinic teacher who grounded his authority in "the mastery of wisdom heard from a chain of teachers." The ideology and theology of Oral Torah given at Sinai, elaborated on by the Amoraim of the third century, serves to explain and celebrate the already oral focus of rabbinic learning, which was based in the inherited teachings and exemplary lives of living Sages.[16]

Oral rabbinic learning *was* sometimes written down. Students of the Sages wrote notes to help themselves study in both tannaitic and later times.[17] In addition, there were some private books of halakhah, sometimes referred to as "secret scrolls," emphasizing their nonpublic nature, and the Bavli also occasionally mentions "a book of aggadah." The official view of rabbinic society, however, was that the oral law should be taught orally. There are Talmudic passages that disapprove committing even brief points of halakhah to writing, for example, in letters,[18] but most passages suggest that the majority of the Sages accepted some use of private books of Oral Law. In fact, one passage deliberately highlights the tension between the normative teaching that Oral Torah should never be written and the actual practice of respected Sages: "Were not R. Yoḥanan and Reish Lakish accustomed to looking at a book of *aggadah* on the Sabbath?"[19]

The same page of Talmud just quoted conveys that what was given in written form (the Written Torah—the Pentateuch) should not be recited from memory, and what is transmitted in oral form (the Oral Torah—rabbinic teachings) should not be read from a book.[20] The meaning of the first part of this saying provides a clue to the second part. The Rabbis and their students never recited written Scripture from memory in public liturgical settings, but they knew it well and must have recited passages from memory in informal teaching situations. The Oral Torah, the mirror image of the Written, was never read from books while teaching or lecturing, but individuals wrote private collections of notes for informal consultation.[21] This made for a complex interplay between oral and written material in which, as Alexander shows, informal legal notes and unofficial midrash collections were more fluidly transmitted than most written texts,[22] and memorized legal dicta were transmitted with greater consistency than most oral traditions.

The language used to describe the activities of the study house provides a useful gauge of the degree to which rabbinic study was conducted orally. Sifrei Deuteronomy, composed at roughly the same time as the Mishnah in 200 CE, states that fluency in oral teachings is precisely what defines a "disciple of the Sages."[23] In *Rabbinic Instruction in Sasanian Babylonia* David Goodblatt surveys the formulae used to describe the teaching, learning, and conversation that took place in rabbinic circles. These fixed forms suggest that the activities of the Rabbis and their disciples were overwhelmingly oral.[24] Goodblatt's commonest "verbs of academic activity" describing instruction by a rabbi or study in his presence are *teni* (תני), to recite a tradition, with more than one hundred instances, and particularly *amar* (אמר), to say, explain, or ask, with thousands of instances. All but one of the remaining formulae necessarily or at least usually refer to oral teaching and learning. The sole exception, not surprisingly, refers to reading the biblical text.[25] And, as Elman points out, the Talmud has no "terminology for copying, arranging, editing, and redaction."[26]

The following passage shows the crucial relationship between oral study and rabbinic discipleship.

R. Ḥisda said to the rabbis "I want to tell you something, but I am afraid that you will leave and go away: Whoever learns from [only] one master will never achieve success." They left him and came before Rabbah. He [the latter] said to them, "That saying applies only to *sevara* [explanations of the sources], but with regard to *gemara* [formulated traditions] it is preferable [to learn] from [only one] master—in order that the traditions remain uniform."[27]

If any official written source of formulated traditions had existed, it would not have been so important to learn formulated traditions from only one teacher.

Careful textual study also indicates that legal material was transmitted orally. Yaakov Elman's study on parallels between legal traditions in the Bavli and in the Tosefta shows that in amoraic Babylonia at least, traditions found in the Tosefta circulated as individual oral units. In fact, Elman writes, they "bear the same relationship to their Toseftan parallels that some English and Scottish ballads do to their more 'literary' forerunners." The Babylonian traditions, in comparison to their parallels, tend to condensed language, "transpositions of phrases and lines . . . variations in names, and substitutions of one word for another," all characteristic of oral transmission.[28] Jaffee's analysis of parallel passages in the Mishnah and the Tosefta leads him to somewhat different conclusions for the land of Israel in the early second century. Here, he holds, oral and written teachings interacted in ways far too complex to reconstruct in specific instances. Rabbinic legal texts were written, memorized, and then transmitted orally, perhaps changing in the process. Conversely, oral texts might be carefully arranged for easy memorization by following written exemplars.[29] Whether Elman and Jaffee's differing conclusions stem from their methods and assumptions or from the different texts they study, both agree that oral transmission played a substantial role in transmitting legal traditions.

Aggadah, nonlegal tradition, traveled orally as well and was performed in both formal and informal oral settings. An important venue for the formal performance of midrashic aggadah was the synagogue. The Targums, copied down from or inspired by the extemporaneous Aramaic translations of the Pentateuch performed in synagogues, are rich sources of aggadah, some of it drawn from folklore.[30] Sermons, too, were occasions of oral performance in which the preacher and his audience had a shared collection of traditions and expectations.

These preachers and audiences could be either rabbinic or nonrabbinic. In Babylonia a rabbinic context for the public performance of aggadic traditions was the *pirka*. This was a public lecture, perhaps including a discussion session, containing both aggadah and parables and attended by ordinary Jews as well as rabbis. Both scholars and ignorant people (*ammei haaretz*), including in one instance a humble laundry worker, are said to have come to hear.[31] In order to make it easy for ordinary working people to attend, these gatherings might be held on holidays; there are also at least five records of a pirka occurring on Shabbat. Altogether there

are about ten references to popular attendance and eighteen references to attendance by scholars. At least some of the time, scholars and ordinary people would
have attended the same pirka, and when they did it may have been an occasion for
the exchange of rabbinic and popular midrash and legends.[32]

There are also references to informal performances of religious and secular narrative in the Talmud, probably reflecting the situations in which storytelling took
place. A teacher might tell jokes before starting his lesson. A cycle of legends about
the destruction of Jerusalem is introduced by a scene in which three rabbis sitting
together ask each other if one of them has heard anything interesting.[33] Ben-Amos
writes that, even when specific occasions of performance are not recorded, "The
numerous quotations of popular proverbs scattered throughout the Talmuds . . . [and]
the many anonymous traditions . . . often repeated in different versions . . . attest
to a dynamic informal exchange of oral tradition."[34]

In short, both the Palestinian and Babylonian Talmuds are written texts that
value orality, and that overwhelmingly record events and situations in which people
speak, rather than those in which they read or write. The idea of "repressed literacy"
a concept used by Ian Henderson to describe the *Didache*, a collection of early
Christian traditions, is also valuable for understanding the Talmud.[35] In fact, reading
certain passages in Henderson's article while substituting *Talmud* for *Didache*, suggests possible reasons for the way in which the Talmud presents its material.

> This singular absence from [the Talmud] of "literacy events" and its contrasting
> emphasis on "orality events"—even in the face of its own . . . textuality—indicate
> not only a strongly oral sensibility: so consistent an avoidance of literary symbols
> must be taken as evidence for a conscious, programmatic option for oral categories.
>
> . . . [The Talmud, in citing multiple individual authorities, presents its sources] as
> voices, audible and to some extent questionable. By implicating the reader in its own
> oral sensibility [the Talmud] suggests the possibility of creating or re-creating an
> atmosphere in which the variety of normative language may be simultaneously and
> cumulatively . . . maintained. This deliberate recreation in writing of a specifically
> oral situation . . . gives [the Talmud] its fictive quality, but the fiction is grounded in a
> genuinely, if relatively, oral attitude. [The Talmud] is not only orally written; it is [in
> part] *about* orality as a normative hermeneutical [and legal] strategy.[36]

Thus the Talmud, in recording countless examples of teaching and study,
social events and informal exchanges, all taking place without reading or writing, implicitly models an oral ideal of learning. This sharpens the image of the

Talmud as orally derived literature, although it cannot be used to prove that any *particular* passage was composed or transmitted orally.[37] While a number of scholars have discussed the Talmud's explicit advocacy of reciting rather than reading the Oral Torah, fewer have considered the implications of its global emphasis on the spoken word. The Talmud's preference for recording oral communication makes the whole document, and not merely selected anecdotes, a testimony to the fundamentally oral culture of the Sages: the Bavli reenacts "Oral Torah" in written form.

The oral nature of rabbinic learning continues in some sense even after texts are fixed in writing. The usually cryptic discourse of the rabbinic texts themselves, their air of being brief mnemonics for a larger dialogue, means they cannot be read fluently and silently. Foley often calls ancient texts libretti, underlining both how static and silent they are in comparison to actual performance and also suggesting the possibility of their imaginative reanimation.[38] In the case of rabbinic literature, as Jaffee points out, the oral reanimation of texts is not merely an aesthetic choice, but an intellectual necessity, the only proper response to the way in which they were composed:

> The written collections of materials were composed in deep interactive relationship to orally performed versions, just as orally mastered, memorized texts, would commonly be tailored for preservation in written documents. . . . The anthologies that reflect the written pole of this process [of movement between composition and performance] function both as mnemonic aids in the preservation of the material and as springboards for restoring textually fixed traditions to the aural/oral world analysis and debate. . . . It is in the return of writing to speech that rabbinic texts achieve their literary purpose and gain completion as "works" that are, of course, constantly being rewritten as they are studied and performed.[39]

Halakhah, Aggadah and Folklore

So far we have considered the oral-traditional roots of rabbinic literature without distinguishing between halakhic traditions and aggadic ones. The previous section established that the halakhah of the study house, despite its technical subject matter and structured transmission, was a significantly oral tradition, but it differs from folklore as it is usually understood. Nonlegal traditions, "aggadah," were transmitted considerably more informally, and folklore studies has different techniques to bring to the study of these traditions.

In rabbinic times the term *aggadah* (or *haggadah*) referred only to nonlegal interpretation of Scripture. By the early Middle Ages, however, the meaning of the term had been extended to include any nonlegal narrative in rabbinic sources, whether a midrashic story, a legend, a fable, or a tall tale, and this is how it is used today.[40] Halakhah and aggadah differ by definition; one has legal significance, and the other does not. This obvious distinction may have bearing on whether they were transmitted with equal fidelity, as halakhah prescribes or forbids behavior while aggadah exhorts and even entertains. Many authors have remarked generally that most aggadic traditions are transmitted more freely than halakhic ones, but, to my knowledge, the evidence for this has never been presented systematically.

In examining questions of transmission, one can distinguish between aggadah and halakhah, and among different types of aggadah, in three ways: one can examine what rabbinic documents themselves say about how traditions were handed down, one can compare variant versions of traditions, and one can examine texts' formal characteristics. In the preceding section we discussed indications of oral transmission in the verbal formulae the Babylonian Talmud uses to describe study, teaching, and preaching. In this section we will examine the Bavli's explicit references to how the transmission of traditions, particularly halakhic ones, took place and then compare the ways in which halakhah and aggadah were transmitted. Some of these differences can be found by observing how halakhah and aggadah were discussed by the Rabbis, but more are evident in the differences between aggadah and halakhah in both content and literary form. Finally, we will touch on the existence of variant versions, both within and between each of the two Talmuds, because that is a good indicator of how much traditions have changed during transmission.

Gerhardsson's *Memory and Manuscript* draws together many Talmudic traditions about the transmission of halakhah.[41] While Gerhardsson's aim was to prove that early Christian traditions were passed down with the same fidelity as later rabbinic ones, in the process he compiled a comprehensive anthology of the Bavli's own description of how legal traditions were transmitted. The Talmud states that all students of the Rabbis ought to know the Mishnah by heart, saying that "if you see a pupil for whom the study of Talmud is heavy as iron, that is because his Mishnah is not fluent."[42] The Tanna, the professional reciter of halakhic traditions, was expected to know more, including halakhic midrashim and extramishnaic tannaitic sources. The Tanna's recited text was not a performance based on a dynamic and fluid tradition, but was critically examined by the rabbi and his students, and at times rejected as invalid and then emended. Gerhardsson observes that the conscious correction or harmonization of tannaitic and amoraic dicta by the Rabbis leads to a distinctive relationship between parallel versions of passages. They exhibit a mixture of extensive literal agreement and sudden omissions, additions, and revisions.[43]

Gerhardsson takes the Bavli's self-report as fact and therefore probably exaggerates both the exclusive orality and the accuracy of halakhic traditions. Nevertheless, his conclusion that halakhic study was conducted orally accords with Goodblatt's portrayal of rabbinic instruction as well as with the conclusions derived from the form criticism of legal material.[44] This relatively faithful transmission of halakhic passages makes it possible to separate traditions by age using form criticism. Baruch Bokser, for example, shows how certain turns of phrase ascribed to early Amora Samuel were preserved remarkably faithfully, though not unchanged, throughout the generations of Amoraim and are still discernible in today's Babylonian Talmud.[45]

The word-for-word transmission of halakhah is comparable to that of memorized traditions in contemporary societies that are predominantly oral. Studies of modern oral history have found that memorized traditions sometimes allow one to reconstruct their original version by comparing the extant variants, just as one does for ancient manuscripts. On the other hand, one cannot reconstruct the original of a tradition that was never memorized, and indeed there often is no one original version. In addition, when the original source of a nonmemorized tradition is available in writing, it often varies widely from the orally circulating version(s).[46]

Most aggadic traditions were not memorized. In fact, the main error that Gerhardsson makes in *Memory and Manuscript* (aside from directly superimposing rabbinic Jewish practices onto prerabbinic Christianity) is that of assuming that *narrative* New Testament traditions—which one might call Christian aggadah—might have been transmitted the way that *legal* rabbinic traditions were. The laborious process of memorization described among the students of the sages was used for halakhic traditions, not aggadic ones.[47] When Morton Smith points out the differences between rabbinic literature and the Gospels in his review of *Memory and Manuscript*, three of his five points also apply to the difference between halakhic and much aggadic material in the Bavli. First, parallels between aggadic narratives, like gospel parallels, "generally show freer divergence, especially in rewording." Second, the longer aggadic narratives are told for homiletic purposes, like the New Testament stories. Furthermore, because both aggadic legends in the Bavli and New Testament stories require at least some resemblance to natural speech to be effective, they make less use than halakhic traditions do of mnemonic formulae: stereotyped patterns of question and answer, numbered points, and so on. Third, aggadic narratives, like the stories about Jesus, are likely to include miraculous material—including, of course, the appearance of Elijah.[48]

If anything, legends about Jesus may have been transmitted more formally and with more attention to accuracy than Elijah legends were. Despite a number of rabbinic traditions about what to learn and how to learn it, few of these passages mention aggadic nonmidrashic learning—and none mention stories of the sages. The legendary catalogue of Rabbi Yohanan ben Zakkai's learning, for example, includes "details of the Torah, details of the scribes . . . analogies . . . the speech of the ministering angels, the speech of palm trees, fullers' parables, and fox fables,"[49] but not legends of the Sages. I know of no statement in a rabbinic text that implies that longer and more complex stories about Rabbis were either formally memorized (like halakhah) or recorded in special written collections (like midrash aggadah) before their inclusion in rabbinic documents.

Numerous scholars have noted this distinction between legal and narrative material in rabbinic literature. Strack and Stemberger compare the rabbinic transmission of aggadic traditions to contemporary societies in which each performance of a tradition is a "'re-creation,'" leading at times to considerable change, especially early in its transmission.[50] Not all aggadah, though, was transmitted with equal freedom. Richard Kalmin notes a distinction between long and short stories. He writes: "Very likely the authors and transmitters of lengthy stories had freedom to . . . distort or invent facts to serve the purposes of their narrative and the moral, religious and polemical message they wished to teach." In contrast, "authors and transmitters of . . . briefer stories . . . worked under more rigid constraints."[51]

Shorter stories were probably transmitted more faithfully because they were transmitted within the context of halakhic traditions, which were, as we have seen, at least intended to be passed on word for word. Such stories generally either report court cases or serve as legally relevant examples of behavior. Some Elijah material appearing in a halakhic context is very brief, including legal dicta transmitted by Elijah to certain individuals, and several stories sketched in bare outline to illustrate points in legal discussions, such as the account of a "certain pious man" whom Elijah stopped visiting after he built a gatehouse and thus denied the poor direct access to his courtyard (Bava Batra 7b). Unfortunately, these briefer passages do not have parallels, so that one cannot check how much their variants diverge.

In contrast to the short passages, the longer Elijah stories, like other longer stories, often vary extensively. The two stories of Nahum Ish Gamzu's trip to Rome for example, found in different tractates of the Bavli, follow the same plot, but are recounted in considerably different language, recalling the freer divergence in rewording noted by Morton Smith in reference to the New Testament (B. Ta'anit 21a and B. Sanhedrin 108b–109a). Variants between texts may differ even more. One story, that of Rabbi Judah the Patriarch's thirteen-year-long toothache and its cure, is woven together in the Yerushalmi with the tradition of rivalry between Rabbi Judah and Rabbi Ḥiyya; Elijah brings peace between the Sages by performing the cure in the form of Rabbi Ḥiyya. In the Bavli, however, this story appears without Rabbi Ḥiyya or Elijah, although Rabbi Judah's interminable toothache and its unusual beginning are the same.[52]

To sum up, legends about the appearance of Elijah, especially the longer ones, were transmitted orally and informally, the way in which folkloric legends in most other societies were and are transmitted. Furthermore, legends like those of Elijah were probably transmitted even more informally than midrash aggadah: rabbinic texts do not recognize such legends as a subject of study, or name them as a distinct genre. Thus we can freely apply the insights of both folklore studies and oral-formulaic studies to the rabbinic Elijah legends because of their informal transmission.

WHY FOLKLORE STUDIES ARE USEFUL IN INTERPRETING RABBINIC NARRATIVE

As we have seen, rabbinic society was significantly oral, and stories such as those found in the Talmud circulated informally, in speech and perhaps writing, just as orally derived traditions did in other ancient societies. Oral-formulaic and folklore studies help us understand the Elijah stories in three basic ways: they help us appreciate the style of the stories; they help us understand their social context in the still significantly oral-traditional society of Jewish late antiquity; and they help illuminate the social, legal, and spiritual role of the Elijah stories within the Judaism of the Babylonian Talmud.

The question of style is crucial to understanding rabbinic stories. One cannot treat the written stories as simple transcriptions of oral material: even if we could prove "oral composition," all we have is the texts before us. In addition, the exact transcription of narrative performance was very rare in ancient times; it is common only in modern ethnography, since the invention of the tape recorder. Rather, the Bavli's Elijah stories are orally derived literature, neither purely oral nor exclusively literary. Oral-formulaic studies emphasize how forms of written

and oral expression overlap when certain genres are sometimes recited and sometimes written. Following this approach, the present work sees Elijah stories as
orally derived in a general sense and analyzes them in light of orally derived traditions and style.

The oral-formulaic school stems from the work of Albert Lord and his students,
such as John Miles Foley, David Bynum, and Ruth Finnegan. Its leading practitioners work with modern folklore, both memorized and recreated in performance,
and also with Greek, Anglo-Saxon, and other ancient texts, which they study as
material with roots in oral composition.[53] Although oral-formulaic studies is concerned with oral performance, its approach differs from that of the performance-
centered school in the material it usually analyzes as well as in its methods. It
tends to study oral forms, such as epic poetry, which are performed by specialized
traditional artists who are conscious of their own rhetorical technique, and generally does not study the most informal oral forms such as jokes.

John Foley, a leading exponent of oral-formulaic studies, is particularly aware
of the paradox of seeking for oral performance in ancient texts. He concludes that
in most cases a text's composition was simply too complex to say in what propor-
tions it is "oral" or "written."[54] Instead, Foley points to the observable differences
between conventional literary texts and those with oral roots. By the standards of
modern literature, with its emphasis on originality, the way that orally derived literature recycles plots and phrases may seem sterile or clichéd.[55] Within Talmudic
narratives, for example, we find sets of stories, such as Elijah appearing in disguise
to rescue a rabbi from Gentiles, that have many close parallels in plot and often in
exact wording.[56] While these parallels may be useful tools for assessing the historical prevalence of particular beliefs or attitudes, it is hard to know what to do with
them in literary analysis.

In Foley's view, metonomy, understood as the traditional connotations of form,
is the key to understanding an oral or orally derived work. Metonomy is generally
defined as the rhetorical device in which one thing poetically stands for a related
one, as in "the pen is mightier than the sword." Foley widens its use to convey how
certain phrases and structures are supercharged with meaning within an oral-traditional context, thus explaining the use and value of patterned repetition in orally
derived works.[57] Form-critical and generic categories help us identify the building blocks, the conventions, with which the creators of the Elijah stories worked.
The repetition of formulaic phrases, motifs, and plot structures are not clichés but
rather evocations of traditional concepts and characters carrying overtones still
barely audible, though clear enough to their original audiences or readers.[58] These

evocations raise expectations the performer or author may sometimes overturn, creating as much shock as complete departure from conventional style can do in a modern work.[59]

Thus Talmudic narrative might better be compared to a traditional lyric form, such as the Shakespearian sonnet, than to modern fiction. In a contemporary short story, original plotting and diction create excitement, whereas in the rabbis' stories, as in Renaissance sonnets, the elegant terseness of language and the witty and poignant play with traditional ideas creates similar excitement. Someone analyzing the religious sonnets of John Donne, for example, needs to know both the strictly formal conventions of the genre—how the ideas developed in three four-line stanzas are summed up, often with a twist, in the final couplet—and also be aware of Donne's startling choice to transform the usual romantic-erotic themes of the genre into evocations of religious faith.

One may ask how reading with attention to metonomy differs from ordinary close reading of rabbinic texts: is it only a new name for something sensitive readers have been doing since before the advent of modern scholarship? No, and yes. One must stress that metonomy differs significantly from literary allusion, which, Bradbury writes, "makes use of [a written] source's network of meanings, its cultural prestige, and perhaps its verbal aptness." Metonymic associations activate a network of meanings the audience experiences in relation to a "multiform tradition" of overlapping associations.[60] To put it another way, metonomy is holographic, each part conjuring the whole, whereas literary references are linear. That is, in identifying literary references, careful readers seek to determine which specific prior text provides the quotation or allusion. In contrast, folklore scholars can bring in a variety of sources from different times and places to grasp how a particular reference calls to mind the "multiform tradition" shared by performer and audience. Thus, reading for metonomy differs significantly from traditional, more linear ways of analyzing literary texts.

On the other hand—the "yes" side—methods of close reading and cross-cultural comparison by scholars of rabbinics from Lieberman in the mid-twentieth century to Boyarin today implicitly reflect many insights explicitly described by oral-formulaic studies. Reading with attention to metonomy builds on the unspoken postulates behind much close reading of rabbinic texts. It also emphasizes how traditional associations create emotional and aesthetic effects as well as intellectual associations, allowing for new kinds of reading.

The opening formula expressing that Elijah often visited someone is an example of metonomy among our stories: It calls to mind all similar stories that go on to say that Elijah temporarily or permanently abandons someone for some fault, generally an ethical one. If a story begins with a phrase expressing frequent visits by Elijah, it always implies he will cease visiting. This is not to say that all these stories are monotonously similar. The Talmud develops narrative conventions in different directions, uses them in different redactional contexts, and sometimes overturns our expectations.

As well as giving an overall approach for analyzing the style of Talmudic stories, oral-formulaic and folklore studies show that many stylistic characteristics of rabbinic stories are also found in other orally derived narrative. Orally derived stories in general, for example, often have sentences with few or no subordinate clauses joined together by *and,* for example, "there is story about a certain scholar who learned a great deal of Mishnah and read a great deal of Bible and served the disciples of the Sages a great deal, and died when half his days had passed" (B. Shabbat 13a–b). Another stylistic marker found in both oral folklore and in the Elijah stories (as well as other stories in the Bavli) is word-for-word repetition. The ubiquitous repetitions of "he said to him . . . he said to him" serve as quotation marks in the traditionally unpunctuated text, but also resemble the style of oral forms. Other stories have word-for-word repetitions even more characteristic of oral narrative, for example, the triple repetition of "a miracle occurred," in the story recounting the rescue of Rabbi Eleazar ben Perata from Roman persecution (B Avodah Zarah 17b).

The longer narratives in the Talmud often have extended dialogue, usually considered a sign of a written work having been influenced by or derived from oral tradition.[61] Furthermore, the way the Talmud presents dialogue is characteristic of folklore or orally derived literature. It involves only two characters at a time (although occasionally one is a corporate body, like the Roman court) and serves primarily to further the plot or provide a setting for a saying, rather than to set a scene or depict character development.[62] Therefore, although dialogue in a Talmudic story may signal a stylistic relationship with legal give and take, it also indicates modeling on oral narrative style. In fact, it may be that the "docudrama" dialogues characterizing halakhic passages are themselves influenced by oral narrative style. I have found that I understand the wit and rhetorical force of the repetition and dialogue form characteristic of these stories better when I read them aloud and best when I memorize them and tell them to an audience.

Another example of orally derived style, this time in the realm of plot motif, is the story of Nahum Ish Gamzu's journey to Rome. It shows how a feckless (and completely faithful) hero triumphs with Elijah's help over those who attempt to deceive him, after which the deceivers are caught in their own trap. Even the casual reader will probably notice how much this plot resembles a folktale. It does in fact clearly follow the narrative structure discovered by Propp in his classic work on folktales, strengthening the possibility that the story of Naḥum was modeled, unconsciously or consciously, on the folktales of its time.[63]

Terseness is another characteristic of Talmudic narrative style. Stories, like legal traditions, are usually expressed with the fewest words necessary to be comprehensible (sometimes, for the modern reader, fewer!). The terseness of Talmudic narrative is undoubtedly part of the Talmud's preferred style for both legal and narrative traditions, a style that itself is influenced by oral transmission.[64] It is also a style that is common when oral prose narratives are reduced to written form. Historical anecdotes, legends, and many folktales, when not embellished by a literary author, are rarely more than several printed pages and frequently only one or two paragraphs long. Prose narrative tends to shrink when written by nonliterary authors (whether amateur or scholarly) because the person who knows the story (whether dictating or writing from memory) concentrates on the main points and skips the details in order to accommodate the slower process of writing.[65] The narratives in the Talmud, for example, or the stories of Jesus's miracles in the Synoptic Gospels, both orally derived, are far more concise than more literary works such as the Septuagint book of Tobit or the Judeo-Arabic retellings of rabbinic works in Rabbi Nissim's *Elegant Composition*. The latter books, although both have folkloric sources, present much longer and more literary reworkings of their oral material than do the two Talmuds or the Gospels.

The oral-formulaic scholar Alain Renoir provides another important tool for analyzing stories in the Talmud and later Jewish sources. He shows that one can often compare similar orally derived texts from distant times and places because oral plot motifs tend to remain stable, even over centuries. He writes, "attestations necessarily accumulate in the records and provide a rich context for works whose immediate context may be poverty-stricken." Renoir suggests the accumulation of attestations as an interpretive rather than historical tool, showing that the shared presence of a particular formula or motif can make works mutually illuminating even if the historical connection between them is unknown and unknowable.[66] The historical context of rabbinic narrative is not so much poverty-stricken as cryptic: Although there are plenty of more or less datable documents, most of them are edited collections of earlier material, and there is little or no extratextual evidence to stand beside them. Thus scholars disagree on how comparable passages in different documents, or even within the same document, are related to one another.[67]

Renoir's insight enables the student of rabbinic literature to move beyond the obvious fact that good stories travel through time and between cultures and start to look at how smaller units of plot, motifs, and stock characters may have circulated throughout the rabbinic world. Thus one can compare stories from, for example, earlier Palestinian and later Babylonian sources while, at the same time, recognizing that their historical connection remains undefined.

Furthermore, certain plots and motifs circulated throughout the Mediterranean sphere and Near East in late antiquity, transforming rabbinic traditions and being transformed within them. As we will discuss at more length in chapter 3, these are usually folktale motifs, but may include traditions of religious elites. Fischel's study of stories about the Rabbis, for example, compares the striking deeds and pithy sayings of rabbis to the striking deeds and pithy sayings of Hellenistic philosophers. This indeed suggests a common Mediterranean genre of stories about sages and holy men.[68] Galit Hasan-Rokem appears to have independently arrived at Renoir's principle in her use of narrative motifs from both the New Testament and later Jewish folklore to explore the implications of Rabbinic stories, such as one in which a woman asks to borrow something from her neighbor.[69]

Renoir's approach bridges issues of style and of cultural context as well as cross-cultural context. Thus he brings us to the second major point in this discussion of "why folklore studies are useful," which is how attention to literary and cultural context illuminates the Elijah stories. Nearly all research on ancient texts takes into account the kind of society that produced them as well as that society's political and cultural challenges. However, oral-formulaic and folklore studies particularly emphasize the way that different texts from the same or neighboring cultures can be read together to illuminate one another's rhetoric and ideas.

To start with, a reading sensitive to the Elijah stories' immediate literary-cultural context inquires how other rabbinic stories treat themes found also among the Elijah stories. It is useful to ask how rabbinic narrative in general recounts miracles, asserts the authority of the Sages and portrays supernatural mediators. Some of these stories share plot motifs or formulaic language with the Elijah stories, showing that the redactors themselves considered them related. Thus understanding of both the concepts and the style of other rabbinic narratives, as well as some non-narrative material, is essential to a full understanding of what the Elijah stories mean. Chapter 3, after beginning with the intra-Jewish context of the Elijah stories, goes on to examine some of their extra-Jewish context in the wider world of late antiquity, discussing in particular Elijah's resemblances to non-Jewish supernatural mediators. This cross-cultural comparison reveals what is unique and what is not about rabbinic viewpoints and their expressions, with occasionally surprising results.[70]

Finally, a better understanding of the social and spiritual role of the Elijah stories, the third issue mentioned at the start of this section, flows from a good grasp of their oral-traditional context within rabbinic society. The best of folkloric or oral-traditional analysis encourages thoughtful examination of the social role of stories while avoiding simplistic *cui bono* readings. Folklore studies, with its relationship to anthropology, and oral-formulaic studies with its literary approach, both recognize that narrative is not equivalent to preaching and still less to propaganda. People tell and write stories to express things that ordinary discourse cannot easily convey. Orally derived stories in some sense reflect societies as a whole: they may express religious belief, social norms, or even religious or class prejudice. Yet they often instead (or also) mirror the elasticity and ambivalence found in all societies and the sorrows, joys, and fears of simply being human.

Furthermore, good stories, and particularly stories as pithy as those in the Talmud, leave room for interpretation. When Rabbi Yossi meets Elijah in the ruins of Jerusalem,[71] their dialogue would have meant different things to a Jew from Palestine who might actually have seen the ruins than to a Babylonian Jew, for whom the destruction of the Temple was more remote. It would also have meant different things to a student of the Sages, who would have enjoyed Elijah's greeting Rabbi Yossi as "Rabbi," than to an ordinary Jew who might have appreciated particularly Elijah's closing statement that God rejoices when he hears his people praying in their synagogues. In fact, this same richness of possible interpretations is part of what makes rabbinic narrative fascinating today. As Hasan-Rokem writes, rabbinic stories "have stimulated generations of traditional interpretation and scholarly research" because of "their capacity to present themselves continually as forceful and condensed signs for multiple concerns and areas of experience and expression."[72]

This is not to say, however, that Talmudic stories are literary silly putty, equally adaptable to any interesting interpretation. Only some homiletic or literary readings will be spiritually and poetically faithful to the originals and only a smaller range of these will be historically sophisticated enough to be faithful to the stories in their redactional context. Folklore studies can be helpful here as well. In addition to freeing Talmudic stories from simplistic readings, folkloric and ethnographic analyses can contribute to situating them in their historical social context.

To start with, rabbinic rather than popular culture provides the social context of many Elijah stories. They can be understood in terms of two overlapping categories, "fringe," and "higher" folklore, defined by Olrick in the early twentieth century. "Fringe folklore" is orally composed—today we would say that it *appears* to be orally composed—but also bears the marks of individual literary creativity. This definition is subjective, as Olrick admits, but at the same time it is undeniable that such works do exist.[73] Insofar as Talmudic stories are fringe folklore, they cannot serve as a clear mirror of the popular tradition of Jewish society, however much they may draw from it. Instead, they are best understood as the product of individual artists and reflections of rabbinic culture. As such, even if they are not fringe folklore, they are unquestionably the folklore of an elite, what Olrick calls "higher" folklore. He describes higher folklore as being discernibly the product of the age in which it is produced, and "characterized by the intellectual traits of the age."[74]

Talmudic Elijah legends are thus higher folklore. This does not mean, however, that they express any one rabbinic party line. As orally derived traditions, they have the variety and indeterminacy of folklore, expressing both the Rabbis' own viewpoints and those of the ordinary people whose stories they retold and, at times, as we will see, even expressing the Rabbis' own critique of themselves. Nevertheless, one must remain aware that the Elijah stories appear in the Talmud because one or more rabbinic authors and editors found them true or useful or witty. It is only a rabbinic view of these stories that we have access to, through study of the stories' rhetorical or halakhic functions in their redactional contexts. Furthermore, folkloric transmission (and redaction as well) functions as a kind of "negative filter" because people do not retell that which does not appeal to them.[75] No doubt there was Jewish folklore the Sages found irrelevant, boring, or offensive. We will never know about it.

In addition, folklore studies and ethnography can shed light on the Elijah stories' social function by showing us how people in various societies understand and use legends. A study from the 1960s of sacred legends told by Israelis from Oriental Jewish communities, for example, shows that both realistic and fantastic legends were in a general sense seen as "true," inasmuch as they were meaningful, regardless of their realism or lack of it. This truth, however, is not the same as unchanging historical truth, since "the narrator's attitude toward his tale is unstable . . . it varies from individual to individual and even from period to period in the lifetime of a single individual." In general, the narrators insisted that all their stories actually took place—"otherwise there would be no point in telling the tales!" Nevertheless, while some legends, such as those recounting miracles performed by famous rabbis of the recent past, were generally seen as objective truth, other legends with more distant settings, such as those set in unnamed Jewish communities in an undefined "once upon a time," were not believed in the same way.[76]

Applying this model to the Elijah stories in the Talmud, one can posit that the Rabbis thought they were true, but did not necessarily believe in their factual accuracy in the same sense that they would if they had heard the stories from eyewitnesses. The more recent in time the story, the more believable its events (even if miraculous), the more closely the Rabbis' conception of its truth would approach a modern definition of historical fact; the farther in time, the more fantastic its events, the further the Rabbis' sense of its truth would be from our own definition of objective truth.

Thus, seeing them as true, the rabbinic tellers and writers of such tales would have tried to transmit them accurately. However, because, as we have seen, the stories were not memorized, rabbinic narrators and writers would also have unconsciously or half-consciously recreated them to make them *more* true, which is to say more meaningful. In this view, the Elijah legends are neither literature as we know it, nor philosophy, nor polemic, although many are indeed literary, philosophical, or polemical. Although this is only a model, I believe that it explains much. Because the Rabbis saw even their longer stories as true, they did not hesitate to use them to prove important legal and ethical points. Because the Rabbis' definition of truth and meaningfulness overlapped, the succession of tellers changed stories significantly over time and inserted certain culturally important motifs into more than one story.

This perspective can also shed light on how best to understand the miraculous or fantastic elements of the Talmudic stories. A folkloric or anthropological approach to traditional stories supports the growing consensus that the supernatural events in many rabbinic legends simply reflect the Rabbis' own belief that "natural" and "supernatural" realities could affect one another. Visions, dreams, providential rescues, miraculous healings, and other phenomena understood as encounters with the supernatural are frequent in oral societies, and indeed in all societies. Even in contemporary North America, people tell of miraculously wise rabbis, rescues by angels, or visions of the Virgin Mary. In significantly oral societies, such stories may gain and retain wide oral circulation, even in the lifetime of their protagonists, because of novel situations they legitimize or explain or because they tellingly express important values or fears. Thus, in general, one ought not to dismiss stories of the miraculous as embellishments of a later age.[77]

My methodology does not seek to somehow arrive at the only or even the ideal reading of the Elijah stories in the Bavli, much less Elijah's role in all of Judaism. Instead, its purpose is to interpret the different "appearances of Elijah" insightfully while remaining faithful to their textual and historical contexts. Chapter 3 is organized by categories that reflect Elijah's roles in the Bavli and other rabbinic texts and the various figures whose roles are somehow comparable. Chapter 4 analyzes the three generic categories of Elijah story, including an in-depth discussion of several stories. Chapter 5 will propose a few general conclusions about Elijah in rabbinic society and then go on to briefly discuss the later life of Elijah in folklore and Jewish rituals: Passover, circumcision, and Motzei Shabbat (Saturday evening following the Sabbath).

Chapter 3's overview of all the Elijah stories has many of the useful qualities described by Boyarin in his discussion in *Carnal Israel* of new ways of doing history. Examining both apparently literary and apparently popular Elijah stories together means working with the hypothesis that "so-called high culture has no essential privilege over 'popular,' and 'mass' culture, nor do the latter more truly reflect society than the former."[78] These postulates are self-evidently useful for approaching rabbinic literature, in that most rabbinic works, including the Talmud, are compositely authored and, as we have seen, often reflect the influence of popular culture. Boyarin's insight that literary works should not be studied in isolation encourages one to examine both more complex and simpler stories, both highly sophisticated and apparently naive stories, in light of one another, in order to see if they may reflect, and help create, the same values and worldviews.

Additionally, Boyarin's emphasis on the idea that narrative can teach us about the ways in which a culture understands itself and the world has encouraged me to concentrate on the risky but interesting questions of how various Elijah stories express and create socially relevant meanings. This idea is in harmony with the other major influence on the methodology of chapter 3, ethnopoetics, in its hypotheses that apparently simple stories can be ways of approaching universal human questions about life and death and the divine, even if they never address these questions explicitly.

Chapter 3 is organized around three of the key functions or roles Elijah assumes in the Bavli. First, he is portrayed as an angelic or semiangelic figure, although one who is clearly different from ordinary angels. Second, Elijah is portrayed as a holy man or rabbi and as a teacher of moral values, proverbial wisdom, and of halakhah. Third, Elijah plays some roles, as savior, trickster, or both at once, which are highly reminiscent of the god Hermes, and could well have been composed in relation or response to pagan myths and stories. The questions that will largely guide the examination of these roles are also inspired by the approach Boyarin outlines, asking what might have been the conscious or unconscious social, ideological, and theological reasons for telling these kinds of stories about Elijah.[79]

Chapter 3, with its catalogue of stories analyzed from the point of view of meaning and social use, is balanced by chapter 4, which describes the three generic groups and provides a more literary treatment of various stories within them. This literary treatment is inspired largely by form criticism used in the service of oral-formulaic studies. Shared formulae and plot structure connect one story to another and make it possible—and indeed necessary—to analyze one story in light of others within the Bavli and, occasionally, from other rabbinic texts. Thus form criticism as a mode of classification and oral-formulaic studies as a mode of aesthetic analysis go hand in hand. As we will see, the literary implications of orally derived motifs and formulae are at times obvious and at times subtle, but almost always relevant to the meanings of the stories. Oral-formulaic criticism can also be used to analyze meanings inherent in the formal categories themselves. The generic groups, in particular, are helpful for understanding the meaning of the Elijah stories and their role in rabbinic society. Because the three generic groups are traditional forms rather than the creation of any one author, they reveal some of rabbinic Jewish society's concept of itself and of supernatural mediation.

Chapter 5 sums up the nature of the rabbinic Elijah and goes on to look briefly at Elijah in later Jewish folklore and ritual. In later stories I analyze recurring plot motifs and morals, discussing both continuities and discontinuities with the rabbinic portrait of Elijah. I consider the meaning of Elijah's presence in ritual and argue that the prophet entered Jewish practice in the Middle Ages through his presence in folklore, leading to developments in popular rituals, practices then explained and made official by the religious elite. The final few pages are devoted to Elijah in the present.

3

ELIJAH IN RABBINIC CULTURE AND THE WIDER CULTURE OF LATE ANTIQUITY

Many aspects of the rabbinic Elijah can be best understood by comparing him to other figures that mediate between the supernatural and human worlds. In this chapter we will see that Elijah is unique as mediator of God's mercy, God's affirmation of rabbinic authority, and God's support for humanity. The first major section of this chapter, "Elijah as Angelic or Supernatural Being," compares Elijah to other supernatural figures within the Babylonian Talmud, bringing his unique role within the Bavli into high relief. The second section, "Elijah as Rabbi and Holy Man," compares Elijah to Jewish Sages as well as to Christian saints alive and dead, showing Elijah's role as ideal teacher. The third and last section, "Elijah as Hermes Figure," examines Elijah in light of that Greek god, finding surprising and revealing similarities among the obvious differences.

Because this chapter will refer to Elijah stories in a number of classic rabbinic sources, not only the Babylonian Talmud, I begin with a brief discussion of the Elijah of the Bavli, comparing its picture of Elijah to that of other rabbinic texts. I originally chose the Bavli as a basis for analyzing all rabbinic Elijah stories because its thirty-eight stories and references to the legendary Elijah are a convenient body to work with: there are enough stories to see subgroups and relationships among them, but not too many to consider each carefully. Analyzing the stories in more depth, I came to see that there are not only more Elijah stories in the Bavli, but that its collection is special in other ways. It includes many individual stories that have no parallel in other works, and there is even one generic group, the one in which Elijah appears in disguise to rescue Jews from Gentiles, that is unique to the Bavli among rabbinic texts, though later folklore does have Elijah appearing in disguised form. The Bavli's other two clearly definable generic categories, the one in which Elijah imparts special information, and the one in which Elijah refuses to visit someone, do appear elsewhere. The Bavli, however, marks these categories with unique formulaic language. Furthermore, the motif of Elijah providing wealth to the poor, so popular in later Jewish folklore, first appears in the Bavli.

The largest number of unique Elijah stories outside the Bavli are found in two rabbinic sources, the Yerushalmi, or Palestinian Talmud, which precedes the Babylonian Talmud, and the Pesikta de Rav Kahana, a homiletic midrash redacted at roughly the same time as Bavli (we will cover rabbinic texts from the early medieval period in chapter 5). The Yerushalmi, redacted about the mid-fourth century CE, presents a very rabbinic Elijah. In three out of the Yerushalmi's four Elijah legends Elijah performs no miracles, but only teaches, in one instance theological aggadah, in another a moral lesson, and in the third a halakhic point. In the fourth story, Elijah heals Rabbi Judah the Patriarch while taking the form of Rabbi Ḥiyya.[1] The ability to heal is not unique to Elijah—the episode's key point is that Rabbi Judah is reconciled to Rabbi Ḥiyya. Thus, in the Yerushalmi, Elijah performs only one miraculous action that is uniquely and characteristically his: appearing in the form of a living person.

In contrast, the later Pesikta de Rav Kahana presents Elijah as a more supernatural figure.[2] In the three stories first found there Elijah attempts to introduce the living Rabbi Joshua ben Levi to the saintly dead Rabbi Shimon ben Yoḥai, but is rebuffed. He becomes a miraculously heavy rider on the back of Rav Eleazar bar R. Shimon, persuading him to leave off collaborating with the Romans and study Torah. He even rescues a Jewish boy from a foundering ship so that he can show Rabbi Joshua ben Levi the supernatural red *kadkudaya* stones of which the turrets of the future Temple will be built.[3]

In contrast to the Yerushalmi and the Pesikta de Kahana, the Bavli has a more varied picture of Elijah's activities. Although the greater number of Elijah traditions in the Bavli may be part of the reason for their greater variety, the range of variation is significant. The Bavli's Elijah is both rabbinic and angelic, both an educator and a supernatural being.[4] This makes the Bavli the richest source for understanding rabbinic beliefs about Elijah and how they developed in later Judaism.

While it is useful to compare the Bavli's Elijah to his other rabbinic portrayals, it is even more fruitful to compare Elijah to other heavenly and human figures that also mediate between natural and supernatural. Within the Bavli, Elijah is clearly distinguished from any other holy being. He appears in some ways like an angel and in more ways unlike an angel. At times Elijah relays information from God much as does the *bat kol,* the "divine voice," but the bat kol has much more specific and limited functions. And of course the "divine voice" does not *do* things, but only speaks. In the second section of this chapter we see how the Bavli some-times portrays Elijah as a rabbi or holy man, but here too there are differences: Elijah is neither a living Sage still constrained by time and space nor a saintly dead rabbi appearing only at his grave site and in the heavenly court. Despite his varied roles, the Bavli's Elijah has important unifying characteristics: more than an angel, bat kol, or rabbi, Elijah comes to help people and affirm human power.

ELIJAH AS ANGELIC OR SUPERNATURAL BEING

The legendary Elijah has angelic powers. He is deathless; he travels freely between heaven and earth; he possesses supernatural knowledge. On the other hand, Eli-jah's roles in the Bavli are very different from the roles that angels play. Angels do things that Elijah does not, and vice versa. In order to better understand Elijah, it makes sense to supply a quick overview of the roles angels play in the Talmud, which are quite different from the roles of angels in the Hebrew Bible or Second Temple literature.

Spiritual beings occupy different niches in the ecology of thought of different religions, niches that may be mapped in various ways in different faiths and at different times. Demons, for example, occupy a niche in rabbinic Judaism dis-tinctly different from their role in Patristic Christianity. While the Jewish demons, *shedim*, are certainly nasty and dangerous, they are not agents of damnation as Christian writers thought demons to be.[5]

Spiritual beings may also have their "niches" change over time in the same faith. Angels are common in Jewish literature from Second Temple times, but less com-mon in the later rabbinic sources. The Rabbis believed that the angels helped the righteous in biblical times more often than they did the Rabbis themselves, as we see in angels' larger role in midrash than in legends about the Rabbinic present. The Bavli, for example, has no stories of angels helping or rescuing righteous individu-als of its own era, although its midrashim often describe angelic assistance in the Bible.[6] Tractate Megillah, on the Purim festival, is a particularly rich source of such midrashic stories. Angels came to Esther's and Mordecai's aid nine times, even enhancing Esther's charm before her fateful interview with the King of Persia.[7]

While angels do at times reward or punish in the rabbinic present, their rewards (and usually their punishments) are directed to certain behaviors rather than to individuals as such. For example, Rabbi Yossi states that "two ministering angels accompany each man on Sabbath evening . . . one good angel, and one bad. When he comes to his house, and finds the lamp lit and the table set . . . the good angel says 'May it be God's will that this shall be so for another Sabbath,' and the bad angel answers 'Amen' against his will." If, however, the house is dark and dirty, it is the bad angel who calls for another Sabbath like it, while the good angel unwillingly replies "Amen."[8] In this story each angel's blessing or curse seems directed toward the house as much as the people in it. The angel acts as an impersonal agent of God's justice, and it does not seem to matter *why* the house is well or badly prepared for the Sabbath.[9]

The Bavli describes this type of angelic reward or punishment seven times, both in life and after death. In each case the people rewarded or punished are either "the righteous" and "the wicked" or all those who do a specific action.[10] In contrast, Elijah never brings harm to a living person and often rewards or rescues specific people. We will see how Elijah usually rewards or rescues particular individuals more as a person than as an angel, albeit a supernaturally powerful person, appearing to help where he can or perhaps where he wants to.

There are only three brief passages, none of them stories, in which Elijah acts more like an angel, relating to people in general or all who do a certain action.[11] In these passages Elijah, like most angels, appears neutral or negative rather than positive. Elijah is most explicitly compared to various angels following a midrash proving from Daniel and Isaiah that Michael is greater than Gabriel because Michael flies to the prophet with a simple single form of the verb *to fly* and Gabriel in a doubled form, and therefore "Michael in one" as opposed to Gabriel needing two. Then it quotes a tradition: "Michael in one, Gabriel in two, Elijah in four, and the Angel of Death in eight, and in time of plague, in one."[12] "One," "two," or "four," seem to refer to the number of "flights," so to speak, each being needs to reach his goal. Michael is fastest in traveling from heaven to earth, or in performing God's will in the world. In any case, Elijah is here described in the same terms as angels, wherever he goes and whatever he does is in "four."

There is also one instance where Elijah does something otherwise the province of angels: he participates in the punishment of sinners after death. "Any one who marries a wife who is not worthy, Elijah binds him and the Holy One blessed be He flogs him." And, for all who marry unfit wives, "Elijah writes and [God] signs 'Alas for him who . . . blemishes his family by marrying a wife who is not worthy.'"[13] Other than this passage, only angels are described as undertaking the postmortem punishment of sinners. This passage seems connected to traditions about Elijah found outside the Bavli. The scene of Elijah writing and God signing recalls Enoch's role as heavenly scribe in Second Temple literature, suggesting an influence on Elijah traditions because Elijah and Enoch both entered heaven without dying (Gen. 5:24). Elijah's role in punishing those who marry wrongly may recall the identification of Elijah with the zealot Pinḥas (Phinehas) who killed an Israelite man and Midianite woman while they were having sexual intercourse, thus sternly discouraging the surviving straying Israelites (Num. 25:6–15). This identification is not found explicitly in the Bavli, although Elijah is once referred to as a priest, like Phinehas.[14] Nevertheless, it is a tradition of long standing, which both predates and postdates the two Talmuds, and it is likely that it influenced this description of Elijah binding the man who married unworthily.[15]

The third and last non-narrative reference to Elijah also implicitly compares him to an angel, in this case the angel of death. "The Rabbis teach: dogs howling—the angel of death has come to town; dogs frolicking—Elijah has come to town (but this holds [only] when there's no female among them)."[16] The most surprising element of this passage, Elijah's association with dogs, is something to which we will return later, in the section on Elijah and Hermes: it may have been acquired from his being compared to the god of graveyards and the herald of the dead. On the other hand, the implied comparison to the angel of death makes sense in a Jewish context.

Elijah and the Angel of Death

In an number of stories in the Bavli the angel of death and Elijah share a relative freedom of action and a corresponding fallibility in contrast to angels in general. Angels are almost always direct arms of God's will and as such unacquainted with choice and error. Elijah, in contrast, often appears as a free agent and sometimes as less than perfect. The most telling instance of both Elijah's free will and his fallibility is the story in which he tells Rabbi Judah the Patriarch that the prayers of Rabbi Ḥiyya and his sons could force the coming of the Messiah. When this is "heard in heaven," Elijah is punished with burning lashes and required to drive away the congregation by taking the form of a bear.[17] A striking example of free will and error for the angel of death is the story in which he agrees to let the saintly Rabbi Joshua ben Levi hold his knife while being shown his place is paradise and ends up losing the knife to the rabbi, who only returns it at God's command (B. Ketubot 77b). No such human victory over another angel is recorded in the Bavli. Tricking and defeating any other named angel, such as Michael or Gabriel, would seem particularly strange in the rabbinic worldview because a such a victory would seem like an impossible victory over God Himself. However, imagining the angel of death as an independent, and fallible, agent softens the harsh concept of God killing people directly.

In addition to the angel of death's lack of omnipotence, he also has what might be termed freedom of choice in that rabbis can bargain with him, seeking, sometimes successfully, to postpone their deaths. The angel of death's limited free choice also seems to partially disconnect death—at least the death of the righteous—from God's will. Diamond writes, "two notions share an uneasy coexistence in rabbinic thinking. On the one hand, life and death are meted out by a fate unmoved by human righteousness or wickedness; at the same time, members of the circle of sages are said to have a limited power over their destiny."[18] The Talmud expresses the Sages' power to delay their deaths by picturing the angel of death, although created by God and subservient to God's will, as a partially free agent. Thus it is the angel of death whom the Rabbis contend with, not the direct decree of the Blessed Holy One, which it would be both sinful and impossible to oppose.

The fallibility of the angel of death raises the possibility that Elijah's relative freedom of action and corresponding possibility of error come from his function within the rabbinic world view as well from as his mortal origins. If the angel of death—no more mortal than any other angel—displays the human characteristics of fallibility and free will for specific reasons that might be called both emotional and theological, then we can also look farther for the reasons behind Elijah's fallibility and free will. In so far as Elijah is like an angel, what aspect of the Sages' experience of God or of the holy do his activities portray? Two aspects of Elijah's role as helper or rescuer in the Bavli are key to answering this question. First, Elijah does not come to everyone who needs help, but sometimes appears and sometimes does not. Second, no one ever requests Elijah's help (as opposed to his presence), nor, in the Bavli, does Elijah appear in response to prayer to God for rescue from a difficult or dangerous situation. Because Elijah's help is both unpredictable and unlooked for, he might be said to embody the aspect of divine mercy, which is also unpredictable in this premessianic age.

Baruch Bokser, in "The Wall Separating God and Israel," restricts the tradition of an "iron wall" separating God and Israel at the Temple's destruction to the obstruction of petitionary and intercessory prayer, not to the obstruction of all relationship with God. He argues that this passage sees the block as particularly applying to praying for oneself, as opposed to praying community prayers of praise and thanksgiving that are appropriate service to God.[19] Bokser's analysis is borne out by other rabbinic passages that reveal a decidedly ambivalent attitude to individual petitionary prayer. If not wrong, such prayer may sometimes be inappropriate; if not impossible, it may often be ineffective. One passage says that people should not pray for their personal needs if they expect to have their prayers fulfilled, which opens the door to "hope deferred [that] makes the heart sick." In three cases of successful prayer for personal benefit, two intercessory and one petitionary, the prayer somehow turns out wrong and has to be reversed.[20] In addition, rabbis and Jewish holy men rarely heal dangerous illness through prayer. Such prayer was not characteristic of the Rabbis, as it was of Christian holy men and women.[21] Even intercessory prayer for the community can be fraught with difficulties: the stories in Bavli Ta'anit on praying for rain show that success in such prayer is often difficult and is not necessarily guaranteed.[22]

The Talmud is even more skeptical of petitionary prayer for rescue from individual danger. Elijah rescues those who are in danger of death at the hands of the Gentile authorities, but never because someone has called on him or prayed to God for help. One story dramatically illustrates that those in the greatest danger behave most admirably by submitting to execution as the will of the Righteous Judge. At the time the Temple was destroyed, Emperor Trajan mocks the martyrs Lulianius and Pappus by asking them why God did not rescue them as he delivered Ḥananya, Mishael, and Azaria from the hands of Nebuchadnezzar. Lulianius and Pappus declare that he, Trajan, is a common tyrant, and thus unworthy that a miracle should be performed through him and, moreover, that they, the victims, have been already condemned by God and will be killed by some wild animal if Trajan does not murder them first.[23]

In the light of the preceding, one sees how it might have been problematic for rabbinic concepts of theodicy if God were seen to directly rescue some endangered people and let others die. In several places in the Talmud, people are said to die young for their own sins or those of their contemporaries. Young children die because of the sins of their parents, and righteous people or their children are taken because of the sins of their generation.[24] If all must die, and untimely deaths arise from God's justice, individual or collective, then it could easily appear to impair God's justice and impartiality if God himself were to rescue people capriciously, without the mediating personality of Elijah.

This is analogous to the theodicy problem of making God kill people directly, without the mediating personality of the quasi-fallible angel of death. Without the angel of death as mediator, God would appear too much the merciless destroyer. Without Elijah as mediator, God's mercy would appear too random or else overly swayed by personalities. If God rescued all righteous people in danger, that would be congruent with omniscience and omnipotence, but a God who personally rescues only some righteous people might appear unsettlingly random or biased. Without Elijah as mediator, it would be God himself, for example, who rescues Rabbi

Eleazar ben Perata from martyrdom by the Romans, while at the same time allowing the even more worthy Rabbi Akiva to be tortured to death. In that case, the question the Talmud puts in the mouth of the angels, "Such Torah and such reward?"
would be even more disturbing, perhaps too disturbing to contemplate.[25]

Elijah in his very unpredictability thus in some way reflects the experience of
the rabbinic community—that God's mercy is unpredictable *in the present*. Rabbis often recount how people of biblical times were helped by angels, the direct
arms of God's will, help that was both mercy and justice because of the virtue of
those like Esther or Moses. In contrast, rabbinic—and later—Jewish sources often
express the uncertain action of divine mercy in their own times by recounting stories of the humanly fallible Elijah. Elijah's unpredictable favor is in accord with
the Sages' own experience, while their descriptions of rescue by angels in Scripture is in accord both with the Bible itself and with their view that their biblical
ancestors were far more deserving than anyone alive in rabbinic times.

How Elijah Differs from the Angels More than He Resembles Them

Elijah, like an angel, moves freely in and between heaven and earth, unlike a saintly
dead rabbi who is present only at his grave site and in the heavenly court.[26] Elijah is
also, in a broad sense, angelic in knowing what God is doing in heaven and being
able to tell people. However, Elijah differs from the angels in the use he makes of his
freedom of movement and his knowledge of heaven. One could say that Elijah occupies a very different set of literary and religious niches from those angels occupy.

As we have seen, Elijah is seems most like an angel in three brief descriptive
passages. The *stories* told about the legendary Elijah are almost entirely different from those told about angels in the rabbinic present. Although Elijah's power
resembles the angels', he does not act as they do. For example, in the Bavli angels
rarely bring word of God's will in the rabbinic present, as opposed to biblical times.
In the present, Elijah or the bat kol, the heavenly voice, fulfill this role. Elijah differs even more significantly from the angels in being fundamentally beneficent.
Despite his fiery character in Scripture, Elijah is not portrayed as dangerous to living
people—although, as we will see, he occasionally appears in a frightening form.

Angels, on the other hand, are often dangerous. A story set in the early amoraic
era describes how an angel plans to kill two students of the Sages who forsake their
studies on account of poverty.[27] Later in amoraic times there is the story of how the
Shekhinah, the Lord's indwelling spirit, filled a synagogue in Nehardea as once it

filled the Temple, and people had to leave. When Rav Sheshet, who was blind, did not go, the angels sought to harm him, and Rav Sheshet had to appeal directly to God.[28] In these stories, the angels act as the servants of God, but emphatically not as the allies of humankind. If one compares God to a mortal ruler, as the Rabbis do, the angels seem like ministers or palace guards who are more concerned for the king's honor than the king is himself.

In contrast, there is only one story in the Talmud in which Elijah harms a living person.[29] Even this story is unevenly supported in variant editions and manuscripts. In it Elijah testifies in Roman court against an unfaithful Jew who was punished by a rabbi and then took revenge by reporting him to the Roman authorities.[30] The manuscript evidence for Elijah's presence in this story is very mixed, and this may be in part because the scribes were uncomfortable with the idea that Elijah does even indirect harm, even to an enemy of a rabbi. In any case, in this story, Elijah's concern is not the angelic one to protect the honor of God, but a more human desire to protect a rabbi in a dangerous spot with Gentile authorities.

This story aside, Elijah punishes only by staying away (either temporarily or permanently) because of a person's lack of respect for others or his unkind or unethical behavior. The misdeed is always slight, because Elijah will only appear to a righteous person in the first place. In fact, Elijah appears benign not only beside the angels, but even in comparison to living rabbis, as we will discuss in more detail in the next section. Whereas angels are pictured as willing to violently vindicate the honor of God, and living humans are capable of cursing in defense of God's honor and causing harm to others because of their own personal jealousy or wounded feeling.[31] Elijah only stays away. Elijah's absences are basically personal, not based on set rules like angelic punishment. He seems to refuse to visit either because he chooses to avoid people who are not righteous, kind, and generous or because he is disappointed in the actions of someone he regularly associates with.

While Elijah is not dangerous, he cannot be expected or compelled to help in ways that angels can be. The Bavli states that angels automatically blessed anyone who did specific virtuous actions, like preparing for the Sabbath, but never states Elijah does. Jews who were contemporaries of the Rabbis—though they did not share their views—wrote magical texts that call on angels for help in various ways. Even the Talmud recommends invoking angels as a cure for certain diseases. One passage in the Bavli includes several incantations to cure illness, one of which says, "Sherlai and Amarli are those angels who were sent forth from the land of Sodom to heal boils and aches."[32] Elijah, however, was not often mentioned in magic and never requested by prayer.

In some mystical Hekhalot literature, whose relationship to rabbinic Judaism is uncertain, and in definitively nonrabbinic magical texts such as *Sepher HaRazim*, angels are invoked for more than curing illness. Hekhalot Rabbati provides those who wish to master all the Written and Oral Torah a long invocation ascribed to an angelic being called the Prince of the Torah. This is to be followed by adjurations of "each individual heavenly prince" given by name.[33] *Sepher HaRazim*, a Jewish magical text reconstructed by Mordecai Margaliot from fragments and translations, is essentially a handbook of angel magic. Each subdivision describes a particular class of angels and the purposes they can be made to serve—including afflicting an enemy, binding oneself to the heart of a wealthy woman, driving away an evil spirit from a woman in childbirth, and picking a winning chariot team—as well as the rituals and incantations necessary to get results.[34]

Thus we see a widespread Jewish belief that skillful use of angelic assistance could compel results, a belief found to a limited extent within the Talmud itself. The Rabbis, however, in their strong desire to affirm the omnipotence and freedom of God, also try to discourage people from calling on angelic powers. The Bavli both explicitly condemns magic praxis and implicitly discourages people from calling upon angelic powers. It explicitly states that anyone who sacrifices to existing beings, such as the heavenly bodies, mountains or rivers, or "Michael the great prince" should be considered as one who makes sacrifices to the dead.[35] *Sepher HaRazim* confirms that what the Bavli condemns really was done, giving instructions for magic to get help from angels as well as for sacrificial rituals to gain knowledge from the "moon or the stars" or from the dead.[36]

The Bavli's use of angels to affirm rabbinic values also implicitly discourages people from calling on angelic powers. In stating that angels reward people predictably in response to specific actions, the Bavli presents these actions as in some sense magical—doing them guarantees angelic blessing. In contrast to magical rituals, however, these actions are also intrinsically right: halakhically mandated and pleasing to God. Perhaps in a context in which people thought that magic could compel angelic assistance, rabbis used or even created traditions about automatic angelic blessing to help reinforce rabbinically approved behavior. At the same time, when they emphasized that angels bless those who keep the Torah, they implicitly discounted and discouraged nonrabbinic magical praxis that makes the angels serve the practitioner's material interests. Presenting angels as dangerous serves the same implicit purpose. Beings who are risky to encounter, and who serve to enforce God's justice strictly construed, are not beings you want to call upon with demands to marry a rich woman or pick a winning chariot.

Just as the Bavli discourages seeking earthly results from invoking angels, it discourages seeking knowledge of the heavenly angelic realm, associating angels with mystical knowledge that could be dangerous. Unprepared people who arrived at a spontaneous understanding of heavenly knowledge could come to serious harm: A child who read Ezekiel's vision suddenly understood *hashmal*, the radiance that surrounds God's chariot, "and a fire went out from *hashmal* and burnt him up."[37] Since mystical experience and esoteric knowledge are associated with angels in early Judaism, by presenting the mystical and esoteric as dangerous the Bavli also in effect discourages knowledge and personal experience of angels.

Taken as a whole, one sees that the Bavli seeks to deter calling on angels for help or knowledge on many fronts. It describes the dangers of mystical visions of the angels of the Chariot. It discourages magical praxis using angels, except for specific illnesses. Most significantly, it portrays angels as dangerous when acting on their own and, when beneficent, as automatic agents of divine blessing without free will.

This rather lengthy treatment of angels in the Bavli throws into high relief the ways in which the Bavli's portrayal of Elijah is profoundly different. The Bavli presents Elijah as free, unpredictable, inaccessible through prayer, hardly ever the agent of harm, and helpful to the righteous. In the context of beliefs about angels that many people hold today, these attributes are positive, even inspiring, but not terribly remarkable; in the religious universe of ancient Judaism, however, these attributes made Elijah unique among supernatural beings. The Bavli does not ascribe free beneficence to angels, only to Elijah.

In another contrast to its treatment of angels, the Bavli welcomes human contact with the free and beneficent Elijah. There is no hint that people may be tempted to worship Elijah or try to compel him by magical practice. There are no warnings that the appearance of Elijah is risky or statements implying that Elijah only appears to the well-schooled mystical initiate. In one instance, Elijah appears to a widow, and another passage tells how Elijah was accustomed to appear to a "certain God-fearing man."[38] Elijah is a unique figure who has angelic powers, but is more human than angelic, and who differs from both angels and rabbis simply by his beneficence.

Elijah and the Bat Kol

Elijah also differs from another angelic or quasi-angelic phenomenon, the bat kol, the "echo," "reverberation," or "divine voice" mentioned in rabbinic literature, although here too there are certain points of connection. The term *bat kol*—literally "daughter of a voice"—has two distinct senses, the first unrelated to the appearance of Elijah. In this sense it refers to words overheard by chance that are considered an indirect indication of distant events or of God's will. This meaning is relatively rare in the Babylonian Talmud, occurring only five times among the Bavli's more than thirty references to the bat kol in Hebrew or Aramaic.[39] The bat kol in its other sense serves as a messenger of God as Elijah sometimes does. In these instances it is best translated "divine voice," a supernatural voice from heaven, often expressed by the formulaic phrase, "a heavenly voice went forth and said" (יצתה בת קול ואמרה).

The exact nature of this kind of bat kol is uncertain.[40] One passage implies that the bat kol is produced by an angel,[41] but it often seems to be the first-person voice of God, like the "Thus says the LORD" of biblical prophecy. Prophecy, though, came to an individual for the sake of the group, whereas the bat kol usually goes forth— generally to more than one person—in reference to an individual.[42] At one point, for example, a bat kol goes out from Mount Horeb and laments "the whole world is sustained for the sake of Ḥanina my son and he eats only carob pods from one Sabbath to the next."[43] For me, the best analogy for the bat kol as divine voice in the Bavli is that it is God's words filtered through an angelic or cosmic loudspeaker. It is like the herald of an emperor who walks through a city and shouts out the emperor's exact words, as it would clearly be inappropriate for the emperor to do himself.

As well as serving as God's messenger in a general sense, the bat kol has two characteristic functions in the Bavli that are not shared either by angels referred to as such or by Elijah. The first and most common of these functions is announcing that someone has gained eternal life, by saying that they have "inherited the life of the world to come" or that they are "called" (מזומן) to life of the world to come." Most of the times that the bat kol makes one of these announcements are occasions of sudden death, sometimes martyrdoms. Rabbi Akiva is perhaps the Bavli's quintessential martyr. He goes to death open eyed and even glad that he is now loving and serving God to his last breath, with all his soul. Not one but two *benot kol* (the plural of bat kol) go forth to mark his death: "Happy are you, whose soul departed with [the word] 'One' [of the Shema]"; and "Happy are you who are called to life in the world to come."[44] Sometimes, in contrast, the bat kol heralds the sudden deaths of people who do not, on the face of it, seem likely candidates for the world to come, but who become so by the manner in which they die or by repentance just before death.[45] These latter stories teach that eternal life is strictly God's business and that God forgives whom he wills.[46]

Elijah (once) and saintly mortals, rabbis and biblical heroes can all say a person is "a son/child of the world to come" (בר עלמא דאתא), but this is different from the bat kol's statement that someone has "inherited the world come." Five times, for example, the phrase appears in the question "Who is the son of the world to come?" with the answer specifying someone who does a particular praiseworthy action.[47] Elijah and others who use this phrase mean that someone is especially pleasing to God or perhaps speak of the *likelihood* that a person will eventually enter the world to come, whereas the bat kol announces a fact about someone who has just died. When Rabbi Joshua ben Levi asks Elijah if he will attain life the world to come, Elijah can only answer cryptically (saying, "if this Lord wills"), until he knows that Rabbi Joshua has found the Messiah and the latter has said "Peace be with you." Then Elijah can tell Joshua that the Messiah has promised him life in the world to come—but Elijah cannot on his own authority guarantee eternal life.[48] In this respect Elijah is more like a human being than like the divine voice—apparently he does not know who will be chosen for eternal life.

The second characteristic function of the bat kol is to publicly rule on the moral worthiness of various people.[49] In contrast to Elijah, it has nothing to say about halakhic matters, with one exception: the famous bat kol that adjudicates between the House of Hillel and the House of Shammai. Although the content of the divine voice is legal—the law will henceforth be decided according to the house of Hillel—the story is simply one of those in which the bat kol rules on human worthiness. In this case, both houses are worthy, both teach "the words of the Living God," but, because it is even more virtuous, the law will be framed according to the decisions of the House of Hillel.[50]

The bat kol as loudspeaker can rule on human merit or announce that someone has inherited the world to come because God alone has final say over the worthiness of human beings, whether in life or in death. Elijah may choose to visit someone because that person is worthy, but only a bat kol can reveal God's will about ultimate fate or comparative worth. In addition, there is a public quality to the bat kol not shared by Elijah. The usual phrase a "bat kol went forth" does not specify a single person to whom the divine voice is directed. In many instances the bat kol is heard by a group of people, sometimes defined, more often undefined. Elijah, in contrast, always appears to individuals, except when he appears disguised.

Another helpful way to look at the differences between Elijah and the bat kol is to use the concept of metonomy utilized in oral-formulaic studies. As discussed in chapter 2, certain recurring phrases and plot motifs can evoke whole categories of traditional meaning. The bat kol's "so-and-so is called to life in the world to come" contains an enormous wealth of meaning in few words, including the whole idea of God's control of each person's destiny at the moment of death. In addition, because it is a formula and not the work of any one author, it indicates that the bat kol was connected in the popular mind with the moment of death, as Elijah was not. The same holds true for the other characteristic functions of the bat kol, but not as strongly insofar as they are not expressed in such standardized language.

In a few stories, however, the functions of Elijah and the bat kol overlap, with Elijah bringing a message to someone about what he can or should do. Elijah's messages, however, come in support of human power much more than the bat kol's. One story, that of Shimon ben Yoḥai, is particularly interesting because in it both Elijah and the bat kol appear. When the rabbi is hiding from Roman persecution in the cave, Elijah comes first and says, "Who will inform the son of Yoḥai that the emperor is dead and his decree is canceled?" When Rabbi Shimon and his son leave the cave, however, Shimon is so angered by ordinary human activity—the life of the moment as opposed to eternal life—that whatever he turns his eyes on is immediately burned up. A bat kol then orders him to return to the cave. Later a bat kol announces that he should now leave, and this time it works out for the best: for where Rabbi Shimon wounds, his son Rabbi Eleazar heals (B Shabbat 33b).[51] In this case Elijah functions exactly as the bat kol does. Interestingly, however, here Elijah is ineffective while the divine voice is effective: Elijah's invitation to leave the cave is premature and leads to misfortune. The prophet may be intentionally portrayed as jumping the gun a little in support of the rabbi—he was so anxious to let Rabbi Shimon know that his time of self-imposed imprisonment was over that he led him to leave the cave before he was ready.[52] In general, Elijah affirms the power of human beings, whereas the bat kol often limits that power.

Elijah's Unique Role as Supernatural Mediator

We have shown how the characteristic functions of angels and the bat kol are different from those of Elijah. The converse is true as well: Elijah's most characteristic functions are not shared with other supernatural beings. This is true particularly for functions associated with specific generic forms of plot and language. Reviewing the generic groups, which were the common property of the Talmud's redactors—and perhaps of other contemporaneous Jews—we see how Elijah differs profoundly from other supernatural mediators. Table 3.1. sums up how much Elijah differs from heavenly figures, and, as we shall see, he differs from earthly supernatural mediators as well.

TABLE 3.1 Elijah, Angels, and the Bat Kol

LEGENDARY ELIJAH IN RABBINIC SOURCES	ANGELS, INCLUDING THE ANGEL OF DEATH, IN THE BAVLI	THE BAT KOL AS "DIVINE VOICE" IN THE BAVLI
Responds to the questions of individuals about what God is doing.		
Something of a trickster, and not a respecter of authority, Elijah helps rabbis challenge God. Also sometimes rescues rabbis from trouble in embarrassing ways.		
Associated with God as supporter of human (that is rabbinic) initiative—never punishes chutzpah in relation to God.		
Benefactor/protector of poor/powerless; rescues rabbis from Gentile courts.	In occasional passages, angels collectively lament human suffering but do not help.	
Characteristically appears in disguise to help people.	Once angels appear as boatmen with sacks of grain, foretelling the end of a famine.	
Frequent source of wise teaching and also solves difficult questions.	Angels occasionally teach esoteric information.	
Supports the *human honor* by refusing to visit haughty or unjust Jews in power.	Angels are protective of God's honor—even threatening those who disrespect it.	

TABLE 3.1 Elijah, Angels, and the Bat Kol (*continued*)		
LEGENDARY ELIJAH IN RABBINIC SOURCES	ANGELS, INCLUDING THE ANGEL OF DEATH, IN THE BAVLI	THE BAT KOL AS "DIVINE VOICE" IN THE BAVLI
Elijah *unpredictably* gives money or other benefits to the deserving.	Angels *automatically* bless those who observe certain commandments.	The bat kol brings word of God's special blessing.
Occasionally brings God's message to individuals.		Characteristically relays God's words to groups of people.
On one occasion heralds a rabbi new-come to paradise.		Characteristically brings word that the righteous or repentant sinners have "inherited the world to come."
Once stated that Elijah punishes those who marry an unworthy wife.	Angels punish human sin, both automatically and on specific occasions.	At times reproves human arrogance.
Is flogged in Heaven for trying to help Rabbi Judah bring the Messiah before his time.	The angel Gabriel is flogged in heaven for not fully obeying God's order to destroy Jerusalem (see note 17).	
Very occasionally heals.	Healing incantations involving angels appear, but they *never spontaneously* heal.	
Sometimes fallible.	Angel of Death is some-times fallible.	

The type of story in which Elijah appears in disguise to help or rescue is unique to the prophet. The Bavli has only one instance of angels appearing in disguise to people in the rabbinic present, and even there they are of no direct benefit.[53] Some other supernatural beings (even Satan, as we will see in chapter 4) do appear in disguise, introduced with the same phrase used to introduce

Elijah, but they come to do harm. In fact, in disguise or out of it, Elijah is the only supernatural being other than God who rescues and benefits specific individuals in the Bavli.

The second generic group, in which Elijah refuses to visit, is often introduced with a phrase occasionally used in stories of rabbis. There are no stories of angels not visiting or ceasing to visit anyone. In part this is because angels are not portrayed as the special companions or teachers of the Sages; in the rabbinic present they rarely appear at all. However, while they do not appear visibly, they also do not stay away: guardian angels are said to be always with everyone, good and bad alike. In addition, the principle moral of this generic group, that people must treat one another with respect and kindness beyond the legal requirement, does not fit well with the Bavli's other passages on angels. They are portrayed as far more concerned with the honor of God than with the relationship between people and their neighbors.

The third common generic pattern used for Elijah's appearance is introduced with the formula "Rabbi So-and-so found (or met) Elijah."[54] This pattern, like the first two, is not used in reference to angels or to any other supernatural being. However, it is frequent in purely human contexts, often introducing an exchange between two Sages (and occasionally a Sage and another person) who meet outside the house of study. This pattern will be discussed in depth in the next section. All that need be said here is that this generic pattern represents Elijah as more like a rabbi than like any other supernatural beings.

The existence of Elijah, a supernatural mediator who is at the same time a human being, is both unique to later rabbinic Judaism and also part of a contemporary shift in the religious imagination. The belief in human beings as mediators of God's power is one that appeared throughout late antique culture, even though the legendary Elijah himself is unique to Judaism. Baruch Bokser describes how this trend affected rabbinic Judaism's understanding of holy men and miracle workers. Earlier, tannaitic, sources are reluctant to portray wonder working spiritual "stars" because they undermine the early rabbinic claim that holiness is open to all who practice Torah study and live a pure life. Later sources, however, such as the Babylonian Talmud and aggadic midrashim, recount many legends of miracle-working rabbis because of "developments within Judaism joined with the political and social changes in the Jewish and general society."[55] As a result, rabbis became more open to drawing upon the biblical imagery of specially endowed leaders in stories of Jewish wonder workers and in stories of Elijah as well.[56]

Not only did the spiritual powers of individual holy men rise to the fore in this period of late antiquity, but, within Christianity, the martyrs and saints in heaven began to take over roles previously held by angels within Christianity. Brown documents this phenomenon in *The Cult of the Saints*. He writes how Paulinus, for example, transfers to the heavenly Saint Felix "all the sense of intimate involvement with an invisible companion that men in previous generations had looked for in a relationship with the *non*human figures of gods, *daimones*, or angels."[57] More generally, the martyrs of the Church gradually take over all the intercessory functions that belonged to angels in the apocalyptic literature, such as carrying prayer, helping in salvation, coming to comfort or help in time of danger, and conducting faithful souls to heaven.[58]

The parallels to Elijah are obvious. Elijah, who once lived on earth, takes over, as we have seen, the role of mediating God's help held by angels in Second Temple literature. A brief story that exemplifies the rise of the holy man and the eclipse of angels describes "one of the rabbis that Elijah used to frequent." Elijah tells him that he may witness the holy Sages of the past ascend in their chariots to the heavenly court or academy. Most of their chariots are lifted by angels, but Rabbi Ḥiyya ascends in a chariot that moves by its own power (or his), and Elijah warns the living rabbi not to gaze at it. But he does gaze and is half-blinded by the sight, only recovering his vision when he goes to Rabbi Ḥiyya's grave and asks for help (B. Bava Meẓia 85b). Angels, in this story, are merely means of transportation, and not the most prestigious ones. Elijah is a guide or adviser, and the saintly Rabbi Ḥiyya is by far the most powerful figure.

Elijah's secondary or subordinate position in this story is unusual; generally, when he is portrayed as a colleague of the Rabbis, it is as a senior colleague. However, this story reminds us that, in the Bavli, angels do not rescue people and rarely teach them: human beings do so, whether they are earthly Sages or Elijah. In imparting special or secret information, Elijah sometimes operates as a senior rabbi teaching subordinates, and sometimes, as here, he functions the same way as a wide range of supernatural beings who instruct the Rabbis. Perhaps Elijah's secondary status in this story flows from the fact that here he is not really portrayed as a colleague of the Rabbis—as a *human* figure—but as an all-purpose source of supernatural information.

To sum up, despite the clear parallels between the legendary Elijah and the angels—immortality, traveling between heaven and earth, possessing supernatural knowledge—the roles Elijah plays within the Bavli are distinctly different. In many ways Elijah in the Bavli moves into the angelic role of helper and comforter of the righteous that the angels play in biblical and Second Temple texts. Elijah, however, has relative freedom of action and corresponding fallibility unknown to most angels, except the angel of death. In their exilic age (as in the twenty-first century) the Rabbis saw that only a few righteous people were saved in times of national disaster, and a God who personally saved some and not others might appear capricious or even unjust. Elijah in his very unpredictability thus preserves God's consistency.

Elijah's unpredictability also affects how people relate to him in stories. People do not request Elijah's appearance by prayer, and no human action can ensure that he will show up. While the Bavli attempts to limit deliberate invocation of angels, its legends of Elijah see his appearance as nothing but good. Elijah cannot be compelled, and the Bavli does not hint that people may be tempted to worship Elijah or try to control him by magical practice. It seems the Bavli is not concerned that his power could detract from or be confused with God's power, as it is at times with angels. Furthermore, the Bavli does not warn that the appearance of Elijah is risky, nor imply that Elijah only appears to the well-schooled mystical initiate. Elijah stories, far more than stories of angels, express intimacy with the supernatural realm.

Finally, the great majority of the stories about angels and the bat kol are different from those told about Elijah. Angels reward obedience or punish disobedience impersonally. The bat kol characteristically speaks to groups, not to individuals, announcing who will inherit the world to come or ruling on individuals' relative worthiness in God sight. Elijah, in contrast, always appears to individuals when he appears in recognizable form. Elijah's characteristic functions, particularly those associated with specific generic forms of plot and language, are not shared with other supernatural beings. In short, while Elijah is a "supernatural mediator" figure, he is also a human character. He is best defined over against angels, rather than in relation to them. Closer analogies to Elijah are found among Sages and wonder workers, both among the living and among the holy dead, Jewish and sometimes Christian. Among these powerful figures, Elijah is one of the most comforting.

ELIJAH AS RABBI AND HOLY MAN

I have argued that Elijah's apparent free will makes him similar to the angel of death and that Elijah's unpredictability may express God's unpredictable mercy. These ideas, though, do not detract from the obvious: Elijah's freedom of decision is a human characteristic, and his connections to the Rabbis are in many respects closer than his connections to other supernatural beings. As we will see, the formulaic language used to introduce Elijah stories indicates that the rabbinic storytellers or redactors themselves made this connection. The formula "Rabbi N met Rabbi X" is identical to the formula "Rabbi N met Elijah" and is used in many of the same ways. A rabbi never "meets" an angel. In addition, the statement that some figure "was accustomed to converse with" another person, expressing a special honor not easily achieved, is found only for Elijah . . . and certain illustrious rabbis.

As we have seen, the Bavli does not seem concerned that veneration of Elijah might dilute people's understanding of God's power or role in salvation. In this, too, Elijah differs from the angels and resembles the Rabbis. The Sages rarely concern themselves that too much respect might be paid to one of their own number: that a respected miracle worker, for example, might be seen as a salvific or magical intermediary between his fellow people and God. Although saints alive and dead played such a role in late antique Christianity, Judaism then and now is more skeptical of human claims to perfect or exclusive relationship with God.[59] It is possible that Judaism's early rejection of Christian claims for Jesus inoculated it, so to speak, against making strong salvific claims for any being other than God alone. While Judaism rejected Christianity's beliefs in human mediators of salvation, the Bavli is fairly enthusiastic about human supernatural powers. Elijah does possess miraculous powers, and rabbis in the Bavli do too. Although they cannot do some things Elijah does—such as miraculously appearing in disguise or flying through the air—Elijah himself does not do many kinds of miracles that rabbis are said to accomplish.

Stories of rabbis concern two kinds of supernatural events. Rabbis, like other righteous folk, may automatically attract the blessings and mercy of God because of their ethical merits and, as rabbis, also because of their Torah study. In addition, they intentionally bring about miracles and do magic through their power of Torah and knowledge of its secrets. The line between miracle and magic is notoriously fuzzy, but, according to Urbach's commonsense definition, rabbinic miracles are those supernatural events that testify to the power of God and the value of the commandments.[60] Magic, on the other hand, defines supernatural actions that do not emanate directly from God, but rather are performed through secret knowledge or magical technology and testify more to the power of the individual rabbi-magician than to that of God. This is not to say that the Rabbis would have made this distinction. They had no particular word for their own miraculous/magical powers and considered magic as what their enemies did.[61]

There are many examples of rabbis successfully praying for miracles or believing that miracles would be performed on their behalf. For example, in two different stories a rabbi reassures people that a broken-down building will not collapse so long as he is in it. The rabbi does not perform any magical action; he simply knows that God will hold up the building because God recognizes his learning and piety.[62] Although rabbis' protective powers in these stories may seem somewhat "magical" in a loose modern sense of the word, they are rewards for qualities they have. When, on the other hand, Rav enters a graveyard and by certain incantations discovers who among the deceased died at their proper time and who by the evil eye, he seems more a skilled magician (B. Bava Meẓia 107b). His supernatural knowledge testifies to his own power rather than to God's blessing.

Elijah in the Bavli occupies an interesting place in the realm of the miraculous. His uniquely close relationship with God makes it unnecessary for him to use magical incantations to change the world. He acts as the intermediary of God's miraculous help for the righteous, although not generally as a direct agent of God in the way angels do. One might compare his powers to those of Rabbi Yoḥanan when he comes to Rabbi Ḥiyya bar Abba's sickbed (though Elijah rarely heals). Rabbi Yoḥanan asks, "Are your sufferings dear to you?" When the latter replies, "Neither them nor their reward," Rabbi Yoḥanan simply puts out his hand and raises him up.[63] In this case Rabbi Yoḥanan is acting by his own power, rather than petitioning God for a miracle through prayer. Nevertheless, he is not doing magic. He performs no ritual or incantation, and the story is told—at least in part—as a testimony to God's power, power He lends, so to speak, to the Sages. Rabbi Yoḥanan acts independently but in accordance with God's will rather than apart from it. This is also how Elijah acts.

Nevertheless, Elijah's God-given supernatural abilities are different in kind if not in degree from those of an earthly rabbi or holy man. Because he ascended to heaven without dying, he routinely travels freely between heaven and earth, appearing instantly (or at least at very short notice) anywhere he wants. Although the Rabbis' powers may be as remarkable as Elijah's, the specific wonders Elijah accomplishes—miraculous rescues, miraculous gifts, miraculous changes of form—are, in rabbinic tradition, uniquely his own—as much part of who he is as what he does. In the context of the Bavli, these powers do not make Elijah godlike or even precisely angelic; they simply make him a particularly valuable friend and adviser. While it is an honor for certain rabbis that Elijah appears to them as a senior colleague, it is not an inordinate or improbable honor.

Elijah most resembles the Rabbis in the details of his teaching and in the ways in which he interacts with specific Sages, greeted by them as one of their own. When

Elijah meets Rabbi Yossi in the ruins of Jerusalem, he says, "Peace be with you, my master [that is, Rabbi]," and Rabbi Yossi responds, "Peace be with you, my master and teacher." In this instance Elijah accords Rabbi Yossi the respect due to a Sage, and Rabbi Yossi in turn salutes Elijah as a senior Sage. These were ritual salutations owed to men of rabbinic rank. A disciple greets a master, "Peace be with you, my master and teacher," whereas a master greets a disciple, "Peace be with you."[64]

Elijah functions as a colleague of the Rabbis in many instances, and encounters with him are often expressed with the same formulae as encounters between rabbis and sometimes follow similar patterns. There is, for example, a form of exchange in which one rabbi meets another person (usually a rabbi or Elijah) and asks him a question the second person answers.[65] One subgroup of such stories has rabbis meeting Elijah, but there are other generic subgroups that use this formula. In seven instances, for example, a Babylonian rabbi "goes up" to Palestine and asks a local rabbi about a legal tradition or practice of the Land of Israel.[66] Stories such as this share a framing plot structure with Elijah stories in the same generic category: in each case a rabbi meets someone who has access to specialized information and asks a question the other answers. When rabbis meet Elijah and ask him what God is doing in the heavenly court, or when the Messiah will come, they are behaving like other rabbis who question a colleague on matters about which that colleague has unique knowledge.

The specific information that rabbis request from Elijah is not always about God or the Messiah. Once a rabbi meets Elijah and asks a midrashic question, "Why is woman called man's helper?" (in Gen. 2:20), receiving a highly practical answer. Elijah replies, "A man brings wheat—does he chew on [grains of] wheat? Flax—does he wear [stalks of] flax? Doesn't she brighten his eyes and stand him on his feet?"[67] Elijah's witty answer, with its two rhetorical questions, makes his response memorable. Like the Rabbis, Elijah can also teach proverbs. Elijah tells Judah, brother of Rav Sala the Pious, "Do not get boiling hot [angry] and you will not sin; do not get soggy [drunk] and you will not sin, and when you depart on a journey, acknowledge your Creator as king and depart."[68] In another instance, Rabbah bar Abbuha meets Elijah and asks three halakhic questions, and Elijah answers these questions not with a message from heaven but with biblical proof-texts such as any rabbi might use.[69] In teaching proverbs and halakhah, Elijah is clearly more like a rabbi than an angel. Whereas an angel teaches halakhah only once in the Bavli, and other supernatural beings never do so, Elijah imparts legal or homiletic teachings that fit rabbinic norms.[70]

Elijah differs from the Rabbis also introduced by the form "he found him," not so much by the miraculous infallibility of his knowledge as by its breadth. He knows what occurs on heaven and on earth; he knows halakhah and midrash. Still, Elijah's knowledge has limits. These limits appear, for example, in a passage in which Elijah speaks to a rabbi with no preamble (which is, of course, the pattern of most rabbinic interactions recorded in the Bavli).

> Elijah said to Rav Judah the brother of Rav Sala the Pious, "The world will not exist less than eighty-five jubilees, and in the last jubilee the son of David will come." He asked him, "At its beginning or its end?" He replied, "I don't know." "Will it be completed [the last jubilee] or won't it be completed?" He replied, "I don't know."
>
> (B. Sanhedrin 97b)

Here Rav Judah is not an awed witness of revelation from a godlike figure, but Elijah's junior colleague. Elijah can tell him only so much and freely admits his ignorance when asked to be more specific. In sum, the Bavli portrays Elijah in his human aspects as more a rabbi than a rabbinized holy man, more a teacher than a miracle worker or healer.[71] He shares information on matters halakhic, midrashic, and eschatological.

Elijah, unlike the angels of midrash or the righteous of biblical times, is very much a figure of the rabbinic present. He provides the Rabbis a human face for the supernatural world, an image of a being not unlike themselves who is close to God and possesses God-given miraculous powers that they themselves aspire to. Elijah forges a link between human creatures and God, the heavens and the earth, by both his activities and his very existence. The other luminaries of biblical times, the patriarchs, Moses, and David, are lovingly remembered in midrash and are sometimes spoken of as existing at their tombs or with God in paradise; only Elijah is free to travel anywhere and serve as teacher, helper, and model.

Elijah as Ideal Teacher

Elijah's functions as ideal teacher and model are key aspects of his role in rabbinic life. To see why this is so one must step back and examine the teacher's role in rabbinic Judaism. The whole system of rabbinic education and piety was intimately bound up with the practice of discipleship. As Neusner writes, "It was the 'service of the disciples of the sages' that ultimately separated the true sage from the merely learned man." In imitating their masters, the disciples of the Sages "conformed to the heavenly paradigm of the Torah."[72] The practice of devotion to and imitation of one's master and teacher was a key aspect of classical and late antique culture. Not surprisingly, both Jewish and Christian piety consecrated service to one's master as way of serving God. Rabbinic texts teach that a teacher is more worthy of his disciple's respect than his own father, for fathers only bring one into this world, but teachers bring one into the world to come. As Jaffee writes of discipleship in general: "In the disciple-community the disciple returns to the psychological situation of childhood to be fundamentally reformed as a human being."[73] Even in the laconic anecdotes of rabbinic writings one can often discern the depth and closeness of the relationship between master and student. In the Bavli this close bond between Sage and disciple is expressed especially in legends of the tannaim, such as the story of Rabbi Meir, who will not abandon his teacher Elisha ben Abuya when he becomes an apostate.[74]

The importance of discipleship within both rabbinic and Christian communities makes it possible to consider whether Elijah's role as master and teacher resembled the heavenly masters of the Christian world, the saints and martyrs. According to Peter Brown, one of the primary social, emotional, and ethical functions of the Christian saints was to provide an ideal model of just and proper authority, a heavenly counterpart and counterpoint to the patronage system of the wider society. For a serious and learned Christian, one devoted to a particular saint, that saint became an ideal model who attracted the "deep warmth that always welled up in ancient Mediterranean men around the figure of the beloved teacher and spiritual guide."[75]

Similarly, Elijah is an ideal teacher for the Rabbis. Not only is he addressed as "master and teacher," but he often acts as an ideal teacher, displaying patience and dispensing encouragement in ways that speak to the tensions between the disciples of the Sages and their earthly teachers.[76] Elijah's encouragement counterbalances other tensions of rabbinic life as well, in particular the ever present competition within the rabbinic subculture in which spiritual and intellectual success were one.

Tensions Between Master and Disciple and Elijah

The strong emotional connections and spiritual aspirations focused by the practice of discipleship brought with them corresponding tensions. Although rabbinic texts exhort the disciples of the Sages to behave respectfully toward everyone, they stress humility toward a teacher above all. A tannaitic source cited in the Bavli states that a disciple who greets his master disrespectfully, who publicly questions his master's decisions in court, or who teaches something that he has not heard from his master's mouth causes the Shekhinah, the presence of God, to depart from Israel.[77] Four later midrashim say that if a disciple quarrels with his master, contends with him, expresses resentment against him, or speaks evil of him, it is as if he had done so against the Shekhinah. In each case the prooftexts are biblical passages in which opposing Moses is identified with rebellion against God.[78] One can easily imagine how difficult it would have been for a sensitive student to reconcile himself to the inevitable feelings of resentment that would arise in him against his teacher, especially if the teacher were arrogant or abrasive.

The strict hierarchy between disciple and master existed throughout the master's life. The designation "disciple of the Sages," as a general term for rabbis as well as students, not only indicates the importance of discipleship in rabbinic society but also implies that a rabbi was in some sense a disciple, a student, throughout his life. Even after Abaye, for example, becomes a teacher in his own right, the hierarchical distinction between him and his teacher Rabbah is maintained consistently. So, too, Abaye never teaches in declarative statements in the presence of his other teacher, Rav Yosef, although he often voices strong and sometimes successful objections to the older Sage's statements. This pattern is characteristic of an inferior teacher in the presence of a superior; a man who is both a disciple and a teacher can and does object to his teacher, using logic or traditional sources, but never teaches or rules independently in his master's presence.[79] The Sages' passion for the truth was inevitably both spiritual and self-interested. This passion, and their need for accurate legal decisions as well, must have made the relationship between master and more advanced disciple particularly problematic.[80] The rabbinic tradition was not quietistic; competition in the search for truth was open, even between senior and junior teachers, and mutual respect and traditional sanctions could only go so far in smoothing out the tensions inherent in rabbinic dialogue.

Serious problems arising between masters and disciples and between Sages in general are sometimes expressed in the Bavli with the difficult to translate phrase ḥalash da'atei "his/her mind became sick" (חלש דעתיה\ה). "He became heartsick," is a more idiomatic translation, because it does not suggest we would call mental weakness or illness, but heartfelt pain or shame.[81] In an interpersonal context, "he became heartsick" refers to a powerful mixture of humiliation, bitterness, and anger. The person who has these painful feelings can be dangerous to the person who has hurt him or her, casting a sort of unconscious curse. When, for example, a certain student of the Sages is mocked by others and becomes heartsick, a senior Sage implores him not to bring down punishment upon his colleagues—not by anything he might do but by the consequences that will result from the way he feels unless he forgives those who disrespect him (Ḥagigah 5b).

Of the twenty appearances of the term in the Bavli, six refer specifically to conflicts between masters and disciples.[82] In these conflicts, it is always the teacher who becomes heartsick at his student's disrespect and the student who is endangered. The tragic end of the friendship of Rabbi Yoḥanan and Reish Lakish comes because Rabbi Yoḥanan the teacher could not control his hurt and anger at his student's insult until it was too late. When Reish Lakish dies and Rabbi Yoḥanan realizes at last the cost of his unforgiving bitterness, he becomes inconsolable and dies himself. Even when one leaves behind the mythic atmosphere pervading legends from early generations of amoraim, one continues to encounter the notion that a teacher's humiliation and anger are dangerous for a student. When the apparently highly irritating Rav Adda bar Ahavah dies unexpectedly, no less than five Sages claim responsibility for his death, four of them because he offended them personally.[83]

In light of the rabbinic view that undertaking a master-disciple relationship opened one to both emotional pain and physical danger, the simple fact that Elijah does no harm becomes unusual and important. In relationship to the disciples of the Sages, the worst that Elijah ever does is refuse to visit someone whose behavior displeases him. Elijah never takes personal offense and thus exposes others to danger, as living masters may. Rabbis of medieval and later times have left written testimony that they experienced themselves as personal students of Elijah, blessed with his presence by God's grace and their own spiritual excellence. We do not know if any such existed in Talmudic times, only that people told stories about Elijah visiting others. These stories present Elijah as a heavenly teacher to which all disciples of the Sages may turn, envisioning themselves as potentially his students.

Even more vitally, Elijah brings word of, and thus represents, God as ideal Master, a Teacher who has infinite dignity and honor and who thus can neither be offended nor, needless to say, shamed. For example, in the oven of Akhnai story, in which the Sages assert their right to legislate according to the majority in the face of miracles and even a bat kol in support of the minority view, Elijah crowns the tale by later telling Rabbi Natan that God was laughing when the Rabbis contradicted him, laughing and saying, "My sons have defeated me." In a story less known but perhaps even more powerful, Elijah carries Rabbah bar Shila's message to God that He should be reciting the traditions of Rabbi Meir even though Meir learned Torah from Elisha ben Abuya the apostate, and Elijah returns with the news that God has agreed and is now doing so (B. Bava Meẓia 59b and Ḥagigah 15b).[84]

Elijah's role in these stories is dramatically different from that of angels and the bat kol, through which God often speaks to discourage human presumption. Elijah supports human power, relaying news from God's heavenly court, which is understood, on the human model, to be at least as much a place of study as of judgment, a place where God and the Sages of past generations study Torah and recite legal traditions. Thus Elijah as teacher and adviser of the Rabbis reveals God to be an ideally accepting master and teacher, one who encourages rather than takes offense at students who challenge his authority—at least in certain matters.

Elijah Stories and the Tensions of Rabbinic Society

Another aspect of Elijah's role as an ideal teacher is his ability to adjudicate between Sages of more or less equal rank. In so doing, Elijah helps resolve another tension of rabbinic society, the constant competition for rank. The limited egalitarianism of the rabbinic community of Torah study meant that high rank depended not only on birth or wealth but also on having one's scholarly accomplishments recognized as superior to those of others. The stories of various Amoraim who come off well when in the company of one rabbi but appear as idiots when in the company of another indicate not only divergent sources but a lively rivalry between rabbis and between their circles.[85] Kalmin writes:

> Contemporaries and near-contemporaries [those separated by only one generation] express not only anger or surprise in response to specific statements or actions, but also the conviction that a particular sage is fundamentally flawed or inadequate. The accusation will be made, for example, that a rabbi's traditions are untrustworthy, that he violates halakhah . . . that he has not served as an apprentice rabbi and is therefore not a full-fledged member of the rabbinic community and the like.[86]

Even when relations among rabbis were not strained to the breaking point by rivalry for scholarly renown and the authority accompanying it, relative rank inescapably structured their interactions [87] One should read the stories that confirm rabbinic rankings with supernatural support within the context of rabbinic competition. Establishing rank was so important, and sometimes stressful, that rabbinic sources bring in miracles or supernatural revelations simply to confirm the superiority of certain Sages or resolve conflicts between rabbis or their schools. The tension between pride and humility, between serving God by study for its own sake and seeking human renown, seems so great that establishing proper rank was an existential problem for the Rabbis. The bat kol is usually God's messenger when the issue is eternal life or fundamental worth; when the issue is who is correct, Elijah steps in. In either case, the supernatural mediator, like a good teacher of contentious students, often affirms the fundamental value of both parties.

Unlike the bat kol, Elijah does not rule on a person's absolute "greatness" or worthiness; that is a role fittingly reserved for a divine voice that speaks more directly for God. Instead, these Elijah stories address an issue almost as loaded for the Rabbis: "who is right?"—that is to say, who is the more effective, the wiser, Sage? Issues of rank and of halakhic authority are clearly bound up in this issue, as we see from the story of Rabbi Aviatar.[88] Rabbi Aviatar sends a legal ruling to Rav Ḥisda, and Aviatar's authority is brought into question by Rav Yosef on the grounds that he wrote Bible verses improperly, without underlining them. Abaye rejoins that this rule is simply a tradition Aviatar had not heard, ignorance of which does not impugn the rabbi's legal authority. Furthermore, Abaye (or perhaps an anonymous voice) continues, Rabbi Aviatar is the one "whose master confirmed his opinion." Then follows a story of Rabbi Aviatar meeting Elijah and finding out from him that God is reciting two interpretations of the story of the concubine of Gibeah, his and Rabbi Yonatan's. Aviatar says in effect, "God forbid that God should be uncertain," and Elijah replies that both are "the words of the living God," using the same words as the famous bat kol resolving the dispute between the houses of Shammai and Hillel.[89]

This story could easily have followed a pattern like that of the bat kol stories, especially because it shares a memorable phrase with one of them. In this pattern Elijah would have explained how both rabbis are right, but that one is somehow more worthy of having his view adopted. But Elijah does not rank the two views, rather including them both in God's words, even though the introduction to the story, with its concern for legitimate authority, seems to be leading up to a ranking. This inclusiveness is even more strongly expressed in a similar story in which Elijah speaks purely on his own rather than transmitting God's view. A midrash in Bavli Megillah gives the teachings of twelve (!) different rabbis on why Esther invited Haman to her banquet with the king. When Rabbah bar Abbuha meets Elijah, he asks him whose reasoning Esther shared in doing what she did. Elijah replies that her thinking was "like all Tannaitic and all Amoraic views" (B. Megillah 15b).

One could see this as inclusiveness raised to the point of absurdity. Both these stories, however, are much more than rabbinic jokes. They fulfill an important function as commentary or counterpoint to the rabbinic competition for legitimacy. They say, in the clearest way possible, that on some issues — and one notes that these are not practical halakhic issues — everyone's teaching can be true.[90] These stories reinforce the stories above in which Elijah, and God as Elijah presents Him, are teachers more tolerant of challenges and apparent disrespect than many earthly teachers are. Both sets of legends invoke the highest authority to encourage confidence and self-respect in their hearers amid the rabbinic struggle to be recognized as right for the sake of both God's truth and human recognition. In light of research showing that rabbinic Judaism had not yet become normative in the amoraic era, such stories may also "reflect a need to legitimize rabbinic authority" in the face of challenges by nonrabbinic Jews.[91]

Elijah Compared to the Christian Saints

As noted above, the relationship Brown describes between educated Christians and their patron saints sheds light on the relationship between the Rabbis and Elijah. In both cases, the heavenly human being serves as an ideal teacher for the disciple on earth. This correspondence makes it appropriate to look for other possible resemblances between Elijah and the saints. It is also true that both Elijah and the saints are part of the phenomenon by which human figures replace angelic ones as heavenly mediators. Aside from these two important similarities, however, Elijah is distinctly different from the Christian saints. The core of this difference lies in Elijah's resemblance to the Sages; he is in many respects a rabbi writ large. Rabbis' social and religious roles were quite different from those of the living Christian holy people who were their contemporaries, and Elijah differs correspondingly from Christian saints in heaven.

The most striking disparity between the Sages and their Christian counterparts lies in the kind of supernatural mediation they offer. The Byzantine Christian world had in practice come to doubt the direct access to God traditionally attributed to all the baptized. By the fourth and fifth centuries, "the ordinary Christian layman no longer had confidence that his prayers were acceptable to God." Instead, most Christians relied on holy men and women who by ascetic practice had won free access to God and thus served as mediators of healing and divine blessing, and of salvation.[92] In contrast, the Rabbis had a relatively sporadic and insignificant role as healers or mediators of God's blessing. One must stress the word *relatively*, because the Rabbis did sometimes heal, and they could successfully request God's help for their communities—particularly rain in times of drought. The Rabbis, however, did not serve as healers for their communities, do not appear to have performed exorcisms, and (unlike Elijah) very rarely brought about miracles for specific individuals, all characteristic functions of Christian holy men and women. Most significantly, the Rabbis never served as mediators of salvation, whereas human beings did mediate salvation in Byzantine Christianity. Some traditions describe how when the devotee of a holy man died "the spiritual father would draw up and place in the hands of his son a safe conduct to heaven."[93]

The Rabbis' negligible role as spiritual mediators is mirrored by Elijah. Elijah's spiritual mediation is limited to supplying information about God's will or God's activities in heaven. Furthermore, Elijah is never a mediator of salvation. Within the rabbinic tradition, there are no real mediators of salvation, at least in part because of the tradition's emphasis on strict monotheism. While the bat kol often supplies the assurance of salvation, it announces God's decision at the time of a person's death rather than in any way bringing it about.

In contrast, both rabbis and Elijah, like the saints, protect against physical calamities, although in this case Elijah is rather more like a Christian saint than like a rabbi: rabbis usually benefited the community as a whole, whereas Elijah bestows help on specific individuals in crisis. Sages bring rain and may also avert communal disasters through their prayers. Rabbis and other pious folk are also described as automatically protecting their communities from harm by their good deeds, as when a woman who heated her oven and let others cook in it prevented a fire from burning down her neighborhood.[94] Elijah, in contrast, works on an individual basis. The one time Elijah seeks to benefit the Jewish community (and the world) as a whole, he advises Rabbi Judah the Patriarch that the prayers of Rabbi Ḥiyya and his sons will bring the Messiah and encounters a resounding failure. God hears what Elijah is doing, punishes him, and has him stop the attempt (B. Bava Meẓia 85b).

Though Elijah resembles Christian saints in coming to rescue individuals, he differs in the kind of danger he comes to remedy. Elijah mediates God's saving power in situations where one human being is in trouble with other people. He rescues Rav Kahana when the latter throws himself off the roof to avoid being forced into sinful sexual intercourse. He convinces Rabbi Ishmael to stop acting as an informer (B. Kiddushin 40a, B. Bava Meẓia 83b–84a). Most characteristically, he appears in disguise to rescue Jews when they are menaced by Gentiles. The this-worldly and human dangers from which Elijah saves people emphasize the prophet's own humanity. In many respects, Elijah in the Bavli acts as a supernaturally powerful political patron. Just as one expects a human patron to help with human-caused problems, the Bavli has Elijah coming to rescue those threatened by other people. In this respect, Elijah differs markedly from Christian saints, who mediated more aspects of divine power, interceding in all sorts of individual and community misfortunes.

To conclude, Elijah often interacts with the Sages as a senior Sage. As we have seen, many stories about a rabbi meeting Elijah use the same formulaic language as stories describing the meeting between two Sages. Like a Sage, and unlike a Christian saint, Elijah does not help his disciples achieve eternal salvation or effective prayer. Rather, he provides insight, halakhic knowledge, and news about God. This information about God often presents God Godself as a Sage writ large, one who supports and delights in the Rabbis' assertion of truth as they understand it. In so doing, the Elijah of the Bavli serves as an ideal teacher, providing unlimited support and intellectual validation to anyone working faithfully within the rabbinic way of life.

Finally, Elijah is often also an intermediary of God's saving power in times and places where Jews are troubled by other people, usually Gentiles. As shown, when Elijah rescues individual people from practical difficulties, he is not operating on the model of the Sages, nor, as we saw before, on an angelic model. While Elijah's powers to rescue somewhat resemble those of Christian saints, I will argue that there are also interesting connections between Elijah and the god Hermes, connections that strongly suggest some interreligious borrowing of motifs. To support this somewhat outrageous claim, the next section will include a longer explanation of why cross-cultural comparison is useful tool for analyzing rabbinic texts.

ELIJAH AS HERMES FIGURE

As we have seen, some Elijah stories in the Bavli and later draw from the prophet's role in Kings and in Malachi, as herald of the last days, and from midrashim on the biblical Elijah. Other Elijah legends express rabbinic aspirations and values. However, in addition to these intra-Jewish ingredients in Elijah's character, Hermes too plays a role. Although we are focusing on the stories in the Bavli, a legend from a later midrash very clearly underlines how different Elijah's role in the rabbinic present can be from his role in Scripture. In this story Elijah appears in dream to help a man with money troubles.

There is a story of a certain man who was carrying his money on a Friday. Near sunset he entered a synagogue. He found a man praying with tefillin still on his head. The man with money said to himself, "Shouldn't I deposit this money only with this person who is crowned with the commandments?" He got up and deposited it with him. [But when] he came at the end of the Sabbath, the other denied [he had] it.

He [the first] said to him, "It was not you that I put my trust in, but the holy Name that was on your head." He wrapped himself in his prayer shawl and stood up to pray in the same place, before Him, "Master of the Universe, I put my trust in nothing other than the holy Name that was on his head." After he prayed he lay and slept. Elijah of blessed memory appeared to the man. He said, "Go tell the wife of that man [with the tefillin], 'This is the sign that you have—On Passover night we eat leaven, and on the Day of Atonement, some of that stuff.' Then say, 'Give me the valuables left with you.'" And she went and gave him [the money].[95]

I argue that this picture of Elijah, seen here and in certain legends in the Bavli, was created under the influence of, or in competition with, attributes of the Greek god Hermes. Hermes, like Elijah, was the protector of travelers, patron of financial success, and master of clever stratagems of all kinds.

One cannot now know whether the figure of Hermes influenced the character of the legendary Elijah from the earliest stages. What I seek to show is that at some point Jews noticed similarities between Elijah and Hermes and deliberately constructed stories about Elijah in which he performed functions similar to those of Hermes (but better, of course). From that point on, some developed the comparisons consciously for polemical purposes, while others may have made them unconsciously. Eventually, probably still in Talmudic times, the connection was forgotten, but Elijah retained certain characteristics of the Greek god.

Several authors have noted Elijah's resemblance to Hermes in a general way. Wiener's Jungian study of Elijah notes that the prophet has aspects in common with the god. Hermes, like Elijah is "a spiritual leader who . . . symbolizes the reconciliation of opposites," the human and divine realms.[96] Segal writes that Elijah "became what the folk wanted him to be. . . . He is at times the sublime prophet, at times a shifty Mercury," and so on.[97] Segal ascribes Elijah's Hermes-like character to the material aspirations of poor folk, invoking ordinary human desires for healing, help, and success. Neither considers that Jews may actually have taken motifs or functions from the cult of Hermes and transferred them to Elijah. Ben-Amos, on the other hand, admits the possibility of historical connection. Observing that Hermes is both at times a savior figure and a shape-shifter, characteristics Elijah shares, he adds that further study might reveal some historical connection between the two figures.[98]

Although we have no rabbinic sources that explicitly contrast Elijah to Hermes or otherwise connect the two figures, there is a wealth of suggestive resemblances between them. Some of these resemblances are general and obvious: both are liminal figures, existing between heaven and earth, both messengers of the divine, and sometime shape-shifters. Hermes is the quintessential trickster, and Elijah can be one too. Other resemblances are more occasional and more obscure. They carry cumulative weight when taken together and with the more general similarities.

But how did Jews come to hear and adapt stories about Hermes? Contemporaneous cultures and religions frequently connect at three points: in their basic worldviews and common preoccupations; in their magical practices; and in their use of narrative themes and motifs. We have discussed Elijah in light of the shift in worldview in which human beings tended to became supernatural mediators, replacing angels and so forth. This section will be more concerned with magical practices and especially with narrative themes and motifs. Magical practices provide evidence for Jewish knowledge of Hermes; narrative and mythological details supply evidence for the resemblances between Elijah and the Greek god. First, however, it makes sense to evaluate the validity of cross-cultural comparison in itself and examine evidence of opportunities Jews had to hear about Hermes.

The Possibility of Cross-Cultural Comparison

Social connections between Jews and Gentiles provide the most likely source of correspondences between Jewish tradition and that of surrounding cultures. Word-of-mouth communication can never be proven, and the Talmud's written tales of Jewish-Gentile conversation are of dubious historicity at best, but evidence for these connections is to be found in numerous highly specific resemblances in religious thinking and storytelling across East-West and Jewish-Gentile boundaries. Many scholars have worked with the concept of a Mediterranean and, to a significant extent, a pan-Mediterranean *and* Middle Eastern cultural koine to elucidate the religious and magical beliefs of late antiquity. Lieberman's *Hellenism in Jewish Palestine* and related works are eloquent testimonies to the value of this approach in rabbinic studies.[99] On the Patristic side, Peter Brown writes of "a *koine* which by the end of this [late antique] period had already spilled far from the shores of the Mediterranean, to the Nestorian hagiography of Sasanian Iran and the Celtic holy men of Northumbria."[100] Brown does not shrink, for example, from using the Persian Mani, founder of the Manichaean religion, to illustrate the close relationship to a guardian spirit or angel that is characteristic of many third-century religious leaders from "Iran to Northumbria."[101] Daniel Boyarin, writing more recently, cites connections between Hellenistic culture and the Babylonian Talmud in both a humorous anecdote and a fundamental change in scholarly approach.[102]

One does not usually, however, find the clearest manifestations of this common religious culture in its more esoteric expressions, in the finer points of rabbinic halakhah or Patristic theology. Rather they appear in the aspects of culture common to most people and closest to most people's daily needs and preoccupations. The commonest correspondences between religions and regions come in three areas: in social beliefs such as gender roles and postulates about the supernatural, such as belief in human supernatural mediators; in magical practice; and in mythical and legendary narrative themes that speak powerfully to people of a given age.

Magical material is strikingly similar across geographical regions. Most charms, amulets, and incantations survived more or less by chance. Our largest contemporary sources for late antique magical texts are papyri from Egypt, because of the dry climate, and magic bowls from Syria and Babylonia, because of the bowls' durable material. Both these sources exhibit connections to material in Palestinian and Babylonian rabbinic literature. Lieberman notes that the Bavli and Babylonian magic bowls shed light on the popular practices of oath taking in Palestine.[103] Even Jewish and Hellenistic texts may be mutually illuminating. Daniel Sperber writes that "in the study of Hellenistic magical and Gnostic material, rabbinic lore may at time[s] illumine an obscure point, just as a puzzling passage in the Midrash may find its solution in a Greek or Coptic magical text."[104] One sometimes cannot even determine whether a particular magical text has Egyptian or Babylonian origins. The translator of *Sepher HaRazim*, Mordecai Margaliot, writes that it has more or less equally close similarities to Egyptian magical papyri and Babylonian magic bowls.[105]

The third common point of contact between religions, cultures, and regions is found in narrative motifs and whole plots that are irresistibly retellable. For example, rabbinic sources from Palestine and Babylonia have two stories with the same basic plot about two famous miracle workers, Ḥanina ben Dosa and Pinḥas ben Yair. In each of the stories the daughter of a cistern maker falls into the water and the rabbi predicts her survival on the grounds that her father's meritorious profession will protect her. In the story about Ḥanina ben Dosa the daughter is rescued by a "an old man leading a ram," whereas one of the versions of the other story says that she was rescued by an angel in the form of the rabbi who predicted her survival, Pinḥas ben Yair himself.[106] Patristic literature contains a very close parallel to the second rabbinic story. In this story a pious woman welcomes the saintly monk Julian Saba to her house and her only son falls into a well. Though she assumes the child is drowned, they find the little boy "sitting on the surface of the water, striking the water playfully with his hand." On being brought up out of the well, he runs to Julian and says that he had seen Julian himself supporting him above the water.[107]

Another striking plot motif found in both rabbinic and Patristic material is that of a serpent enforcing the will of God. In *Lives of the Monks of Palestine* a monk who attempts to steal from the monastery is prevented from claiming his buried treasure by a snake that blocks his way. When, however, he confesses his crime, others have no difficulty getting the money.[108] This role of the serpent as an agent of justice is in striking contrast to the usual place of wild animals in stories of Middle Eastern monks: they are generally either killed, frightened away, or tamed by the monk's God-given charisma.[109] Rabbinic literature shares the same contrast: serpents, usually seen as entirely pernicious, on three occasions enforce the will of heaven, guarding the entrance to a holy rabbi's tomb. Twice the snake moves aside, when properly requested, and once a bat kol comes to explain why it does not.[110] Here the connection between Christian and Jewish stories is a shared plot motif rather than an entire plot. Nevertheless, the stories have telling points in common. In both the snake guards the "underworld," be it a tomb or buried treasure; in both the snake's presence is a miracle directly from God.

Thus we see how many connections there were in religious thinking and storytelling within and across religious boundaries in late antiquity. Pagan Greco-Roman ideas and culture, like Christian, also influenced rabbinic tradition, apparently from popular knowledge of mythological motifs. Jews of the rabbinic era, especially in Roman Palestine, would have been familiar with pagan symbols and probably the stories that went with them. Seth Schwartz, in his *Imperialism and Jewish Society*, cites the strong archaeological evidence that third- and fourth-century Tiberias and Sepphoris, with apparent Jewish majorities, "were normal Greco-Roman cities, with a full range of institutions and public buildings and spaces" and had much apparently pagan iconography, public and private. Schwartz argues that the majority of Jews at this period were only very loosely Jewish and participated in the official pagan rites of their cities.[111] His claim is controversial: other scholars hold that it goes much too far for the majority of Jews.[112] However,

Schwartz is on firmer ground when he emphasizes the "ubiquity" of pagan mythological motifs in cities with Jewish majorities.[113]

I suspect that Jews of the rabbinic era had many different responses to images of pagan gods in public and private decoration, including grudging toleration and aesthetic enjoyment; some must have interpreted them in Jewish ways, as somewhat later Jews must have interpreted the astrological mosaics on synagogue floors. In any case, the omnipresence of pagan images and the social connections between Jews and their neighbors makes it likely that Jews had a rough sense of what these images represented.[114] Several examples of Greco-Roman mythology entering Jewish storytelling are found in midrash. For example, the Procrustean bed, on which travelers were cut or stretched to fit, turns up in the arsenal of the people of Sodom, who were legendary for their cruelty to poor strangers.[115]

Rabbis might also deliberately choose to borrow an idea or practice from the wider non-Jewish world. While the Procrustean bed seems to be merely a good story, Elman, for example, argues that the fourth-century Babylonian Sage Rava accepts part of the Zoroastrian model of theodicy, arguing that life span, the survival of one's children, and one's material sustenance are dependent on an individual's astrological fate assigned at birth, a conclusion rejected by later Sages.[116] Even the quintessentially Jewish ritual of the Passover Seder was informed by the surrounding Greco-Roman culture—and in more than the obvious custom of reclining. S. Stein argues that several details of the Haggadah—two examples being the discussion about the food and the extravagant rhetorical augmentation of the plagues from 10 to 50 to 250—were influenced by the classical *symposium*, a formal dinner that might be either cultured or raucous. Stein concludes, "The compilers of the Haggadah have made their own contribution to sympotic writings. It is, in fact . . . an unanswered challenge to its models."[117]

The Elijah story at the beginning of this section may descend from earlier versions that contained a similar challenge, although probably a more popular one. One of the subtexts of these tales might easily have been, "You deluded pagans hold that Hermes protects travelers, but our Elijah can and does do what you only *think* that Hermes does." Nevertheless, the key supernatural actor in the story is not Elijah but God, who sends Elijah in response to the defrauded man's challenge that he had put his trust only on God's Holy Name. Furthermore, in context, the story is brought to prove intra-Jewish points, one being that hypocrites can pretend to be pious by wearing tefillin. This story's effortless integration of pagan and Jewish motifs is characteristic of Jewish folklore's use of non-Jewish elements. They quickly become fully incorporated, with their non-Jewish origin forgotten.[118] This is true for most of connections between Elijah and Hermes explored here: though they may well have begun in conscious opposition to pagan beliefs, probably in Palestine, they probably were quickly assimilated into Jewish tradition.

Jewish Knowledge of Hermes

Although we know little about the popular worship of Hermes, the god was still respected in late antiquity. Mercury, the Roman name for the god, was the protector of peddlers and merchants, and statues of Hermes presided over marketplaces throughout the Greco-Roman world.[119] In addition, what rabbinic literature calls *merkolis*, busts of Hermes on pillars surrounded by cairns of stones, were found in both Palestine and Babylonia as market guardians and road markers.[120] In fact, the Bavli's mention of these cairns is one of the few indications of a popular Hermes cult in Babylonia itself.

The ancient story of Hermes' childhood was still retold by writers such as Apollodorus in the early centuries of our era. In it, the infant god, child of Zeus and a nymph, slips out of his swaddling bands and steals Apollo's cattle. When Apollo catches up with him, he must take him before Zeus to demand justice before Hermes finally confesses. Hermes then promises to return the cattle — less the two that he has sacrificed to the twelve gods, including himself! Zeus laughs, amazed and amused by his child's presumption. When Apollo goes off with Hermes to claim his herd, Hermes shows him the lyre that he has just invented, playing a sweet song praising Apollo's intelligence and generosity. Apollo not only forgives him but trades all his cattle for the new musical instrument. When they return to Zeus, Zeus makes Hermes his messenger and herald and the god of commerce and travel, giving him a herald's staff and extracting a promise that he will be better behaved.[121]

This story captures the freedom of action and skill with words that were associated with Hermes. Despite his trickiness, Hermes retains the innocent chutzpah of a child, disarming his opponents and allowing them to forgive him. Of course Hermes' functions did not stop there. He was patron of the art of rhetoric and, like Apollo, associated with divination, as well as being the god of merchants and thieves. He also has another side, as the psychopomp who leads souls to the underworld. In fact, Hermes has so many roles that Lucian, a second-century skeptic and satirist, has Hermes complain that he is the gods' put-upon slave of all work: "It is not enough that I must be busy all day in the wrestling-ground and the Assembly and the schools of rhetoric, the dead must have their share in me too."[122] In fact, Hermes resembles Elijah in his many roles and the trouble one has determining his key defining characteristics.

Although Hermes had few major cult centers in the ancient world, his worship is well attested in classical and late antique times, and the history of Syro-Palestine reveals literary and archaeological traces of Hermes. Hermes was known in the area long before rabbinic times. Excavations at a Hellenistic fortress in lower Galilee, built about 250 BCE, found a knucklebone from a sheep or goat, often used in gambling, inscribed with *Hermes* in Greek letters.[123] Statues or coins depicting Hermes have been found in Baalbek-Heliopolis (not far north of Upper Galilee), Caesaria Philipi, Antioch, Sidon, and Tyre.[124] Nor was the worship of Hermes unknown in Babylonia. Excavations at Tyre revealed a statue of Hermes from the Parthian period.[125]

There are two categories of Jewish sources that refer directly to Hermes, rabbinic and magical. Rabbinic texts notice Hermes as a problem—the problem of unavoidable contact with pagan worship. Magical texts see Hermes as a resource. The discussion of the merkolis, the roadside shrine to Hermes, in the Mishnah and the Talmuds' accompanying commentary are among the most extensive treatments of named pagan deities. Saul Lieberman holds that Hermes was regarded as a typical pagan god, at least insofar as being the favorite representative case of pagan worship.[126] This was probably because the images of the merkolis were common, public, and unavoidable—not hidden in pagan temples—and yet definitely worshipped—unlike decorative images on mosaics or statues in bath houses. The magical references to Hermes appear on an apparently Jewish Babylonian magic bowl and in *Sepher HaRazim,* the collection of magical texts from the Cairo Geniza.

To start with the earliest rabbinic source, the merkolis appears twice in the Mishnah. Mishnah Sanhedrin states that among those guilty of idolatry are "one who uncovers himself before Baal Peor; one who throws a stone at a *merkolis*: this is its worship."[127] Here the merkolis are linked to the idols of Baal Peor, mentioned in the Bible, as unusual cases, because both are worshipped in apparently disrespectful ways, by exposing oneself to them or tossing rocks at them. Mishnah Avodah Zarah deals with whether Jews can benefit from a merkolis or offerings left by it, given that benefiting from idolatrous worship is forbidden. One ruling holds that stones that "appear to be with it are forbidden; those that do not appear to be with it are permitted. If coins, clothing, or useful items were found on its head, behold they are permitted; but bunches of grapes . . . or anything whose like is offered on the altar, [these are] forbidden."

Most of the discussion of these passages in the Bavli is conceptual, responding to the theoretical questions they imply. For example, if a person tossed a stone at a merkolis not intending worship, perhaps even intending disrespect, is that person still guilty of idolatry?[128] This discussion, despite its theoretical aim, reveals that there were merkolis in Babylonia. Rav Menasseh, a late third-century Amora, was going to Bei Torata, a town in Babylonia. When they told him there was an idol by the road, he threw a stone at it. Then they told him it was a *merkolis* and, therefore, he had "worshipped" it.[129] Whatever the historicity of this story, it suggests that there were merkolis in Babylonia, but not in all localities. Thus the local people were familiar with it, but the visiting Rav Menasseh was not.

If rabbinic Sages in Babylonia were familiar with the merkolis as idols to be avoided, other Babylonian Jews had a higher opinion of Hermes. A magic bowl found at Nippur seeks to protect the life and property of Yezidad bar Izdandukh in the name of God, referred to by the characteristically Jewish titles of Shadda El and the Holy One and in the name of numerous angels and good spirits, the first listed being "Gabriel, Michael, Raphael . . . the angel Asiel, and Hermes the great lord (מריא רבא)."[130] In this text Hermes is simply granted the status of an angel, one standing only a little below the archangels, surprising as this might seem in a text whose first appeal is to God with his Jewish titles. Another Jewish text, one mostly dealing with angels, also includes an invocation to Hermes. *Sepher HaRazim* has an invocation of Hermes as god of graveyards and the dead:

> If you wish to question a ghost; stand facing a tomb and repeat the names of the angels of the fifth encampment (while holding) in your hand a new flask (containing) oil and honey mixed together and say thus: I adjure you O spirit of the ram bearer [קריפורייא, i.e., Κριοφορος, which is a Greek name for Hermes] who dwell [*sic*] among the graves among the bones of the dead, that you will accept from my hand this offering . . . and bring me (the spirit of) N son of N who is dead.[131]

Jewish knowledge of Hermes' epithet "ram bearer" raises an intriguing possibility. In the previously mentioned story a cistern maker's daughter falls into the water and is rescued because of her father's worthy profession, saved by a "an old man leading a ram."[132] In later Jewish tradition, and possibly in the Bavli as well (although in general we are not concerning ourselves with the possibility), an unknown "old man" often stands for Elijah. Perhaps, in this case, the unknown rescuer is Elijah, identified by an attribute borrowed from Hermes. While reasoning from such an odd little detail may appear frivolous in isolation, it is the first brick of possibility among a number of other odd little details, bricks that can support the weight-bearing structure of argument.

Returning to aspects of Hermes of which Jews might have been aware, we come to the cult of Hermes Trismegistus. For non-Christian Gentiles in late antiquity, Hermes often took on the characteristics of Hermes Trismegistus. Developing from an Egyptian fusion of Hermes and Thoth, the Egyptian celestial scribe, god of wisdom, and judge of the dead, Hermes Trismegistus developed an influential cult of his own whose beliefs were disseminated in the Hermetic writings, which ranged through magic, astrology, and theosophy to a philosophy with resemblances to both Gnosticism and Neoplatonism. One belief expressed throughout the Hermetic corpus is that Hermes, or at least *their* Hermes, author of all the Hermetic books, had once been a mortal man, now divinized.[133] This belief that Hermes was a mortal who had been promoted to godhood is probably the pagan form of the increasing emphasis on human mediators of supernatural power in relation to Christianity and Judaism.

The human origins of Hermes in the Hermetic texts may have made it easier for Jews to compare him (unfavorably of course) with Elijah. Then, in becoming better than Hermes, Elijah becomes in some ways like him. This process is analogous to that described by VanderKam for Enoch in Second Temple times when he writes that the Second Temple tradition's authors "enlivened . . . Enoch with a variety of mythological traits and thus created for Judaism a primeval hero who outshone the legendary supermen or even divinities of any other people."[134] In this process, though, Enoch took on roles, such as that inventor of civilization, not played by the biblical Enoch. A similar process took place for at least one Hellenistic writer, apparently Jewish, who assimilated Moses rather than Elijah to the Egyptian Thoth-Hermes, whose cult was associated with the origins of Hermes Trismegistus and who was far more respectable than the Greek god of wayfarers and thieves.[135]

But would the Rabbis have known of Trismegistus? Knowledge of the cult of Trismegistus was probably widely distributed in Syria. A Syriac Christian commentary on Acts 14:12, which says that Gentiles in Lystra think that Paul is Hermes, identifies the New Testament's unqualified "Hermes" as Hermes Trismegistus. "They called Hermes one of the gods who was more rational and skillful and intelligent than all of the gods; and they called him Trismegistus . . . and because of this they called Paul Hermes." Given this wide distribution of Hermetic traditions throughout Syria, it is likely that Jews would have picked up the fact that some pagans held that Hermes was or had been a human person.

Elijah as heavenly scribe and righteous ascended human being has affinities with Hermes Trismegistus, while as trickster and guardian of travelers he is more like the Greek Hermes. This suggests that the Jewish picture of Hermes came from extensive but superficial knowledge of pagan cults, which is what one would expect in an environment in which Jews had pagan neighbors and learned about their beliefs in a casual piecemeal way. *Sepher HaRazim* suggests that at least some Jewish practitioners of magic knew more and appear to have seen Hermes as a sort of angel to whom it was appropriate to appeal.

Correspondences Between Elijah and Hermes

Some of the points of contact between Elijah and Hermes are fairly direct, others are more complex. Elijah has roles, especially those of herald and divine messenger, which resemble those of Hermes without in any way needing to have been borrowed from him, though they might have suggested the resemblance. Elijah's role as financial benefactor makes more sense in the context of Olympian myths than of Jewish traditions because neither the original prophet Elijah nor any other Jewish supernatural figure dispenses cash gifts, although the biblical Elijah does provide miraculous sustenance to the widow with whom he stays. Still other characteristics, such as a group of legends, discussed later in this chapter, in which Elijah saves Jews in Gentile court settings, probably arose in conscious dialogue with stories about Hermes.

The "origin myth" of the legendary Elijah—the biblical narrative and the rabbinic commentary on it—also has resemblances to the character and myth of Hermes. Some of these are general similarities that Jews may have noticed but that did not arise through borrowing. When Elijah runs before Ahab's chariot like a herald after the sacrifice on Mount Carmel (1 Kings 18:46), it is not because of borrowing from Hermes! Similarly, the biblical Elijah's great independence of character, even toward God, was elaborated on by the Rabbis without any necessary influence from Hermes.

One midrash, though, significantly resembles Hermes' origin myth. In the Yerushalmi, Elijah is metaphorically portrayed as having stolen the keys of the rain and dew from God, so that he (not God!) could bring about the drought that he prophesies on his first appearance. "Rav Yudah ben Pazi said, "[This is analogous] to one who stole a physicians's medicine case. Soon after he went out, his son was wounded. [The thief] went back to him and said, 'My lord physician, cure my son.'

He said to him, 'Go and return my case that has all kinds of medicine in it, and I will cure your son.' Thus did the Holy One speak to Elijah: 'Go and annul the oath concerning the dew, for only with dew can the dead be made alive, and I will bring to life the son of the [widow] of Zarephath.'"[136] The motif of stealing from a god or God and going unpunished appears in both midrash and myth. Each thief, in fact, strikes a bargain with the deity he stole from and gets what he wants: Apollo's cattle or the resurrection of the widow's son.

At the end of his origin myth, Hermes is appointed herald of Zeus. The similarity of Hermes' role as Zeus's messenger to Elijah as God's prophet may have allowed Jews to perceive a relationship between the two. Elijah, however, in contrast to Hermes, is generally not described as bearing messages sent by God. Elijah usually serves as God's messenger by answering rabbis who ask him what God is doing and then sometimes relaying their words back to God.[137] The difference between Elijah's and Hermes' role as messenger may be because in rabbinic Judaism God speaks in Scripture, oral law, and occasionally through a bat kol, and therefore generally does not send a messenger, though one rabbinic source does say that God sends Elijah to tell someone something, the way that Zeus sends Hermes.[138]

Related to his role as messenger, Elijah mediates between the living and the dead and travels between earth and paradise, sometimes leading people on brief visits to supernatural realms. In one instance Elijah leads Rabbah bar Abbuha to paradise so that he can collect some of his future reward while still among the living.[139] In showing a living rabbi the saintly dead ascending to the heavenly academy, or reporting what is done there, Elijah creates a connection between the living and dead representatives of the rabbinic tradition. Similarly, Hermes appears in the classical tragedies as mediator between the living and their ancestors.[140]

One of the most suggestive among these parallels to Hermes is the passage in which Elijah heralds Rabbi Joshua ben Levi on his arrival in paradise (B. Ketubot 77b). Elijah generally does not lead souls to heaven; this role belongs to the angel of death. In this story Rabbi Joshua has just triumphed over the angel of death, defeating him so totally that God must intercede and ask the rabbi to return the angel's knife so that death will not pass from the world prematurely. Elijah goes before Joshua to announce his entrance to heaven very much as Hermes, in his role of psychopomp, leads all souls to the after world. Perhaps, however, this story is even more resonant of Hermes' role as helper and companion to the heroes of classical myths. Elijah is the one who sets the narrative seal on Rabbi Joshua's triumphant ascension to heaven without dying, just as he, Elijah, once did.

Of all the legendary Elijah's roles, the one that is least prophetic and most like Hermes is that of financial benefactor. Hermes granted prosperity and riches—a valuable windfall was called *hermaion*. The original point of connection may have been the endlessly renewed flour jar and oil jug of the widow in Sidon with whom Elijah stayed, though in Scripture these were arguably God's gifts for the prophet more than for the widow (1 Kings 17:16). Though the legendary Elijah does not bestow any magically renewed resources until much later folklore, the rabbinic Elijah does provide wealth. In Kiddushin 40a Rav Kahana is selling baskets door to door. Propositioned by a matron, the rabbi prefers death to dishonor and throws himself off a roof. Elijah comes and catches him, but complains that he had to come four hundred leagues. When Rav Kahana retorts that the whole problem was caused by his poverty, Elijah gives him a bushel of dinars.

Another significant role that Elijah shares with Hermes is that of traveler and patron of travelers. In the first story in this section, Elijah advises a traveler who was cheated out of his money. In the Bavli this one of Elijah's traits does not appear as the main point of any particular story but emerges out of many different details. On two occasions Elijah provides advice on how to pray when traveling. In one instance he teaches Rabbi Yossi to say a shortened form of the Eighteen Benedictions when on the road and in another he tells Rabbi Judah, brother of Rav Sala the Pious, to pray to God before setting out on a journey.[141] In Tana Devei Eliahu, a late rabbinic or early medieval work, written pseude-pigraphically in the voice of Elijah, the narrator several times begins, "Once I was walking," on the road, through a market, or in the Babylonian Diaspora.[142] When Elijah advises a widow as to why her husband has died, he is lodging in her house as a guest.[143] In Pesikta de Rav Kahana 11.22, Elijah appears to Rav Eleazar bar R. Shimon as an old man traveling. Even the common formula that begins many Elijah stories, "Rabbi Ploni met (אשכחיה) Elijah," implies that they met in public space, not in someone's home or in the house of study. One also recalls the stories in which Elijah reports what God says and once relays a rabbi's opinions back to God. He appears as a traveling messenger between heaven and earth, somewhat like a supernatural version of the rabbis who travel back and forth from Palestine to Babylonia.

In addition to these major parallels, there are a number of other fascinating correspondences between Elijah and Hermes. Many of them appear only once or twice, but their cumulative weight suggests that at least some if them were consciously or unconsciously borrowed from Hermes. The first of these was mentioned above, the possible identification of Elijah as "the old man leading a ram."[144] More substantially, Elijah's association with cemeteries and tombs recalls *Sepher HaRazim*'s invocation of Hermes for communicating with the dead. Once Rabbah bar Abbuha finds Elijah in a Gentile cemetery. On another occasion, Rabbi Joshua ben Levi finds Elijah standing at the entrance to Rabbi Shimon ben Yohai's tomb, and either sees or hears from Rabbi Shimon when in Elijah's company.[145] One of the oddest correspondences between Elijah and Hermes is that they are both associated with dogs. The Bavli states, "When the dogs howl, the angel of death has come to town; when the dogs frolic, Elijah has come to town,"[146] a relationship that recalls the iconographic connection between Hermes and dogs.[147]

Three Elijah legends could well have been created in polemical dialogue with the myths of Hermes. All tell of occasions when Elijah saves a Jew who is in danger from a Gentile court, once the royal court of Caesar, in another case an unspecified Roman court, and in the other case a Roman court in Palestine during the persecution after the Bar Kokhba revolt. As already mentioned, Hermes is the patron of rhetoric in classical mythology, and the autobiography of Libanius, a fourth-century rhetor, suggests that this also was true in rabbinic times. He recalls an occasion on which he was called to give a speech before Emperor Julian, one that went very much in his favor: "People insisted that Hermes in the care for his servant stirred every member of the audience with his wand, so that no single expression of mine should pass without its share of admiration."[148]

In these Elijah stories the prophet is a rhetorician of a sort, but more of a trickster. Elijah appears in Gentile disguise, in two cases looking like a member of a Gentile court. In one instance he works or announces a miracle, and in another two seems to help one along. Not only does the Elijah of these stories display Hermeslike attributes of savior and trickster, but in so doing he indirectly engages Hermes the patron of rhetoric and law courts on his own ground and proves as effective in defending Jews as Hermes was supposed to be in helping his devotees.

The first of these legends is the story of Rabbi Eleazar, which I will analyze at length in chapter 4. It comes just before the heartbreaking martyrdom legend of Rabbi Ḥanina ben Teradion, arrested at the same time, who was burned alive wrapped in a Scroll of the Torah, and perhaps serves as a sort of comic relief to that tragedy. In the first act, Rabbi Ḥanina prophesies to Rabbi Eleazar, when the two meet in prison, that Eleazar will be saved on account of his charitable deeds. Because there is no suspense around Rabbi Eleazar's safety, the irony that makes this story a comedy in juxtaposition with the tragedy of Rabbi Ḥanina comes to the fore.

They brought Rabbi Eleazar ben Perata [to trial]. They said, "Why have you taught, and why have you stolen?"

He said to them, "If one is a robber one is not a scholar and if one is a scholar one is not a robber, and since I am not one I am not the other either."

"Why do they call you 'Rabbi?'"

"I am a master of the weavers."

They brought him two coils of thread and asked, "Which is for the warp, and which is for the woof?"

A miracle occurred for him, [and he found out the answer]. . . .

They asked him, "Why don't you go to the meeting place?"

He said to them, "I am an old man and I am afraid that I might be trampled underfoot." They asked, "And up until now, how many old men have been trampled?"

A miracle occurred, and that very day an old man was trampled.

"Why did you free your slave?"

He replied to them, "These things never happened."

One of them got up to testify against him.

Elijah came [and] appeared to him as one of the great men of the empire.

He said to him, "Since a miracle occurred for him in all [the rest], in this one too a miracle will occur for him, and you [lit. "that man"] will show your bad nature."

He did not heed him [Elijah] and rose to speak to them [to denounce Rabbi Eleazar].

[At that moment] there was a letter that was written by important men of the kingdom to send to Caesar's court, and they sent it by that man [who wanted to testify against Rabbi Eleazar].

Elijah came and tossed him four hundred leagues.

He went and did not come [back].

(B. Avodah Zarah 17b)

There is an element of the trickster in Rabbi Eleazar's imaginative self-defense. His series of excuses is particularly incongruous compared to the usual rabbinic story of martyrdom. Rabbi Ḥanina, for example, when asked why he occupied himself with the Torah simply says that he did "as the Lord my God commanded me" and is immediately taken out to be killed. And there is an element of the trickster getting tangled in his own schemes in the way that, even with miracles to aid him, Rabbi Eleazar's excuses become more and more lame, until he must simply deny the last charge. Even Elijah's persuasion fails to convince a hostile witness, and Elijah must resort to helping the last miracle along. Nevertheless, nothing can prevent the saving of the man whom God has seen fit to save, and no cleverness of a Gentile court can match the rabbinic cleverness of Rabbi Eleazar, with some help from the master trickster Elijah.

In the second story, Rabbi Shila sentences to flogging a man who has sex with a Gentile woman. The man informs on him to the Roman court, accusing him of inflicting punishment without judicial authority. To save himself, the Rabbi Shila testifies that the man committed bestiality with a donkey, and Elijah appears in disguise as an anonymous witness to support the claim (B. Berakhot 58a). Elijah here resembles Hermes as god of liars and fast talkers in general. The Iliad says that Hermes bestows "skill at the oath" on his son Autolycus, also mentioned as an arch-thief. Elijah as trickster certainly displays "skill at the oath" in this story, testifying to the truth of a midrashic metaphor: when his accuser comes to complain that Rabbi Shila lied, the rabbi cites Ezekiel saying that the personified adulterous Jerusalem sought the pagan kingdoms, whose "members" were "like the members of asses" (23:20).[149]

The third story is one of the stories in the Talmud that most closely resembles a folktale, with plot motifs common in international as well as Jewish folklore. "Why did they call him Naḥum of Gamzu? Because, everything that happened to him, he said, 'this too (gam zu) is for good.'" When he was sent off with a chest full of gold and gems as a gift for the Roman emperor, thieving innkeepers stole the treasure and filled it with dust.

> The next day when he saw them he said, "This too is for good."
>
> When he got there [before the emperor], they unfastened his bags, and they were full of dust.
>
> The king wanted to kill all of them.
>
> He said, "The Jews mock me!"
>
> He said, "This too is for good."
>
> Elijah came and appeared to him as one of them. He said to them, "Perhaps this is some of the earth of Abraham their father . . .
>
> There was a country which they could not conquer; they tried some of it [the dust] and conquered it.
>
> They took him to the treasury. And he filled his bags with precious stones and pearls. And they sent him [on his way] with great honor.
>
> When he returned, he stayed at that inn.
>
> They said to him, "What did you bring there that they did you such great honor?"

He said to them, "What I took from here I brought there."

They tore down their inn and brought it to the court. They said to him, "That dust he brought here was ours.

They tried and did not find it [so], and they killed those innkeepers (Ta'anit 21a).[150]

In this story Elijah functions very much as a conventional fairy-tale helper, rewarding the honest holy man who looks at the best side of things, while the wicked innkeepers, like Cinderella's evil sisters, fall victim to their own greed. Propp, in his classic work on folktales, describes the characteristic plot motifs and their order in the standard folktale. The story of Naḥum Ish Gamzu contains many of these folktale motifs in Propp's order: the description of the hero; the hero's leaving home; the villain finds out about victim; the villain—here, the innkeepers—tries to trick the hero to take possession of his belongings; the victim submits to deception; the hero is "tested, interrogated, attacked, etc. which prepares the way for his receiving . . . a magical helper"; the hero receives a magical gift—the magic dust; the initial problem is overcome; the villain is punished.[151] This Jewish use of folktale form indicates that the theme of Elijah before a Gentile court was part of the popular imagination.

Although Hellenistic and Roman sources also describe Hermes as the god of rhetorical eloquence and wisdom in a more positive sense, in these stories it is Hermes' trickiness in a good cause that Elijah borrows. This power, it is important to note, is never used against rabbis, certainly not in Jewish court settings. In these three stories a Jew faces unequal Gentile opponents with the power of life and death. These stories, or some earlier stories they drew from, were created, I think, by Jewish storytellers who were already aware that their prophet had powers that pagans attributed to Hermes. This being so, they delighted in making Elijah outwit the Gentile authorities. In these Roman settings Elijah may be said to surpass the pagan god on his own religious turf.

Genesis Rabbah's story of Elijah appearing in a dream also presents an ironic challenge to pagan beliefs about Hermes. For Greeks and Romans, Hermes was the messenger of dreams, and Elijah appears to a Roman emperor on one of the two Rabbinic instances he appears in dreams. "Rabbi Levi said, 'Something happened to a certain ruler in Rome who was squandering his father's treasures. Elijah appeared to him in a dream [and] said to him, Your father saved and you squander. He did not move until he filled up his treasury.'" This story is told in the context of the tradition that the rulers of Rome are destined to store up wealth for the King

Messiah. Elijah comes like Hermes (perhaps even disguised as or mistaken for Hermes?) to tell the leader of the Jews' enemies to store up wealth for the future messianic age when the Jewish people will triumph.[152]

Thus we see that resemblances between Hermes and Elijah may arise in several different ways. Sometimes, as when Elijah and Hermes function as divine heralds, the cause is in parallel development, rather than influence. Elijah was the herald to God's new order in Malachi, long before close contact between Greek and Judean culture occurred. However, once parallel development produced enough points of contact between two traditions, the spark of imagination could sooner or later leap the gap and influence could occur. Sometimes this cross-fertilization was due to the unexamined adoption of an attractive motif across cultural lines, as with the "old man leading a ram," if indeed he is Elijah. At other times the Jewish tradition seems to enter into polemical dialogue with the Gentile culture, consciously absorbing or co-opting the virtues of Hermes into the persona of Elijah and thus presenting Elijah as more powerful and authentic than his Gentile counterpart. Once these stories existed, they then became part of the tradition and allowed other Elijah legends to be created along similar lines. It is difficult if not impossible to prove whether any given resemblance between Elijah and Hermes is due to parallel development, unconscious assimilation, or conscious rivalry. However, in some cases, such as the court legends and the emperor's dream, a good case can be made that the original creators of the motif, and perhaps the composers of these particular legends, were aware of the correspondence between the two and exploited it (see table 3.2, "Elijah and Hermes," which shows that the legendary Elijah of the Rabbis had more affinities with Hermes than with the biblical Elijah included for comparison).

What is lacking, and what will probably never be found, is any explicit literary trace of the connection. Some Hellenized Second Temple Jews, seeking to prove the value of Judaism in a Greek context, argued that ancient Jews taught the culture heroes of the Greeks or called the Sibyl Noah's daughter. The Rabbis, in contrast, sought to distance themselves—or at any rate to present themselves as distant—from the surrounding cultures' traditions and beliefs. Nevertheless, the Rabbis did not and could not live in a closed world. In this chapter we have examined some of the ways that the rabbinic Elijah is dependent on the wider culture of late antiquity, despite the rabbis' choice not to acknowledge any such debt. In particular, Elijah exemplifies the movement from angelic or demigodly supernatural mediators toward those who were originally human, a movement that is found in both Christian and Hermetic literature. We have also found many suggestive

TABLE 3.2 Elijah and Hermes

LEGENDARY AND MIDRASHIC ELIJAH	BIBLICAL ELIJAH	HERMES
Herald of the Messiah or End of Days.	Will come before "the day of the Lord."	Herald of the gods.
Messenger of God, answers when asked what God is doing; associated with God as supporter of human (that is, Rabbinic) initiative—never punishes chutzpah in relation to God, though angels do.	Prophet and, as such, God's messenger. He is also a prophet who feels free to complain to God, but is intolerant of others.	Messenger of Zeus, but one who is not afraid to speak boldly before him, as he does in his origin myth.
Protector of poor/powerless, appearing in disguise to fool Gentile courts or refusing to visit haughty or unjust Jews in power.	Performed two beneficent miracles for individual widows, both of whom helped him.	With Zeus, blesses Philemon and Baucis, who welcome them in disguise.
Gives money to the deserving unpredictably and not because specifically appealed to.	Gives a bottomless flour jar and oil jug to the widow of Sidon.	God of financial matters: a windfall was a *hermaion.*
Source of wise proverbs and solves difficult questions. Later, the word *unresolved* in the Talmud is taken to be an acronym for "until Elijah will come and solve it."		God of rhetorical arts and wisdom when connected to Thoth, Egyptian god of wisdom.
Travels between Earth, Eden, and the heavenly court/academy.	Ascends to heaven without dying.	Travels and mediates among realms.
Occasionally heals.	Heals and revives from the dead.	Associated with Asclepius, patron of healing.
Sometimes portrayed as an angel.		At times identified as an angel by Christians authors and Jewish magical texts.
Sometimes appears in dreams.		Appears in or brings dreams.

TABLE 3.2 Elijah and Hermes (*continued*)		
LEGENDARY AND MIDRASHIC ELIJAH	BIBLICAL ELIJAH	HERMES
Helps travelers in several stories; gives advice for prayer when traveling; is met while traveling.	Has no fixed address.	Patron of travelers.
Sometimes fallible in legend, and more so in midrash, which holds Elijah was too harsh.	Definitely fallible in Scripture.	
Will lie or deceive to protect the righteous—especially when appearing in disguise. In midrash it says that Elijah "stole the key to rain," *causing* the drought he prophesied, and had to give it back to revive the dead.		God of fast-talkers and thieves; in his origin myth steals Apollo's cattle as an infant.
In two stories found in a graveyard or at a tomb—both ritually unclean in Judaism.		God of graveyards.
Once in Bavli, and at least once in early medieval sources, acts as God's scribe.		Heavenly scribe, especially when associated with Thoth.
On one occasion heralds a rabbi new-come to paradise.		Guide of souls to the afterlife, heralds heroes.
Once a peacemaker between rabbis.	Peacemaker (in Malachi).	
Not a respecter of authority, helps rabbis challenge God. Rescues rabbis from trouble in clever and sometimes embarrassing ways.		Trickster.

correspondences between Elijah and Hermes, even though there is no proof that any particular detail of Elijah's character was borrowed directly.

Finally, though, it is comparisons within rabbinic literature that most illuminate the Elijah of the Bavli. In fact, exploring how—and how much—Elijah differs from other Jewish supernatural mediators made it possible to consider his connection to Hermes, since parts of his character are not shared by angels or earthly rabbis. Elijah's uniqueness also allows one to start to appreciate his religious function in amoraic Babylonia. In my view, Elijah's most crucial quality is that he provides a sense of greater connection to God without impairing God's authority. He is ideal teacher, benefactor, savior of Jews threatened by Gentiles, yet, with all his powers, he is neither worshipped nor compelled. He points beyond himself, the willing messenger of God. In the next chapter we will use the three generic groups of Elijah stories to expand and refine this picture. The groups suggest a body of commonly held beliefs about Elijah, beliefs that individual stories use as raw material.

4

THE THREE GENERIC GROUPS
OF ELIJAH STORIES

The previous chapter compared the characteristics of Elijah in the Bavli to those of other supernatural beings, seeking to understand what makes Elijah unique. This chapter analyzes the three generic groups of Elijah stories. As discussed in chapter 1, stories in each generic group share close parallels in phrasing and plot and often in theme as well. In the first group of stories Elijah ceases to visit or never visits someone of whom he disapproves, in the second group Elijah appears in disguise, usually to rescue someone, and in the third group Rabbis ask Elijah various questions. This chapter postulates that these generic groups reflect classes of story that rabbinic hearers or readers would have recognized as distinct. Yassif shows that the redactors of the Bavli sometimes used generic groups as the organizing principle of story cycles, strongly suggesting that they recognized the groups as such.[1] As we have seen, Yassif's insight may also be more broadly applied: stories found separately can also be part of the same generic group.

Identifying generic groups helps one recognize the metonymic associations in rabbinic tales, the way a simple phrase or plot motif in orally derived texts can be pregnant with complex meaning.[2] Once a story begins by saying that "Rabbi So-and-so met Elijah," for example, it tells us immediately that the rabbi will treat Elijah as a rabbinic teacher, asking Elijah a question he will then answer. In addition to helping us appreciate the meaning of traditional formulae, the concept of metonomy sensitizes us to the moments when narrators use those formulae in untraditional ways to convey specific points. This kind of oral-formulaic analysis operates in service to literary analysis of a more usual sort when approaching some of the longer and more complex stories.

Each section of this chapter describes and briefly catalogues one of the generic groups before turning to the analysis of particular stories. Reviewing the whole generic group does more than introduce the use of metonomy in individual stories. Each generic group constitutes a traditional ways of speaking and writing about Elijah that were the common intellectual property of rabbinic Jews and perhaps all Jews in amoraic Babylonia. Each group reveals shared rabbinic beliefs about Elijah because it exists independently of the compositional or editorial creativity of individuals. Because of this, the generic groups themselves provide a composite picture of Elijah in the Bavli.

This chapter also analyzes variant readings of several stories. Manuscript readings differ, and we will examine a few variations that affect the meaning of the story significantly. Because there are often differences among the best and earliest manuscripts, especially in longer narratives, it is usually impossible to arrive at a single correct reading. Although I will sometimes advance a theory on which reading is preferable, more often I will simply explore the range of meanings conveyed by the different readings. This approach accords with the theory that there is no one urtext of the Bavli and more than one reading may be "original."[3]

THE GENERIC GROUP OF STORIES IN WHICH ELIJAH CEASES OR REFUSES TO VISIT SOMEONE

This group of stories is marked by two different formulaic phrases that make up a unified generic group: "Elijah was accustomed to come to him" (אליהו הוה רגיל דאתי גביה), in two stories, and "Elijah used to converse with him" (משתעי אליהו בהדיה), in four other instances. The two phrases are parallel in meaning and introduce the same plot motif, that Elijah refuses to appear to someone who is less than virtuous. The plot structure of these stories has two characteristic patterns: in both, Elijah's appearance is juxtaposed with his disappearance. In four stories in the Bavli, Elijah visits someone and later abandons him; in the remaining two stories, Elijah appears to one person and not to another who behaves less well. Furthermore, except for one very brief story, the story first describes the action that makes Elijah stay away and then mentions Elijah. In these tales Elijah acts as a teacher, teaching by his refusal to visit. Their wider form-critical category is that of precedent stories, stories in which the behavior of a Sage conveys a legal or moral lesson.

In the rabbinic culture of discipleship, the daily behavior of the Rabbi was itself exemplary teaching. As Jaffee writes: "The scroll of Scripture was Torah transformed into the code of written human language; the rabbinic Sage was Torah transformed into an embodied form of human being."[4] When Elijah teaches rabbis by his example, he embodies Torah like a Sage. One of the phrases in this group, Elijah "conversed with him," (משתעי בהדיה) underscores Elijah's rabbinic role. In fact, another story uses the same rather uncommon phrase to convey that disciples could lose the privilege of conversing informally with a master Sage. Two students were sitting before Rav; the first student complained humorously about how tired the lesson had made him, making a tasteless reference to pigs, whereas the other more decently referred to goat kids, and "Rav did not converse with the former."[5] Thus teaching was something that Rav offered to all his students, but private conversation was not a disciple's automatic privilege. The story then conveys the same lesson as this generic group: that someone who transgressed nonhalakhic norms might forfeit intimacy with a teacher of Torah, either a rabbi or Elijah.

Good taste, however, is not the transgression at issue in this group of Elijah stories. Most often the moral norm underscored is the need for respect and kindness between people. Furthermore, the need for respect emphasized by Elijah's absence is the respect owed by rabbis or pious men to their social or religious inferiors, whether they are students or servants waiting tables, the poor, or simply the ordinary people of their generation. The message of these Elijah stories is not uncontested. Many other passages in rabbinic literature defend the Rabbis' special privileges or speak slightingly of the unlearned. That makes the message of these stories all the more striking.

The many shared features of this group suggest that it would have been recognized as a set by the Rabbis themselves, defined by metonymic use of formulaic language and stereotyped plot motifs that is a hallmark of the orally derived style found in both Talmuds. Four of the stories of Elijah's absence in the Bavli are exceedingly brief and simple, but gain meaning when one recognizes their relationship to stories of the same generic group. Three of these stories seem to be brought in by the redactors of the Bavli to demonstrate points unrelated to their probable original meaning. They are briefly summarized, rather than having even the modest amount of detail found in longer Talmudic narratives, and yet, because of their metonomy, the stories remain vivid and memorable. For example, two consecutive stories serve to support the medical point that it is unhealthy to see and crave tasty food without being able to eat it. The first story says one man let his waiter eat every dish he served, while the other did not, and Elijah conversed only with the first. The second describes another pair of men, one who let his waiter eat first, while the other made him wait until after the meal, and Elijah, again, conversed only with the more deserving man (B. Ketubot 61a). This pair of stories would lack much of its resonance without the other stories of Elijah's visits. The context of the generic group emphasizes that Elijah stayed away from those who were disrespectful or unkind to those who served them.

A similarly brief story is told about Rabbi Joshua ben Levi. Because a man was eaten by a lion in his neighborhood, Elijah refused to visit the rabbi for a time, knowing that Rabbi Joshua could have prevented the tragedy by praying more for those around him.[6] This one story does not state that Elijah was in the habit of visiting the protagonist. It need not, because Rabbi Joshua ben Levi was well known to be someone whom Elijah visited. In addition to a story in the Yerushalmi, which I will discuss shortly, there are two other stories of Rabbi Joshua and Elijah in the Bavli and two more in Pesikta de Rav Kahana.[7]

The next story is the most deeply embedded in a halakhic sugya (a *sugya* is unified discussion of a particular issue). It interprets the ruling that the residents of a courtyard can be required to contribute to the cost of a gatehouse.

> [The Mishnah appears] to say that a gatehouse is an improvement.
>
> But what about a certain God-fearing man whom Elijah was accustomed to converse with—he built a gatehouse and Elijah did not converse with him again.
>
> [Rashi: because it prevented the poor from calling out . . .]
>
> This is not a problem, this [gatehouse] is inside [the courtyard], and that outside.
>
> (B. Bava Batra 7b)

The discussion eventually makes clear that an appropriate gatehouse should allow entry into the courtyard, and the redactor placed this story at the beginning of the passage to lead into this point. The redactors probably also chose to include the story because the passage goes on to discuss contributing to the welfare of one's community and the nature of righteousness, including care for the poor. Thus the phrase "Elijah did not converse with him" functions as an initial allusion to the later discussion, confident that the audience knows Elijah abandons someone for ethical failures, specifically a failure to respect or provide for the less powerful. Rashi's medieval interpretation comes from a careful reading of the sugya and perhaps of its metonymic context.

This generic group is unique in having an example in the Yerushalmi. The passage preceding it describes how it is lawful to surrender a criminal who was guilty of a capital crime to the Gentile government, but the story goes on to question whether that law is always valid.

The empire sought Ulla bar Koshav.

He escaped and came to Lod, to Rabbi Joshua ben Levi.

They came and surrounded the city.

Rabbi Joshua ben Levi went up to him [Ulla] and persuaded him, and he gave himself up to them.

And Elijah—remembered for good—was accustomed to appear to him [Rabbi Joshua], and he did not appear.

And he fasted a number of fasts and he appeared to him.

He said to him, "And do I appear to informers?"

He said, "Did I not do according to the law [or "according to the Mishnah"]?

He said, "And is this the law of the truly devout?"[8]

This story has almost all elements of this generic group in the Bavli, except for one of the precise formulaic phrases, which is found in a parallel version.[9] As in the Bavli, the story describes the action that causes Elijah to abandon Rabbi Joshua first, before it mentions Elijah. The rabbi's action seems justified, if not ideal, until Elijah passes judgment by abandoning him. Elijah's appearance is juxtaposed with his absence: "And Elijah, remembered for good, was accustomed to appear to him, and he did not appear." Elijah cannot be controlled: he appears only when he wants to.

The story in the Yerushalmi also shares a theme clearly found in the Bavli. Elijah's question, "is this the law of the truly devout?" echoes throughout the whole group. Elijah does not teach halakhah, but rather argues for an ethical standard above halakhah that is incumbent on the fully righteous. In many respects this story is comparable to the story in which a man is eaten by a lion: in both, Elijah is in the habit of visiting Rabbi Joshua ben Levi, but stays away for a time, in one case because the rabbi did something less than right and in the other because he neglected to do something a fully righteous person ought to have done.

This story and several others in the generic group portray an almost collegial relationship between the rabbi and the prophet. Elijah speaks to Rabbi Joshua as a rabbi to his student rather than as a divine messenger to a visionary, responding to Rabbi Joshua's justification of his actions by asking a pointedly leading question, rather than telling him God's will directly. This story in the Yerushalmi and one in the Bavli discussed in the next section have similar teacher-student exchanges when Elijah returns to someone he has deserted. The story in the Yerushalmi, however, is political whereas that in the Bavli is not.

One cannot put Ulla bar Koshav into the category of powerless persons whom rabbis should not disrespect; he is more probably a fighter against Rome, and life and death are at issue. As Daube writes, the story is part of a passage discussing whether specific Jews may be relinquished to Gentiles if the Gentiles threaten to kill many others—perhaps the whole town—if the person is not turned over.[10] The context for this discussion is not response to random terrorism, but, to quote the title of Daube's essay, "appeasement or resistance" to an occupying power. The juxtaposition of Rabbi Joshua's self-justification and Elijah's retort חסידים וזו משנתה, "And is this the law of the truly devout?" speaks volumes about the difficult political situation of Jews in Palestine. Some limited collaboration with Rome was necessary, but how should one draw the line?[11] Is a rabbi convincing someone to turn himself in *that* much better than treacherously informing on someone? While this generic group lacks political themes in the Bavli, other Elijah stories there have political meaning, with the prophet helping Jews against the occupying power, especially in the second generic group in which he appears to rescue rabbis from Romans.

Perhaps this generic group in which Elijah abandons someone is different in the Yerushalmi than in the Bavli, or perhaps the Yerushalmi appropriates the formula to make a new point. We find this in the next two stories, whose creators used this generic framework to convey points different from those the framework serves to express in the more typical cases. We will also see how in one or more variant versions the transmitters or copyists of the Talmud text tried to bring one of these "unusual" stories more in line with other Elijah stories.

Elijah and Rav Anan

This story addresses, among other things, how a judge must act righteously and scrupulously. The stories before it in the Bavli express how fragile a judge's impartiality is and how zealously it must be guarded. Even being offered a gift or favor by a litigant—much less accepting one—should cause a judge to decline to hear a case. Our story continues the theme. A would-be litigant offers Rav Anan a basket of fish, and the rabbi rightly declines to hear the case, but is flattered into accepting the fish. Rav Anan then sends a note to Rav Naḥman asking him to try the case, and Naḥman deduces from the special note that the man who gave Rav Anan fish was the latter's relative. Therefore Rav Naḥman shows the fish-giving litigant so much honor that his opponent is hopelessly intimidated, and the case is not fairly tried. Then the story starts anew, with the mention of Rav Anan's name as in the beginning:

> Rav Anan: Elijah was accustomed to come to him, for he was teaching him the Order of Elijah. Since he [Rav Anan] had done this, he went away.
> He sat in fasting and asked for mercy [from God].
> And [Elijah] came, [but] when he came he frightened him terribly.
> He [Rav Anan] made a box, and sat [in it] before him until he had expounded his Order to him. This is why people speak of the Greater Order of Elijah, the Lesser Order of Elijah [Seder Eliahu Rabbah, Seder Eliahu Zuta].
>
> (B. Ketubot 105b–6a)

What do we make of this story? This is the only story in the Bavli in which someone, like Rabbi Joshua ben Levi in the Yerushalmi, fasts to bring Elijah back, and the only story in which someone prays to God for his return. It is also one of only two rabbinic stories in which Elijah appears in a frightening form. Elijah's frightening appearance, the detail of the box, the added explanation the two Orders of Elijah all rest uneasily within the usually straightforward form of Elijah's refusal to appear.

One likely explanation is that the latter part of the story is an etiological tale grafted onto an Elijah story. Its creator wanted to explain why Rav Anan's Seder Eliahu had two parts, a greater and a lesser. The main point conveyed by our generic form should be that Elijah abandoned Rav Anan because he indirectly caused injustice to someone, but this point is almost eclipsed. Perhaps the creator of the story knew a preexisting tale of Rav Anan's judicial faux pas and Elijah's abandoning the erring rabbi, and added the explanation of why Seder Eliahu has two parts. As it now stands, the story seems odd because its generic form does not quite fit the use to which it was put. It may also be significant that the language used here to describe Elijah's presence is different: the prophet "was accustomed to come," rather than "to converse," with the protagonist, as in most stories of rabbis and Elijah.[12] The story's choice of language, in addition to its several other unique features, makes it possible that it comes from a different source than the other stories do or that perhaps its author or later transmitters recognized it as different in kind.

It is clear that modern readers are not the only ones to find this story difficult. The presence of three widely varying manuscript versions suggest that medieval scribes were also confused. Vatican 113 and 130 have:

Rav Anan was accustomed that Elijah would come to him, for he was teaching him the Order of Elijah. Since he [Rav Anan] had done this, he went away.

He [Rav Anan] sat in fasting and asked for mercy [from God]

And he [Elijah] came,

but even so he [Rav Anan?] would sit in a box, and he [Elijah] taught him.

This is why we speak of the Greater Order of Elijah and the Lesser Order of Elijah.

This version starts the same as our standard edition of the Talmud, but continues differently. Without the statement that Elijah appeared in a frightening form, the necessity of the box becomes even more mysterious. It is remotely possible Elijah returns grudgingly and does not want to let Rav Anan see him directly, but, if so, the story does not spell this out. I think it most likely that the Vatican versions originated with a scribe or scribes who had a version in which Elijah appeared in terrifying form, but left that point out because they could not conceive of Elijah's frightening anyone after abandoning him. The MS Munich simply omits the bulk of the story, perhaps because the Munich copyist was puzzled or embarrassed by the whole incident. The Leningrad MS is the most interesting. It reads:

Rav Anan: Elijah was accustomed to come to him, for he was teaching him the Order of Elijah. Since he [Rav Anan] had done this, he went away.

He afflicted himself and sat in fasting and asked for mercy [from God].

And he came.

When he came, he said to him, "Why haven't you come, Sir?"

He said to him, "Because of this [that you did]."

He said to him, "What about our Order? That which is begun for us—let us finish it."

He said to him, "By my life [let's do it]."

Until that day whenever he [Rav Anan] asked anything of him he would explain it, from that time on he [Elijah] frightened him terribly.

He [Rav Anan] made a box and was placed in it.

One sat in the box, the other outside and finished it.

And this is why they call it the Greater Order of Elijah and the Lesser Order of Elijah.

The creator of this version seems to be trying to bring the story into line with other Elijah stories and also to make it a clearer narrative. Rav Anan asks why Elijah deserted him, and Elijah explains himself and accepts Rav Anan's request that he finish his teaching of the Seder Eliahu. Furthermore, this story emphasizes how strange it is for Elijah to appear in such a form, "Until that day whenever he asked anything of him he would explain it, from that time on he [Elijah] frightened him terribly." It is not Elijah's way to terrify, and the Leningrad version makes the most sense because the rabbi or scribe who created it explicitly acknowledges this with his contrast between "until that day" and "from that time on."

Elijah and Rabbi Yossi

The last story in the group is the only one without the explicit moral lesson that even the story of Rav Anan teaches incidentally. Furthermore, it is the only story in the Bavli that brings the midrashic Elijah into connection with the legendary Elijah. In its redactional context, it follows a number of midrashim about Elijah in Kings, some of which show Elijah in conflict with God over "the keys of the rain," a theme also found in other texts. The Bavli makes it clear that the prophet himself was responsible for the drought in Israel he had prophesied—a mild version of the criticisms of the biblical Elijah found in midrash: that he was overzealous and lacked mercy toward Israel.[13] The story begins with a word that expresses scriptural interpretation:

> Rabbi Yossi expounded [*darash*] in Sepphoris, "Father Elijah was a hot-tempered man." He [Elijah] was accustomed to come to him;
>> he withdrew from him for three days and did not come.
>> When he came, he [Rabbi Yossi] said to him, "Why didn't you come?"
>> He said, "You called me hot-tempered."
>> "It's [now] before us that you *are* being hot-tempered, Sir."[14]

Here the legendary Elijah, kind and generous protagonist of stories in the Bavli and later Jewish folklore, is brought head to head with the hot-tempered zealot of the Bible and midrashic literature, the prophet who was harsh toward Israel and at times in conflict with God. It seems clear that this story was meant to be witty. This story gains its wit—and its force—by following the form of the other stories in which Elijah refuses to visit, then overturning our expectations of that form. As in the other such stories, Rabbi Yossi does something that displeases Elijah, after which Elijah abandons him. He stays away from him for three days, as in the story of Rabbi Joshua ben Levi and the man who was eaten by a lion (B. Makkot 11a). We expect Rabbi

Yossi to be justly chastened by Elijah's abandonment or by some cutting reproof when he returns. Instead, the rabbi holds his ground, pointing out Elijah's hasty and irascible behavior. He does not even say "Why didn't you come, *Sir*?"

This reversal of the generic form may in part be an assertion of the Rabbis' power to interpret Scripture as they please. In this one may compare it to the oven of Akhnai story's assertion of the power of a rabbinic court to legislate according to the majority. In that story it is Elijah who tells Rabbi Natan that God was pleased when the majority of rabbis stood fast to their ruling—despite the miracles and the heavenly voice, the bat kol—supporting the view of Rabbi Eliezer. God was laughing, and saying, "My sons have prevailed over me."[15] Even more, this story makes clear Elijah's pure beneficence as a teacher, a motif discussed in the previous chapter. Elijah is humanly and genuinely angry at Rabbi Yossi's assessment of him, and yet the rabbi is not frightened that Elijah will retaliate in any way. Rabbi Yossi commits no sacrilege in speaking disrespectfully of Elijah, behind his back or to his face. Furthermore, he does not fear that Elijah will be "heartsick" and angry at a perceived insult in a way that might be dangerous. The way in which this story subverts the rules of its form underscores its point: Elijah (and those qualities of God that he represents) tolerates interpretive audacity, even when he is its victim. Read with the other stories in this generic group, this story carries the additional implication that Elijah disapproves more of disrespect and unkindness between person and person than anything said to or about himself.

This generic group, while it upholds kindness and fair treatment for all, also supports the position of the rabbis. They are generally the ones whom Elijah is accustomed to visit or converse with, and they are responsible to pray for and benefit the less fortunate. The merely pious who appear in these stories are also wealthy by the standards of the day—the "pious man" can afford to build a gatehouse and the men who feed (or do not feed) their waiters appropriately, if not rabbis, are men who can afford to have servants or slaves. Thus these stories are more about noblesse oblige than about equality. Still, they present a clear message that respect, as well as charity, is something that the well-off owe to the poor and powerless.

THE GENERIC GROUP OF STORIES IN WHICH ELIJAH APPEARS IN DISGUISE

The generic group in which Elijah appears in disguise is easily identified by the formulaic phrase "Elijah came and appeared to him" or "to them," (אתא אליהו אידמי ליה/להו)

and also by the pattern of its plot. In these stories Elijah appears in the middle of a story to resolve some sort of problem or crisis, which in five out of the seven stories involves a physical threat to a rabbi. Elijah is the only supernatural being who appears in disguise *to help*. Thus this generic group continues a pattern observed in chapter 3: Elijah is uniquely benevolent among supernatural beings and mediators of God's power.

The Appearance of Supernatural Beings in Rabbinic Literature

Rabbinic literature uses passive verbs meaning "seem" or "appear," from the Hebrew root *dmh* (דמה), or the Aramaic *dmi* (דמי), and the noun *demut* (דמות), "appearance," to describe seeming a particular way or appearing in another guise. Certain forms of these words—*idmei*, "he appeared," which occurs seventeen times in the Bavli—express the appearance of a supernatural being in corporeal, usually human, form.[16] However, even though the use of the formula *idmei* is highly specialized, the stories containing it are diverse. A wide range of beings—from God to demons—appear in these stories and do very different things. Still, the stories have certain commonalities. In most of the stories, including those of Elijah, the disguised form is perceptible to ordinary people, not just to rabbis, though the latter *may* recognize the being in the disguise. In Elijah stories ordinary people never realize Elijah's real identity, whereas rabbis sometimes do.

Most beings other than Elijah come to do harm, either deserved or not. In several cases the supernatural being comes to threaten the self-righteous or destroy the wicked. In three stories Satan causes trouble for righteous people who have become self-satisfied or arrogant, in two of them appearing as a woman who so successfully tempts famous rabbis that God must intervene to save them.[17] Righteous figures can appear in disguise to punish the wicked. In a midrash on Esther, angels help bring about the downfall of the wicked vizier Haman by appearing as gardeners who uproot trees in the royal orchard and tell the king that they act on Haman's orders.[18] In some sense Elijah falls into this category when he comes in the form of a bear to end the prayers that might bring the Messiah before his time, although he does so only because he is forced by God.

Purely destructive entities can also appear in disguise. Twice, demons are the subject of *idmei* or *idmu*. An anonymous demon haunting a house of study appears as an enormous snake with seven heads that must be defeated by a rabbi.[19] There is also a general statement that demons can appear in the form of human beings to cause trouble.[20] Finally, the angel of death appears in the form of a beggar to ask Rabbi Ḥiyya for mercy because the rabbi is too virtuous and too immersed in Torah study to leave the angel of death an opening to cause his demise.[21] In all these cases, except for one angelic appearance, supernatural beings other than Elijah are dangerous in disguise, even if doing something entirely just. Elijah, in contrast, nearly always appears in disguise to help the good, punishing the wicked incidentally and rarely.

Elijah in Disguise

In all, Elijah in the Bavli appears disguised in seven stories. Most of these stories have Elijah appearing to many people at once, unlike his usual habit of visiting individual rabbis. Three of these appearances are the court scenes quoted or described in chapter 3. In the first, Elijah helps out Rabbi Eleazar ben Perata when he is accused of teaching Torah during a time of Roman persecution; in the second Elijah testifies for Naḥum Ish Gamzu before Caesar, telling him about Abraham's magic dust (which appears two versions); and in the third Elijah testifies (falsely) for Rav Shila that a certain man committed bestiality with a donkey.[22]

The other stories are a mixed lot. In the one closest to the three court stories the Bavli proposes several alternate ways in which a rabbi could have escaped Roman persecution, one of them involving Elijah. Rabbi Meir rescues his sister-in-law, who was condemned to slavery in a Roman brothel when her father was killed, and Meir's "wanted" picture is posted on the gates of Rome. When Romans see him, Rabbi Meir must disguise himself or be disguised in order to escape. The narrator presents three possibilities: either "they ran after him [and] he ran from them into a house of prostitution" or "some say he saw a pot of idol worshipers' food, dipped this [finger] in and licked that" or "some say that Elijah came and appeared to them as a prostitute and embraced him." When the Romans see whichever of the three it was, they say "Spare us! If it were Rabbi Meir he wouldn't have done that!" (B. Avodah Zarah 18a–b).

The version of Rabbi Meir's story that includes Elijah may have been formulated—before or after it entered the written tradition—to preserve the rabbi's honor, if not his peace of mind. Instead of ignominiously fleeing into a whorehouse of his own accord, or fearfully pretending to taste forbidden food, Rabbi Meir is embraced by Elijah-as-prostitute against his will. Even this scenario, however, is more than faintly undignified. Elijah might perhaps have spirited him away by some miracle and could certainly have appeared to the soldiers as a superior officer and ordered them away. However, the holy Rabbi Meir, who has just rescued his sister-in-law from forced prostitution, must submit to being embraced by a prostitute. Even if he recognizes the prophet, Elijah is putting him in an embarrassing position.

The remaining story, in which Elijah appears to rescue a rabbi from physical danger, does not take place in a Roman court or city but on a roadside in Babylonia. As in the story of Rabbi Meir, however, Elijah appears as a trickster who rescues someone by placing him in an uncomfortable position: "Some say that Rav Shimi bar Ashi swallowed a snake; Elijah came and appeared to him as a horseman, made him eat a gourd with salt and run before him three miles, and the snake came out of him chunk by chunk."[23]

In fact, all five of the stories of Elijah appearing in disguise to rescue a rabbi from danger portray Elijah as trickster and ordinary mortals—sometimes rabbis—as those who are tricked. In chapter 3 we discussed the elements of humor in the story of Eleazar ben Perata. The story in which Elijah testifies for Naḥum Ish Gamzu before Caesar also has elements of a trickster tale. Elijah somehow arranges that perfectly ordinary dirt from the floor of the inn operates like Abraham's magic dust, while asserting (falsely) that it is the real thing. In the stories of Rabbi Meir and Rav Shimi, the objects of Elijah's trickery are rabbis. They are saved, but they are saved in humorously undignified ways.

The last two stories in which Elijah appears in disguise use this plot motif very differently. In the Bavli's version of Rabbi Akiva's origins, Elijah's appearance embellishes the tale of how Rabbi Akiva started out poor and ignorant and rose to be an eminent Sage. Elijah enters the scene shortly after "the daughter of Kalba Savua's son went and married herself to him [Akiva] in winter" and she is disowned by her rich father. They have nothing to sleep on but straw, and Akiva has to pull the straw out of his bride's hair every morning. Then "Elijah came and appeared to them as a man . . . begging at the door. He said to them, 'Give me a little straw, because my wife is in labor and I don't have anything to let her lie down on.' Rabbi Akiva said to his wife, 'See this man, who doesn't even have straw!'" Somehow, the sight of a man even poorer than they are acts as a turning point for Kalba Savua's granddaughter and Akiva. She tells him to go study Torah, and he goes (B. Nedarim 50a). Here Elijah saves the couple not from physical hazard, but from the danger of despair.

This story combines exemplum and a legend. While exempla center on the rewards of study or virtue, legends describe the contact of the supernatural world with the everyday world. The legend generally begins with a lack, or a dangerous crisis, and ends with a positive outcome.[24] Here poverty is the lack that Elijah as supernatural mediator comes to resolve, but, instead of resolving it directly, he sets the exemplum into motion by inspiring Akiva and his wife. Elijah's appearance, expressed in the formulaic language shared by stories of physical danger and rescue, lends metonymic force to the seriousness of Akiva's poverty and emphasizes the role of God's mercy in helping him. This story is also unusual because the powerful Elijah appears in such pitiable disguise and does not act as a trickster or inject obvious humor into the scene. Still, there is an element of hyperbole in a man so poor that he does not even have straw for his wife to give birth on. Whether absurdly extreme or painfully poignant, this situation has a certain dark irony.

The final story containing the expression *idmei* is one in which Elijah visits the academy of Rabbi Judah the Patriarch. Rabbi Judah asks Elijah how to bring the Messiah through prayer, and Elijah tells him that certain rabbis have the power to do so. While they are praying, however, God discovers what Elijah has revealed, punishes him, and Elijah comes down to earth in the form of a bear to scatter the praying rabbis (B. Bava Meẓia 85b).[25] Here Elijah does not rescue anyone; instead he terrifies people. Still, this story does share several characteristics with the rest of the group in which Elijah appears as rescuer. First, Elijah appears in disguise toward the end of the story to resolve a crisis by ensuring that God's will is upheld—even if from a human perspective it was no crisis at all, but an unparalleled opportunity. Second, Elijah acts as trickster in both the beginning and the end of the story. He tries to, in a sense, trick God into the bringing the Messiah before his time, and he scatters the eminent rabbis with embarrassing thoroughness.

This story is also part of the generic group in which Elijah answers a question. It begins with one of this group's two characteristic formulae, "Elijah *was often found* at the court of Rabbi [Judah]," and expresses a messianic theme found in other stories of this group. The story thus combines two groups, taking elements from each. It makes sense that Elijah only appears in terrifying form after being punished and ordered by God to put a stop to the attempt to force the Messiah's coming. He could, presumably, have simply ordered the Rabbis to stop, but chose not to for several possible reasons that may overlap. Perhaps he feared they would not listen, or wanted to disguise his identity while stopping the very prayers he had advised, or he just needed to blow off steam after a taking a beating in heaven.

As these stories have illustrated, metonomy alerts us to the way in which an apparently simple phrase or plot motif in orally derived texts can be pregnant with complex meaning.[26] The phrase *idmei lei*, "he appeared to him," inevitably calls to mind all stories with the phrase, as certainly as the stepmother in Hansel and Gretel calls to mind other stepmothers in European folk tales. When taken apart from their traditional context, some stories of Elijah's appearance in disguise are enigmatically brief, but they become more meaningful when considered in light of the formulae and motifs of which they are composed. For more complex narratives, the perspective of oral-formulaic studies calls the reader's attention to how their creators employ traditional formulae and plot motifs with literary artistry, sometimes modifying or combining them.

What do these stories as a group tell us about how the Rabbis viewed life? More than the other two groups of stories, these stories have concrete real-life precedents: occasions in which help arose for a rabbi from an unexpected — often Gentile — source or occasions where an unlikely person was understood in retrospect to have done God's will. Perhaps rabbis explained unexpected help they themselves experienced as the intervention of Elijah. They certainly appreciated stories of the recent past in which Elijah was revealed as the real savior. These stories encourage trust in God to help the righteous in time of trouble, but not blind faith. They emphasize Elijah's freedom and by extension God's. Elijah's help is never an automatic reward for good behavior: it is unexpected in fact and unexpected in form. In providing help, Elijah does not always respect the dignity of a Sage; he behaves more as a trickster than any other character in rabbinic literature. In short, there is a creative, playful quality to these narratives, a desire to delight and astonish their audience as well as educate and inspire them.

These Elijah-in-disguise stories are legends in the sense that the "supernatural" intrudes into the "natural," suddenly, in order to resolve some crisis. Without Elijah's intervention, if things had followed their "natural" — that is to say, uninterrupted — course, Naḥum Ish Gamzu, Rabbi Meir, Rabbi Eleazar ben Perata, and probably Rav Shila would have been executed by the Gentile government and Rav Shimi bar Ashi would have died from eating that snake. Rabbi Akiva might have remained with his wife, picking the straw out of her hair. Instead, Elijah, as representative of the supernatural, intervenes and saves them. Looking more closely at the definition of "natural" in this context, it becomes clear that in the Bavli Elijah's supernatural intervention is generally within the realm of natural business-as-usual human society as opposed to the nonhuman world.[27] The this-worldly and human dangers from which Elijah saves people emphasize the prophet's own humanity. Because the Rabbis did experience oppression from Gentiles — and probably preferred stories about threats coming from the "other" — Elijah comes to rescue rabbis from non-Jews. Even the Bavli's story of Elijah rescuing someone without appearing in disguise involves an outside threat: he catches Rav Kahana when he throws himself off a roof to avoid the sexual solicitation of a probably Gentile *matrona* (B. Kiddushin 40a).

Thus the stories encourage an optimistic view of life, except in the relationship between Jews and Gentiles. They imply that it is so unlikely that an ordinary Gentile might speak up for a Jew that instead it must have been Elijah who came to the rescue. The tension between Jews and Gentiles, which is explicit in the three stories of legendary court scenes, strengthens this corollary point. In all of them, and especially in the stories of Naḥum Ish Gamzu and Eleazar ben Perata, the hostility of the Gentile court is so intense that some miracle is necessary to overcome it. Within a rabbinic context, a Gentile could not serve as the vehicle for a miracle by God, although he or she might serve as a beneficiary or admiring audience of such a miracle. This discussion of the court scenes brings us to a story that benefits from a closer look than it had in chapter 3, the story of Elijah and Eleazar ben Perata.

Elijah Rescues Rabbi Eleazar ben Perata

This story occurs during the Roman persecutions of the second century, the setting of a number of martyrdom stories, including that of Rabbi Akiva, who died by torture while still praying. Rabbi Eleazar's story, however, is not a martyrdom. It might be called an antimartyrdom, a comedy breaking the framework of the tragedy one expects when rabbinic courage meets Roman violence. Just before Rabbi Eleazar ben Perata is brought to trial, he meets Rabbi Ḥanina ben Teradion in prison. Rabbi Ḥanina predicts that Rabbi Eleazar will be saved, despite five charges against him, because he has busied himself with both Torah and good deeds. Rabbi Ḥanina also predicts that he himself will die, because he has busied himself with Torah alone. Then, after a brief further discussion of Rabbi Ḥanina, the story returns to Rabbi Eleazar:

> They brought Rabbi Eleazar ben Perata [to trial]. They said, "Why have you taught and why have you stolen?"
>
> He said to them, "If one is a scholar one is not a robber and if one is a robber one is not a scholar, and since I am not one I am not the other either."
>
> "Why do they call you 'Rabbi?'"
>
> "I am a master of the weavers."
>
> They brought him two coils of thread and asked,

"Which is for the warp, and which is for the woof?"

A miracle occurred for him, and a female bee came and sat on the warp and a male bee came and sat on the woof.

He told them, "This is the warp and this is the woof."

They asked him, "Why don't you go to the meeting place?"

He said to them, "I am an old man and I am afraid that I might be trampled by your feet."

They asked, "And, up until now, how many old men have been trampled?"

A miracle occurred, and that very day an old man was trampled.

"Why did you free your slave?"

He replied to them, "These things never happened."

One of them got up to testify against him.

Elijah came [and] appeared to him as one of the great men of the empire.

He said to him, "Since a miracle occurred for him in all [the rest], in this one too a miracle will occur for him, and you [lit. "that man"] will show your bad nature."

He did not heed him [Elijah] and rose to speak to them [to denounce Rabbi Eleazar].

[At that moment] there was a letter that was written by important men of the kingdom to send to Caesar's court, and they sent it by [the hands of] that man [who wanted to testify against Rabbi Eleazar].

Elijah came and tossed him four hundred leagues.

He went and did not come [back]

(B. Avodah Zarah 17b)

One can understand this story in the context of rabbinic teachings on suffering as well as on martyrdom. As discussed chapter 3, the Bavli presents diverse views on the causes and meaning of human suffering. Rabbi Ḥanina's prophecy recalls the teaching that the combination of Torah study and good deeds is necessary to stave off suffering and early death. This view of suffering recalls the older rabbinic explanations of suffering as always due to wrongdoing (or at least insufficient virtue).[28] This traditional context provides a framework of divine justice that excuses Rabbi Eleazar's willingness to lie his way out of martyrdom—he is actually bowing to God's will, proclaimed by Rabbi Ḥanina, that his Torah study and good deeds will protect him, whereas Torah study alone is not enough to protect Ḥanina.

Nevertheless, this story is distinctly different from other treatments of suffering because it is, after all, about martyrdom. Other kinds of human and Jewish suffering, even the murder of innocents in persecution, are different from the martyr's path, and stories of martyrdom are also unique. Martyrs die for God, for the sanctification of the Name, as later Jewish sources powerfully express it.[29] Dan Ben-Amos speaks of martyrdom stories as the "fourth category of legend" in which the "supernatural fails to intrude into natural reality." In them, while God does not intervene to save the martyr, "God is not completely indifferent to the suffering of his believers, nor do they expect him to be unconcerned about their fate . . . the whole act of martyrdom is directed toward God." He notes that often a heavenly voice calls out that the martyr has earned eternal life, mitigating God's nonaction.[30] Ben Amos is correct in seeing these stories of God's nonintervention as constituting in themselves an identifiable formal group, linked by both meaning and plot structure. Stories of martyrdom are not only stories of God's refusal to physically intervene to save the righteous; they are also variants of the exemplum, in that they hold up for admiration or even emulation the martyr's willingness to sacrifice his or her life for God and Torah.

Thus our story presents us with both a generic and a conceptual disjuncture. Set during the second-century Roman persecution, and beginning like a martyrdom narrative with a hostile court accusing a rabbi of teaching Torah, it goes on entirely differently. The story of Rabbi Ḥanina's martyrdom directly follows that of Rabbi Eleazar's "antimartyrdom" and underscores how unique the latter is: "They brought Rabbi Ḥanina ben Teradion [to trial.] They said, 'Why are you occupying yourself with Torah?' He said '[I do] as the Lord my God commanded me.' Immediately, they sentenced him to burning, his wife to death, and his daughter to life in a brothel." This is how the Bavli describes the behavior of martyrs, and it is clearly not how Rabbi Eleazar acts. Although Rabbi Eleazar does not agree to break important Jewish laws or renounce faith in God—does not do anything that would make him obviously worthy of divine judgment—he does deny his identity as Sage, lying with as much creativity and consistency as he can. And his lying leads to reward: miracles are done for him because of his good deeds or perhaps simply because God has destined him to live.

Considered outside the wider (and probably redactional) context in which Rabbi Eleazar's lies are rationalized because his rescue is the reward for his virtue, our story seems even more shocking. In its rejection of the value of suffering, it recalls a set of stories in which rabbis are healed of illness after explicitly stating that neither their suffering nor its reward is precious to them.[31] The Bavli is unique among rabbinic sources in the way that it allows, and in fact emphasizes, questions about God's justice, although it generally returns to traditional explanations of why suffering occurs.[32] It is likely that only the Bavli's acceptance of doubt allows it to include Rabbi Eleazar's antimartyrdom, a story that would be even more out of place in other rabbinic works.

Having looked at our story's redactional and theological context, we return to the text. The charge "Why have you stolen?" is the sort of false accusation all too frequent during show trials or kangaroo courts in times of persecution. Blidstein also points out that the charges may go together for the Roman judge to whom "robber" is the conventional label for any rebel against Roman rule.[33] Beginning with the accusation, however, is normal for an ancient Roman trial in which the accused was emphatically considered guilty before being proved innocent.[34] Rabbi Eleazar counters with a bold pun: "If a *sayafa* [a "swordsman" or bandit] not a *safra* [a "bookman"], and if a *safra*, not a *sayafa*—and since one isn't here, neither is the other" (אי סייפא לא ספרא ואי ספרא לא סייפא ומדהא ליתא הא נמי ליתא). His retort is not particularly logically consistent—although one might argue that since the accusations of "teaching" and "stealing" are made together, and rabbi and robber are mutually exclusive occupations, the untruth of one implies the untruth of the other.[35] If the rabbi's answer is a bit weak, it is perhaps because he will not dignify a nonsensical charge with a sensible answer. Indeed, none seems necessary, for the Romans appear to accept it and move on to the next accusation.

The Romans' next demand, "Why do they call you Rabbi?"[36] That is, if you are not a master of Torah, and leader of the Jewish people, why do they call you Master? Here, too, Rabbi Eleazar has an answer, "I am a master of the weavers." Weaving was a low-status trade for men in those days,[37] and in claiming to be a weaver Rabbi Eleazar was both humbling himself by saying he was a mere cloth worker and also making a pun: he was in fact one who wove the webs (the *masekhtot*) of Talmudic discussion.[38] On a more practical note, Rabbi Eleazar picked an occupation that would have explained why he was not tanned or calloused from hard outdoor work. The Romans are still suspicious, however, and bring two coils of thread, demanding to know which is the warp and which the woof. At this point the first miracle is done for Rabbi Eleazar, "A miracle occurred for him, and a female bee came and sat on the warp and a male bee came and sat on the woof." The riddle-solving wisdom of a folktale hero allows Rabbi Eleazar to correctly interpret the miracle: for, as Rashi says, the female bee marks the "passive" warp, and the male bee the "active" woof that is thrust through the warp in weaving.

Then the Romans have another challenge: "Why don't you go to the meeting place?" The literal words here are *bei aveidan* (בי אבידן), "house of their destruction." The Bavli uses this term to refer to pagan or Christian sites of spectacle or worship, and Jastrow plausibly takes it as a cacophemism for *bei va'adan* (בי ועדן), "their meeting place." The Romans want to know why, if Rabbi Eleazar was not a Sage, he had not attended some sort of pagan meeting place. This might have been an actual pagan temple, but there is no other tradition I know of that Jews were forced to attend Roman worship during these persecutions. Instead, the "house of their destruction" probably refers to a theater or, even more, a circus. Worship was offered to pagan gods in these venues, but worship was not their purpose, and some Jews, even some later rabbis, did attend them.[39] A weaver might go to the circus to curry Roman favor or simply to see the excitement; a Sage would not. Rabbi Eleazar's response strengthens this theory. He says, "I am an old man and I am afraid that I might be trampled by your feet." While it is hard to imagine an official public Hellenistic worship service or a theater so rowdy that an old man might be trampled, it is plausible that this might happen in a crowded circus, as men in the cheap seats rushed to cheer their favorites or get a closer view of the carnage.[40] This is not to say that it was common, and the court was skeptical. Here too, however, "A miracle occurred, and that very day an old man was trampled." From the perspective of our story's audience, the old man got what he deserved for attending the "house of their destruction," especially if he were a Jew.

The Romans have yet another accusation: "Why did you free your slave?" Presumably this is a Gentile slave freed by conversion: a sign that Eleazar, if not a Sage, is at least a practicing Jew and in the upside-down logic of persecution deserves to be punished for it. Rabbi Eleazar can find no clever retort and simply blusters, "These things never happened." His flat denial seems to convince most of his accusers. One man, though, is not convinced. At this point, as Rashi points out, the fifth of five charges Rabbi Eleazar refers to in the introduction to our story has already been brought (in order, they are: teaching, stealing, being called rabbi, not attending the meeting place, and freeing a slave). Read in the light of the introduction and Rabbi Ḥanina's prediction, one can see this additional accusation as against God's plan that Rabbi Eleazar escape unharmed.

What is clear is that now Rabbi Eleazar needs another miracle, and this time Elijah must come to his rescue. "Elijah came [and] appeared to him [the accusing Roman] as one of the great men of the empire. He said to him, 'Since a miracle occurred for him in all [the rest], in this one too a miracle will occur for him, and you [lit. ההוא גברא, "that man"] will show your ill will.'" Picture Elijah here, sitting at his ease in a toga, as Rabbi Eleazar stands alone before the court. Elijah speaks to the Roman accuser as an equal, or perhaps a superior, advising him, Roman to Roman, not to make a fool of himself by appearing uselessly bad tempered or vindictive. As the Jewish audience knew, Elijah is actually predicting what he himself is prepared to do: perform a miracle for Rabbi Eleazar. This audience, while marveling at the power of Elijah (and the underlying power of God) could also laugh at the blindness of Rabbi Eleazar's accuser. Elijah was present, but the accuser thought the prophet was a Roman like himself. Therefore, he did not listen to Elijah and rose to denounce Rabbi Eleazar.[41]

Now the expected miracle occurs. In part it is an operation of divine providence comparable to the old man getting trampled at just the right time, but it is helped along vigorously by Elijah: "There was a letter that was written by important men of the kingdom to send to Caesar's court, and they sent it by that man. Elijah came and tossed him four hundred leagues. He went and did not come [back]."

Metonomy in the oral-formulaic sense helps us understand this apparently weird conclusion. The word פתקיה, "he tossed him," always describes the throwing of something light (for the thrower), often casually or contemptuously. In one instance it describes someone spitting, in another throwing a clod of earth at someone as an insulting gesture.[42] Only three beings "toss" humans in the Talmud: Elijah in the story here; Ishbi-benov, the giant brother of Goliath, who throws King David up in the air in a midrash rich in folkloric motifs; and Ashmadai the king of demons, who tricks Solomon into giving up his magic ring and also tosses him four hundred leagues.[43] This last story is particularly relevant to our own, not only because of the motif of "four hundred" but also because Ashmadai does not kill Solomon by throwing him so far.[44] Although Elijah's motives are utterly different from Ashmadai's, and the Roman might well deserve death, Elijah does not kill. Thus this story continues the motif of Elijah's harmlessness as well as his willingness to defend the Rabbis.

In the story of Rabbi Eleazar ben Perata, Elijah, in aligning himself with the rabbi, is aligning himself (and by implication God's will) with someone who prefers life to martyrdom. People perhaps need the fearless example of martyrs, but at most times, including the centuries of the Bavli's composition, Judaism has also honored those heroes of survival who avoid martyrdom and live on to care for others and pass the Jewish tradition to their students. This story celebrates the heroism of survival in the strongest possible terms, beginning the narrative in the same way as a martyrdom story and then breaking the rules of a martyrdom in order to emphasize Rabbi Eleazar's cunning and courage and Elijah's effortless miracles. However, in its context, our story also emphasizes that martyrs and survivors need not be enemies of one another—it is Rabbi Ḥanina ben Teradion, soon to be martyred, who encourages Rabbi Eleazar, predicting he will escape death.

Here, as in most other stories of Elijah's appearance in disguise, Elijah's true identity is unknown to most of those present and perhaps to all. He functions covertly, outside of normal perception and social constructs. For those who do not know, he appears as a pauper, a prostitute, a bear, an anonymous witness, a Roman official. For those who know, the transmitters and audience of these stories, he functions as a potent sign and symbol of God's merciful actions, which change reality powerfully, invisibly, and unforeseen. This particular story, an antimartyrdom in which no one dies, not even the persecutors, is a comedy in the original Aristotelian sense because of the appropriateness and satisfying symmetry of the ending, with the good saved and the wicked punished.[45] The story of Naḥum Ish Gamzu is in a similar sense a comedy, where Naḥum is both saved and rewarded and the wicked innkeepers are punished through their own avarice. The other stories of the disguised Elijah share these characteristics to a greater or lesser extent. Even the story in which Elijah is made to thwart the coming of the Messiah has an element of the comedy insofar as comedy often involves a return to the status quo: no one dies, no lives are ruined, and the good leadership of Judah the Patriarch is maintained.

These stories, however, do far more than maintain the status quo. Peli speaks of Elijah as breaking the "rules of the game,"[46] and that is what happens when Elijah appears in disguise. Comedy as a dramatic form is fictional, but these stories are legends, stories telling the truth about life, and presented as historical. In the real world, especially for an oppressed and colonized people, comedy itself breaks the rules of the rulers' game, in which Romans (or Persians) always win and the Jews always lose. Elijah in disguise opens up the world, introduces unforeseen possibilities and unpredictable freedoms into the imaginative possibilities of rabbinic narrative.

THE GENERIC GROUP IN WHICH ELIJAH ANSWERS QUESTIONS

This generic group of ten stories is the largest and most diverse, because rabbis ask many different kinds of questions and sometimes do different things in response. Elijah specializes in providing information independently, whereas angels or the bat kol more often relay messages from God. Though he occasionally appears to deliver God's words, Elijah more often supplies information on his own initiative—and, in this generic group, in response to a person's questions. The two similar formulae characterizing this generic group of stories simply describe

Elijah's presence or appearance followed by a rabbi asking a question, a question the prophet always answers.

In all these stories, Elijah comes to support the human desire for knowledge and wisdom. As we discussed in chapter 3, Elijah as teacher expresses the value of rabbinic intellectual freedom and, by his presence, implies that God too supports this freedom. Closely linked to freedom of inquiry is power to affect the world. Many of these stories encourage what the Rabbis considered the right and appropriate exercise of human power, both that of the Sages and of other Jews. It is rabbis, however, who always pose the questions, and it their quest for wisdom and power that is most clearly supported, although not without limitation.

The Formal Characteristics of the Group

Seven of stories in this generic group begin "Rabbi/Rav So-and-so met Elijah" (אשכח\יה לאליהו ר' פלוני). In all cases the rabbi immediately asks Elijah a question. Because these stories center around a question and its answer, their dialogue is more important than their action, in contrast to the other generic groups. Most of them are pronouncement stories: they lack a developed plot and instead serve to highlight a memorable saying, usually uttered by Elijah.

The second set of three stories within this generic group state that Elijah "was often found" (הוה שכיח) with someone . These stories also revolve around a rabbi asking Elijah a question and Elijah's answer. Like the shorter stories, these narratives hinge on the exchange of information, but they differ from the first subset because all three of them develop into full narratives that describe how the human protagonist acts on the information Elijah gives him.

THE FORMULA "HE FOUND HIM"   As we saw in chapter 3, the word אשכחיה,"he found him," is characteristic of encounters between rabbis or, occasionally, between rabbis and other folk.[47] In most, the first rabbi asks a question and the second answers it. Many stories with two human protagonists and the similar stories of Elijah describe the encounter between a rabbi and someone who has access to specialized information. In seven instances, for example, a Babylonian rabbi "goes up" to Palestine and asks a local rabbi, usually his senior, for a specific legal tradition or practice of the land of Israel.[48] When rabbis meet Elijah and ask him what God is doing in the heavenly court,[49] they are behaving like other rabbis who question a respected colleague on matters about which that colleague has special knowledge.

The only other supernatural figure whom a rabbi "finds" with the verb אשכחיה is, like Elijah, a biblical figure, Eliezer, the servant or slave of Abraham. Rabbi Bana'ah encounters him at the entrance of Abraham's tomb and asks him what Abraham is doing.[50] Eliezer thus serves as an intermediary between Rabbi Bana'ah and Abraham, as Elijah can serve as an intermediary between the Rabbis and God. It is interesting that Eliezer in midrash, like Elijah in legend, is a boundary-crossing figure, neither quite a slave nor a free man, neither entirely Jewish nor quite Gentile. He is also sometimes a clever trickster, like the legendary Elijah.[51] Eliezer, unlike Elijah, did not ascend to heaven alive, and so can only be found at a grave in the rabbinic present, but his liminal character makes it natural for him, like Elijah, to serve as intermediary between the living and the dead, between his master Abraham and a living rabbi.

THE FORMULA "WAS OFTEN FOUND WITH HIM"   The second formula, "was often found with him" (הוה שכיח גביה), occurs far less frequently than "he found him"—only four times in the Bavli—and has a more specialized function.[52] It always refers to a supernatural figure who visited a rabbi frequently: Elijah in three stories and, in one, the angel of death.[53] The stories with this formula seem to picture a supernatural being visiting certain rabbis regularly and casually, implying that revelations were an everyday thing for them and that the supernatural beings chose to visit them.

The story of Elijah in Rabbi Yehudah's court begins by strikingly emphasizing the rabbi's power, presenting Elijah as a courtier in the patriarch's domain.

> Elijah was often found at the court of Rabbi [Yehudah the Patriarch].
>
> One day it was the New Moon. It became dark and he did not come.
>
> He [Rabbi Yehudah] said to him, "Why were you delayed, Sir?"
>
> He said to him, "[I waited] until I had gotten Abraham up, and washed his hands, and he prayed and I laid him [back] down, and the same for Isaac and the same for Jacob."
>
> "And [why not] wake them up at the same time?"
>
> "I thought that they might become strong in prayer and bring the Messiah before his time."
>
> He said to him, "And does their likeness exist in this world?"
>
> He said to him, "There are Rabbi Ḥiyya and his sons."
>
> (B. Bava Meẓia 85b)

Though Rabbi Yehudah calls Elijah "Sir," he also calls him to account for himself when he does not arrive on time. Rabbi Yehudah's initial authority further emphasizes his dramatic failure in the conclusion in which he runs away with the other worshipers when Elijah appears as a bear.

The Content of This Generic Group

Returning to the seven stories introduced with "Rabbi So-and-so found Elijah," four of them share the theme that God approves of and supports rabbinic midrashic—and in one case halakhic—creativity and innovation. The first of these comments on a group of interpretations of Esther 5:4 in which Esther requests, "Let the King and Haman come to the feast that I have prepared for him." A tradition asks, "What did Esther consider when she invited Haman?" (whom she knew was seeking to destroy the Jews). This question receives twelve answers from twelve rabbis. The answers include suggestions from "So that he would not come to know that she was Jewish" to the idea that she decided to seduce Haman so that he would be killed along with her. After this long list of possibilities, "Rabbah bar Abbuha met Elijah and said to him, 'In accord with whose opinion did Esther decide and act as she did?'" And Elijah responds, "[She thought] like all the Tannaim and like all the Amoraim" who voiced an opinion (B Megillah 15b). Elijah's response is far from self-evident. His point, however, does not assert the probability of the specific suggestions so much as uphold the fundamental truth of non-legal rabbinic midrash. What indeed is the point of midrash if it is not true, as true (in some sense) as the Scripture it interprets? Elijah reassures Rabbah bar Abbuha that despite the abundance of rabbinic interpretations of the same event, all of them are true, which is to say valid and valuable.[54]

This point is sharply underscored by a parallel story in Gittin, another legend in which a rabbi asks Elijah about the truth of conflicting midrashic interpretations of the same passage. The biblical text at issue is Judges 19:2, the prelude to the story of "the concubine of Gibeah," the woman who was murdered by the men of Gibeah. Judges 19:2–3 is normally translated something like, "And his concubine deserted him (ותזנה פילגשו עליו) and went away to her father's house . . . and her husband got up and went after her." The interpretive problem is that the word translated "deserted" literally means, as the JPS translation notes, "played the harlot." If the woman had been unfaithful, however, both biblical and rabbinic mores would have frowned on her husband seeking to take her back. Nor did her leaving him and going back to her father, relatively minor misbehavior, seem enough in itself to merit the term. Both the rabbinic interpretations connect the word with unsavory poor hygiene:

> As it is written, "And his concubine offended him":
>> Rabbi Aviatar said that he found a fly with her;
>> Rabbi Yonatan said that he found a hair on her.
>> And Rabbi Aviatar met Elijah.
>> He said to him, "What is the Holy One blessed be He doing?"
>> He said to him, "He is occupied with 'the concubine in Gibeah.'"
>> "And what is he saying?"
>> He said to him, "'My son Aviatar, he speaks this way; my son Yonatan, he speaks that way.'"
>> He said to him, "Spare us! Is there doubt before Heaven?"
>> He said to him, "[Both] these and those are the word of the Living God. He found a fly and did not object; he found a hair and objected."
>> Rav Yehudah said, "The fly was in his dish, and the hair was in 'that place'; the fly was a disgusting thing, but the hair was a danger."[55]
>
> (B. Gittin 6b)

Here Rabbi Aviatar's question may well be ours: "How can God in heaven uphold two contradictory views?" Elijah's response is prompt and definite, "Both of these are the words of the Living God." These are the words of the bat kol that ends the controversy between the House of Hillel and the House of Shammai.[56] The conflict Elijah addresses, however, is different, and the resolution is different as well. In the case of Hillel and Shammai, the conflict was halakhic, a matter of which faction had the authority to legislate, and the bat kol's answer was that, although "both are words of the Living God," the authority rested in the House of Hillel because of their greater virtue. Elijah's answer here is that because "both are the words of the Living God," both (in their own way) are correct.

The pronouncements of Elijah and of the bat kol serve to underscore the differences—and the similarities—between aggadic and halakhic teaching. In the conflict between the Houses of Hillel and Shammai, only one set of teachings could be normative, and thus only one could be declared authoritative. In weighing aggadic interpretations, however, one finds a large, if not infinite, number of correct answers.[57] Still, the identical wording of the two passages inevitably also creates a comparison between aggadic midrash and halakhah. Rabbi Aviatar's anxious question, "Spare us, is there doubt before Heaven?" may arise partly from a fear that the pluralism of aggadic midrash could infect halakhic midrash and prevent the law from being definitively grounded in Scripture (leaving aside the question of whether most rabbinic law is derived from or supported by midrash). In our story Elijah reassures the hearer that the multiplicity of aggadic interpretation does not mean that God is uncertain. Aggadic midrash has a truth just as valid as that of halakhah, but it is additive; it includes all options rather than specifying only one. Furthermore, God does not merely tolerate aggadic truth. He blesses it by reciting the words of the interpreting Rabbis and calling them his "sons" in their act of interpretive creation.

Elijah also brings word that God calls the Rabbis his children in the famous story of the oven of Akhnai, where the majority of Rabbis decisively reject Rabbi Eliezer's argument that an oven built from detachable sections is not subject to ritual impurity. They remain firm in their commitment to the majority rule, despite Rabbi Eliezer's calling on miracles and even a bat kol to prove his point. Two generations later, "Rabbi Natan met Elijah and said to him, 'What was the Holy One blessed be He doing at that time?' He said to him, 'He was laughing and saying, 'My sons have prevailed over me, my sons have prevailed over me'" (B. Bava Meẓia 59b). Unfortunately, the human side of the story ends tragically. The Sages not only contradict Rabbi Eliezer, they excommunicate him, and Rabbi Eliezer's curse brings death. Rubenstein emphasizes the contrast between human jealousy and divine generosity: God "does not feel his honor compromised. . . . After all, the very sages who 'defeat' him . . . interpret his law and obey its dictates. . . . This happy resolution of the divine-human proves an ironic contrast to the unfortunate outcome of the terrestrial struggle between the sages."[58]

God calls the Sages "sons" precisely in the assertion of their rabbinic authority, even, so to speak, against God. It is no accident that it is Elijah in particular who brings word of this, presenting God as a loving and forgiving teacher. Elijah serves as a bridge between humanity and God and bears witness to human power in relationship to God as no other being does. In all three stories Elijah emphasizes the intimate relationship of the Sages to God in their collective exegetical creativity and legislative assertion. While Elijah appears to individuals, he suggests that the Sages are strongest working together. In these stories the Talmud expresses the conviction that the Sages as a community are doing God's will by picturing God listening appreciatively to their debates and reciting their traditions.

While these stories were probably seen as truth rather than mere literary metaphors, they are far more than naive transcriptions of the earthly house of study into the heavenly realm. Other passages in the Bavli show that the Rabbis were well aware of God's transcendence, God's divine otherness. They often describe the awesomeness of the natural world or of angels and then say how much superior God is to these created things. Ḥagigah 13b, for example, describes the angel Sandolfon as "five hundred years' journey" taller than the already almost unimaginably huge living creatures of the chariot throne of God and yet says that Sandolfon cannot crown God directly because "His Place" is unknown even to the angelic retinue. Rather than limiting or domesticating the divine, stories that present God as, so to speak, a student of the Sages, present truths that are additive, like those of aggadic midrash, which do not deny the other great truth of God's transcendence.

The rabbinic belief that Torah study made them God's colleagues is exemplified in the story in which Rabbah bar Shila meets Elijah. This story is the last in a cycle of stories on Elisha ben Abuya, the early heretic called Aḥer, the "Other." The immediately previous passage says that Rabbi Meir, his student, was right to learn from Elisha because Rabbi Meir had the good judgment to "eat the date"—Elisha's Torah—but "throw away the seed"—his heresy. The Elijah story that follows makes the same point by portraying God as extraordinarily responsive to human critique.

Rabbah bar Shila met Elijah. He asked him, "What is the Holy One blessed be He doing?"

He said to him, "He is reciting traditions from the mouths of all the Rabbis, but from the mouth of Rabbi Meir he is not reciting [traditions]."

He asked him, "Why?"

"Because he learned traditions from the mouth of Aḥer [the Other]."

He said to him, "Why? Rabbi Meir found a pomegranate, ate its flesh, and threw away its skin."

He said to him, "Now He says, 'Meir my son says, When a human being suffers [the penalty of death] what does the Shekhinah say? My head is heavy, my arm is heavy.[59] If the Holy One blessed be He suffers over the blood of the wicked, how much the more so [does He suffer] over the blood of the righteous that is poured out?'"

(B. Ḥagigah 15b, citing M. Sanh. 6.5)

In this surprising and poignant story, Rabbah bar Shila appears to change God's mind as only biblical heroes like Moses did. Elijah's role here is crucial, for the prophet reveals a "second view" of God's will.[60] If Elijah had not told Rabbah bar Shila what God was doing, the rabbi would not have made his comment to God.

If Elijah had not told Rabbah bar Shila of God's changed opinion, he would not have known of it. Elijah, as a specifically human intermediary between heaven and earth, facilitates human critique of God. Elijah's role both legitimates and limits intimacy between the Rabbis and God. Human comments were and are addressed to heaven, but Elijah alone can supply the answers to specific human questions. Thus this story supports the rabbinic contention that prophetic revelations directly from God have ended—Elijah must now serve as intermediary.

All the stories discussed so far are pronouncement stories or mixtures of pronouncement story and legend. Whereas, in the previous two generic groups, Elijah's actions generally drive the plot, in these cases Elijah's words and the pronouncement that concludes the story convey the story's main meaning. In the story of Rabbah bar Shila, for example, the rabbi protests God's neglect of Rabbi Meir's traditions, but there is no physical action as in an ordinary legend. Rather, Elijah mediates an exchange between the rabbi and God, an exchange containing two memorable sayings: Rabbah's statement that "Rabbi Meir found a pomegranate, ate its flesh, and threw away its skin" and the concluding teaching of Rabbi Meir that the Shekhinah suffers when a condemned person is put to death.

In contrast, two stories with the formula "he met him" (אשכחיה) and the three stories containing the phrase "he was often found" (הוה שכיח) all involve a rabbi who *acts* on something Elijah tells him. These five stories, one discussed in detail later in this section, show that while Elijah may impart special truths he does not necessarily give people power to change the way in which the world functions. Though, for example, Elijah "was often present at" the court of Rabbi Yehudah, he cannot help him force the coming of the Messiah.

Another messianic story, in which Elijah tells a rabbi how to find and speak to the Messiah, shows that the Messiah's coming cannot be predicted. As we have seen, the protagonist, Rabbi Joshua ben Levi, encounters Elijah in a number of rabbinic legends. One story has him ascending to paradise without dying, aided by high virtue and low cunning worthy of Elijah himself.[61] This story, on the other hand, records not success but moving failure. The story begins with an encounter between Rabbi Joshua ben Levi, Elijah, and (in manuscripts) the saintly dead Rabbi Shimon ben Yoḥai at the entrance to Shimon ben Yoḥai's tomb. Rabbi Joshua asks Elijah, "Will I enter the world to come?" and Elijah replies, "If this lord wishes." This cryptic remark may be explained by what Rabbi Joshua says next, "I saw two and heard three." The rabbi sees Elijah and Shimon ben Yoḥai, and "this lord"—the mysterious "third" he hears—is the bat kol, the only supernatural mediator to rule on matters of salvation. Then Rabbi Joshua asks Elijah:

"When will Messiah come?"

He said to him, "Go ask him."

"And where [is he]?"

"He sits at the gate of Rome."[62]

"And how will I know him? [lit. what are his distinguishing marks?]"

He sits among the poor who suffer from diseases, and all of them loosen [their bandages] and tie up [their bandages] all at once; [but] he loosens one and ties one [at a time]."

He says, "Perhaps I will be needed [at any moment], so I should not be delayed."

[Rabbi Joshua] went to him.

He said to him, "Peace be with you, my master and teacher."

He said to him, "Peace be with you, son of Levi."

He said to him, "When are you coming, Sir?"

He said to him, "Today."

[Rabbi Joshua] came to Elijah.

He said to him, "What did he say to you?"

He said to him, "'Peace be with you, son of Levi.'"

He said to him, "He promised you and your father the world to come."

He said to him,

"He surely lied to me, for he said he would come today, and he did not come."

He said to him,

"This [is what] he said to you, 'Today, if you will hear His voice' [Ps. 95:7]."

(B. Sanhedrin 98a)

A more vivid portrait of a waiting Messiah is hard to imagine. He is faithful in his suffering, but hopeful, perhaps impatient, "Perhaps I will be needed, so I should not be delayed." The place where the Messiah sits is far from casually chosen. Rome itself was both embodiment and symbol of the day-to-day oppression of the Jews as well as of the unredeemed nature of reality. Furthermore, Rome was a grossly overcrowded and callous city.[63] So, "at the gate of Rome," the Messiah was not only suffering, but suffering in a hostile city, with only the anonymous poor and sick for company.

Rabbi Joshua asks, "'When are you coming, Sir?'" The Messiah replies, "Today." Several things alert the audience of this story that this answer is not as straightforward as it seems. We know that the Messiah himself does not know when he will be needed and we know that the Messiah has not in fact come.

Furthermore, the word "Today," is in Hebrew in a mostly Aramaic text. This, as Elijah later explains, is because the Messiah is in fact quoting Scripture: "Today, if you will hear His voice." The Messiah will come when the Jewish people hearkens to the voice of God. But Rabbi Joshua does not yet understand this.

When he meets Elijah again, Joshua recounts his brief exchange with the Messiah, hears that both he and his father have been assured the world to come, and then—apparently uninterested in personal salvation—exclaims, "Surely he lied to me! For he said he would come today, and he did not come."[64] There is agony and anger in Rabbi Joshua's outcry. Neither awe of the Messiah nor respect for his suffering prevents him from accusing the Messiah of lying—to Elijah, if not to the Messiah's face. In several manuscripts Rabbi Joshua is unable to contain his feelings and cries, "Surely he lied to me!" the moment he meets Elijah, before the prophet asks him what the Messiah said. Elijah, as herald of the Messiah, must explain the real meaning of "today": "Today, if you will hear His voice."

Oral-formulaic analysis can help illuminate Elijah's role in this rich story. Both the structure of traditions starting "Rabbi So-and-so met Elijah and asked" and their metonymic evocations are crucial to its understanding. It is fitting that only Elijah (the Messiah's herald and one who has access to heavenly knowledge) would know where to find the Messiah and how to interpret his answer to Rabbi Joshua. Futhermore, only Elijah would answer when asked, as he always does. Just as Elijah knows what God is studying in the heavenly court, enabling an otherwise impossible intimacy with God, Elijah enables an otherwise impossible encounter with the Messiah. It is consistent with Elijah's character that he does not reprove Rabbi Joshua for his angry accusation against the Messiah and instead simply answers his implied question.

As in other contexts, Elijah's generous response to questioning legitimates and encourages the human thirst for knowledge that is no mere quest for information. It includes two sometimes contradictory desires: desire to understand God and the world and desire to change the world. In trying to force the coming of the Messiah, Rabbi Judah the Patriarch seeks power, but, in bitter hindsight, gains only understanding. Rabbi Joshua ben Levi seeks clear predictions and receives open-ended answers. Even with Elijah's teaching and assistance, the timing of the Messiah's coming cannot be controlled or predicted.

In both these Messianic stories, Elijah stands between human and heavenly reality, but participates more on the human side. In the story of Rabbi Judah, Elijah, struck with "sixty fiery lashes," suffers more than anyone from the ill-timed attempt to force the coming of the Messiah. In the story of Rabbi Joshua and the

Messiah, perhaps Elijah himself does not know how the Messiah will answer the rabbi's question, and that is precisely why he sends Rabbi Joshua off to ask it. Elijah's only superiority over the Sage is in knowing where the Messiah is and being able to interpret his answer. Thus the story becomes that of three people waiting for the coming of the Messiah: the Sage, the prophet, and the Messiah himself. Elijah's participation in these failed messianic quests suggests that human pain at the delay of the Messiah is not a merely mortal failing. It is a heavenly restlessness, but one God does not yet allow to bear fruit.

The remaining two stories that begin "Elijah was often found" (הוה שכיח) also have a rabbi asking a question and acting in response to the information Elijah provides. However, they each differ considerably from the messianic stories and from one another. One story is an exemplum, the other is a legend focused on the saintly Rabbi Ḥiyya after his death, rather than on Elijah. In the exemplum, Rabbi Beroka Ḥoza'a asks which people in the market are "sons/children of the world to come" (בני עלמא דאתי), and Elijah points out several unlikely people, none of them Sages.[65] The rabbi acts on Elijah's information, going to speak with the people he has pointed out, finding out from them why they are worthy of reward. The first man is a righteous jailer who conceals his Jewish identity in order to protect women, particularly Jewish women, from rape and to alert the Rabbis of Gentile decrees harmful to the Jews. The other people pointed out by Elijah are a pair of men who are both merrymakers and peacemakers; they cheer up the sad and reconcile those who are quarreling.

This is a classic exemplum: a story in which a moral or spiritual value motivates the main action of the plot, rather than merely being implied by the narrative. The subcategory of exemplum it represents shows how righteous action gives apparently lowly people rewards of various kinds: wealth, the power of effective prayer, or, as here, the assurance of God's special favor.[66] The preceding story conveys a similar moral: it recounts how Abba, the barber-surgeon, received greetings from the heavenly court more frequently than Abaye the rabbi. When Abaye asks why, people say that Abba preserves the modesty of his women patients, treats poor people for free, and gives generously to young scholars. The moral of both stories is that a common person who is uncommonly virtuous may be more pleasing to God than a learned Sage.

Still, Elijah's role in our story is significant. For one thing, only Elijah has access to the heavenly knowledge necessary to tell Rabbi Beroka which people are "children of the world to come" without such evidence as a bat kol or greetings from the heavenly court. Furthermore, in teaching a rabbi about righteous common people, Elijah's actions are consistent with his refusal to visit someone who has neglected the needs of the poor and unimportant. In addition, Elijah shares certain qualities with those whom he points out. Like the righteous jailer, Elijah appears in disguise in Gentile legal settings, and, like the merrymakers, he will reconcile people, turning "the heart of fathers to the children, and the heart of the children to their fathers" (Mal. 3:23). Finally, the plot structure in which Elijah gives Rabbi Beroka information that he then follows up connects this legend to other stories beginning with "was often found" in which a rabbi's active response to Elijah's information is essential to complete the narrative.

In chapter 3 I used the next story to show how holy men rose in power as angels declined. It begins by saying that Elijah was "often found" (הוה שכיח) and, like the story we have just discussed, does not focus primarily on Elijah. It is the only Elijah tale framed as a story someone tells, giving it the vividness of news about a friend of a friend: "Rav Ḥaviva said, 'Rav Ḥaviva of Surmaki told me a story: I saw one of the rabbis with whom Elijah was often found'" whose eyes looked red and burned. When Ḥaviva of Surmaki asks him what happened, the latter tells him that he asked Elijah to show him saintly Sages ascending from their tombs to the heavenly court. Elijah does so, but warns him not to look at the chariot of Rabbi Ḥiyya, which he will know because it rises by its own power, while the other Sages ascend in chariots lifted by angels. But the rabbi does gaze, and is half blinded by the sight, only recovering his vision when he goes to Rabbi Ḥiyya's grave and pleads for help (B. Bava Meẓia 85b).

Here, as he often does, Elijah teaches heavenly knowledge inaccessible to ordinary mortals. Perhaps there is an association between the Rabbis' chariots and the chariots at the biblical Elijah's ascension. In any case, the liminal Elijah is a suitable figure for giving a living person access to the saintly dead Sages of generations past. Thus Elijah acts as a permissive teacher as well—granting the unnamed rabbi's request, even though it is potentially dangerous. On might say that Elijah encourages human freedom, even the freedom to run risks. Nevertheless, our story reveals ambivalence toward the practice of seeking mystical revelations. It stresses the dangers of seeing Rabbi Ḥiyya and implies no spiritual or practical reward—other than satisfied curiosity—for witnessing the Sages ascend to the heavenly court. The story's conclusion describing the rabbi's cure also deemphasizes esoteric practice. When he goes to Rabbi Ḥiyya's grave to plead for healing, the rabbi says, "it is your legal traditions I repeat" (מתנייתא דמר מתינא), stressing his role of disciple to Rabbi Ḥiyya as master teacher rather than as master mystic.

This generic group of pronouncement stories and legends based on Elijah's answers to a question expresses central convictions of rabbinic Judaism. In the first group of stories Elijah assures Sages that they are deeply pleasing to God when exercising their proper rabbinic authority, whether doing midrash or legislating according to the majority. The oven of Akhnai story in particular often serves as a paradigmatic example of the theme of human freedom in rabbinic thought. In this generic group, Elijah also expresses rabbinic values conveyed by other genres of story. Elijah's response to Rabbi Beroka, for example, sets up an exemplum in which apparently ordinary or unrighteous people are revealed to be outstandingly virtuous.

This generic group as a whole expresses encouragement and appreciation for what the Rabbis considered the right and appropriate exercise of human power. Elijah particularly encourages rabbinic authority, but also teaches about the hard work of women (in Yebamot 63a) and the righteousness of unlearned men. This latter theme of respect for ordinary people is in harmony with the previous generic group in which Elijah abandons those who fail to respect or protect the powerless.

The double emphasis on the authority of Jewish leaders and the virtues of common folk is in harmony with Jewish values today. To modern eyes Elijah's messages do not seem special, perhaps because they were successful: they helped form today's values. Rabbinic stories, however, often convey other messages. The Talmud has many accounts (some disapproving and some apparently approving) of how rabbis asserted their superiority over common people. In addition, the Rabbis frequently emphasize the need for humility before God, and they often express anxiety over human vulnerability to punishing angels, demons, and uncaring fate. None of these themes appear in Elijah stories. The only human limitations conveyed by Elijah stories are the riskiness of esoteric mystical knowledge and the impossibility of forcing the coming of the Messiah. These stories imply that people have certain limits that even Elijah, humanity's advocate, cannot help us overcome.

Elijah's actions support the appropriateness of rabbinic authority in the human realm, but also make it clear that rabbis are not morally superior to women or to uneducated men, defining the right relationship between the Rabbis and the people they seek to lead. The need for the Rabbis to have humility before God is expressed through other mediators. Perhaps this is also reflected in the fact that, of all mediators of the divine—angels, the bat kol, the angel of death, and even Satan—only Elijah is human.

Elijah Brings Rabbah bar Abbuha to Paradise

This story is distinctly comic, beginning with halakhic discussion and ending with a strange, but finally successful, journey to paradise by Rabbah bar Abbuha. Unlike most longer Talmudic stories, it appears in a legal rather an aggadic context, in the middle of a long section on the competing rights of debtors and creditors. A key question for the discussion is this: if a debtor owes as much or more than he owns, does one assess what he pays his creditor so that he retains some possessions beyond the few that are legally mandated? The midrashic argument given for leaving the debtor some possessions is an analogy to the ritual law concerning "valuations" in Leviticus 27:2–8. When someone vowed to give a large donation to the Temple and could not afford it, he was assessed by the priest to determine what he could pay. The Talmud discusses the issue three times, in two long pages, and never completely settles it. Then, without any specific introduction:

Rabbah bar Abbuha met Elijah standing in a graveyard of the Gentiles.

He said to him [Elijah], "What is the law concerning whether they assess debtors?"

He said to him, "Learn it from the use of the root 'poor' in the law of valuation. Concerning valuation it is written, 'But if he is *poorer* (מָךְ) than your valuation' [Lev. 27:8]; concerning the debtor it is written, "And if your brother becomes *poor* (יָמוּךְ)' [Lev. 25:35]."

"What is the scriptural source saying that a naked person should not separate *terumah?*"

"That he should not see in you any improper thing" [Deut. 23:15]. [67]

He said to him, "Aren't you a priest, Sir? Why are you standing, Sir, in a graveyard?"

He said to him, "Haven't you studied 'Purities,' Sir?

"As it is taught in a beraita, Rabbi Shimon ben Yoḥai says, the graves of the Gentiles do not make one impure. As it is said, 'But you are my flock, the sheep of my pasture; you are human beings' [Ez. 34:31]. You are called human; Gentiles are not called human."

He said to him, "I cannot manage four [orders of Mishnah] how can I manage [all] six?"

He said to him, "And why [not]?"

He said to him, "I am poor."

He led him and brought him up to the Garden of Eden. He said to him, "Spread out your cloak—pick and take some of these leaves."

He picked and took.

As he was going out he heard that which said, "Who uses up his eternity as Rabbah bar Abbuha does?"

He shook out [his cloak and] threw them away.

Even so, he took his cloak—his cloak absorbed the scent.

He sold it for twelve thousand denars [that] he divided among his sons-in-law.

(B. Bava Meẓia 114a–b)

Despite their strange meeting place, Rabbah bar Abbuha's first two questions are no different from questions any rabbi might ask another. They are, in fact, typical examples of the kind of encounter between rabbis beginning with the phrase "he met him." This story also echoes an exchange between Rabbah bar Abbuha and Elijah previously discussed in which he meets Elijah and asks a question about interpretations of Esther. Rabbah bar Abbuha may have held public administrative roles in the exiliarch's court. Neusner holds that our story was created to explain how the rabbi suddenly got rich: he conversed with Elijah and the prophet helped him.[68] While our story does provide an explanation for Rabbah bar Abbuha's wealth, it has much more to say about Elijah as a rabbinic teacher.

At first sight it seems like a random miniature anthology of Elijah traditions, but on closer analysis its structure becomes meaningful. Although the three brief pronouncement stories probably come from different sources, they all relate to one another and to the concluding legendary ascent. The first question on debtors is thematically connected to the narrative conclusion because Rabbah bar Abbuha is himself poor, perhaps a debtor. Elijah's answer that one does assess them follows directly from the preceding legal discussion. The majority of preceding legal opinions lean against assessing debtors and toward confiscating their property. Elijah, in asserting that the penniless debtor should be left with some of his possessions, is speaking against the flow of the argument and very much in character in his role as champion and helper of the poor (including Rabbah bar Abbuha).

The second question, requesting a prooftext on not separating *terumah* naked, may have a thematic link to the following question about standing in a graveyard in that separating terumah while improperly naked resembles teaching Torah on the impure ground of a cemetery. This second question also resonates with Elijah's prooftext on "valuations": terumah, the portion of agricultural produce still sometimes given to priests in rabbinic times, was the equivalent of offerings to the

Temple. Last, the question serves to emphasize Elijah's role as teacher in this story and was probably also included in our story in part because it is a *halakhic* midrash associated with Elijah.[69] While stories in which rabbis meet Elijah include a number with midrashic themes, our story has the only legal midrash taught explicitly by Elijah in the Bavli.

Finally, the third question, "why are you standing in a graveyard?" is necessary to the plot: Rabbah bar Abbuha needs to ask why Elijah is in a cemetery because he has not studied the Order of Purities; he has not studied Purities because he is poor, and Elijah leads him to the heavenly Garden of Eden so that he can acquire riches. The question vividly presents Elijah as a rabbi like other rabbis, following the form of a typical exchange in which one rabbi meets another and finds fault with what he is doing. This formulaic interchange between rabbis occurs more than a twenty times in the Bavli with the phrase "he met him" (אשכחיה), and many more times without it. Sometimes, like Elijah, the second rabbi has a legal justification for his action.[70] The use of this form in an interaction with Elijah metonymically reinforces Elijah's resemblance to an ordinary rabbi. Since questioning the halakhic fitness of another rabbi's actions is abrasive even by rabbinic standards, it makes sense that the Munich and Florence manuscripts have Rabbah bar Abbuha say "Sir" twice: "Aren't you a priest, Sir? Why are you standing, Sir, in a graveyard?"

But why should Elijah teach in a graveyard? It has a practical role in the plot, sparking Rabbah bar Abbuha's question, but it also expresses Elijah's role as a liminal figure, one who mediates between life and death. In different manuscripts of the story of Rabbi Joshua ben Levi and the Messiah, the Rabbi Joshua meets Elijah either at the tomb of Rabbi Shimon ben Yoḥai or at the gate of the Garden of Eden. In that story, being at the threshold of the mundane world prefigured Elijah's ability to put Rabbi Joshua in touch with the more-than-mortal person of the Messiah. In this story, Elijah's location in a graveyard prefigures his Hermes-like ability to transport a living man to the heavenly Garden of Eden.

Rabbah bar Abbuha's question is the only place in the Bavli that references a widespread tradition that Elijah was a priest. The source for this could well be the offering he made in biblical times on Mount Carmel in his contest with the priests of Baal.[71] In any case, given that Elijah is a priest, the question is well warranted: even today observant Jewish men from priestly families never visit graveyards. On the other hand, Elijah's surprised or reproving response implies the question is rather elementary, that it was well known that rabbinic laws of impurity applied differently to Gentiles. Elijah quotes Rabbi Shimon ben Yoḥai, saying that the graves of Gentiles cannot make one ritually impure because dead Gentiles are not considered human in conveying impurity as dead Jews do.[72] This "insult" to Gentiles is in harmony with Elijah's role in helping Jews against their non-Jewish enemies, and the prooftext fits well with the story as a whole, describing God as shepherd of Israel. It implies that Elijah's care for Rabbah bar Abbuha is in its final source also God's care for one of his flock.

At this point in the story, though, Rabbah bar Abbuha does not feel well cared for. He responds defensively that he cannot master four orders of Mishnah, so how can he be expected to know all six? Rather than being offended by the complaint, Elijah responds in a practical way, asking him what the problem is. Rabbah responds that he is poor, using an idiom—"things are narrow for me."[73] This last exchange resembles the meeting between Elijah and Rav Kahana quoted in chapter 3. Rav Kahana, selling baskets, was propositioned by a matron (possibly Gentile, certainly married) whom he could not safely refuse. He threw himself off the roof to avoid sinning, and Elijah came and caught him. When Elijah complains that Rav Kahana has forced him to come four hundred leagues in a hurry, Rav Kahana complains in his turn that poverty has forced him to adopt the unsafe occupation of salesman. Elijah, rather than being offended, makes Rav Kahana rich by giving him a bushel of denars. Both there and here, Elijah has a impressively practical response to the difficulty.

In our story, Elijah brings Rabbah bar Abbuha up to the heavenly Garden of Eden. In the language of the Vilna text, "He led him and brought him up to the Garden of Eden. He said to him, 'Spread out your cloak—pick and take some of these leaves.'" The disparity between the halakhic genre of the beginning and the legendary genre of the ending is striking. As we have seen, however, most Elijah stories are carefully constructed, and this is no exception. A good case can be made that the very thing that seems incongruous about this story—the union of two disparate genres—is the best key to one of its implications. Elijah never appears more like a colleague of the Rabbis than he does in the beginning of this story. He answers three halakhic questions by means of legal midrash, just as a Sage would, without any apparent recourse to special heavenly knowledge. Then, again like a rabbinic teacher, he helps Rabbah bar Abbuha his student, but does so by the miraculous expedient of bringing him up to the Garden of Eden. This movement from legal instruction to miraculous assistance seems intended to evoke wonder and appreciation of Elijah's double identity: is it not marvelous that Sages have met and learned from a previously mortal man who is at once clearly their senior colleague and also a supernatural mediator who can transport a rabbi to to heavenly Eden before his death?

After the two arrive in the Garden of Eden, however, things do not go precisely as Elijah has planned. Rabbah bar Abbuha picks the leaves from the trees and fills his cloak with them. Then, however, "As he was going out he heard [something] saying, 'Who uses up his eternity as Rabbah bar Abbuha does?'" At this implied warning, "He shook out [his cloak and] threw them away." Nevertheless, the cloak absorbed the scent of heaven, and he was able to sell it for a vast sum of money that he shared with his sons-in-law and, by implication, his daughters and grand-children. Although for a while his gain seems to be lost, Rabbah bar Abbuha seems able to enjoy part of his heavenly reward without using it up.

Odd as the idea of "using up" one's heavenly reward may seem to us, the Bavli implies this idea is several places, and one other story clearly says that this is possible. It is part of a collection of seven stories on Rabbi Ḥanina ben Dosa, his poverty, his virtue, and his wonder-working powers. Fed up with their hard life, his wife asks him to pray "that they will give you something." Rabbi Ḥanina prays, and something in the form of a hand gives him a table leg made of pure gold. Before they can sell it, however, they see in a dream that in heaven the rest of the righteous will eat off three-legged tables while he and his wife eat off a two-legged table. Rabbi Ḥanina prays again and the table leg is taken away.[74] This story seems to imply that it is impossible for people to request miracles to change their basic life situation—at least without reducing their future reward, which recalls Baruch Bokser's argument, described in chapter 3, that individual petitionary prayer was seen as blocked after the destruction of the Temple.[75] Stories such as this reveal an ambivalent attitude to individual petitionary prayer: such prayer, if not impossible, may be inappropriate.

All these caveats are forgotten, however, when Elijah appears. He does not come in response to prayer; he simply arrives and proceeds to change the ordinary way of the world dramatically for the better. Stories like that of Rabbah bar Abbuha and Rav Kahana have a thematic connection to some of the stories in which Elijah appears in disguise to rescue those in hopeless situations. The anti-martyrdom of Rabbi Eleazar ben Perata, in which Elijah rescues the Sage from otherwise certain death, resembles our story in that both Elijah and the mortal hero of the narrative act to bring things to a happy conclusion. We have in a sense come full circle back to the liberating, sometimes mischievous, Elijah of the stories in which he appears in disguise. In both cases those he helps need to think on their feet to receive Elijah's blessing. Rabbi Eleazar loudly claims not to be a rabbi, with some success, and Rabbah bar Abbuha wisely discards the heavenly leaves he has picked.

There are, in fact, some versions of our story that may indicate that Rabbah bar Abbuha has to do something that requires even more independent judgment: discard leaves Elijah himself picked. The Munich manuscript reads:

> He brought him to the Garden of Eden. He filled his cloak with leaves.
>
> As he was going out, he heard the guardians of the Garden of Eden who were saying, "Who goes ahead and uses up his eternity as Rabbah bar Abbuha does?"

This version of the passage could mean either that Elijah both led Rabbah to heaven and filled his cloak with the leaves or that Elijah simply led him to heaven and Rabbah did the rest. Both ways of reading it serve to emphasize Elijah's relative equality with Rabbah. If Elijah simply leads Rabbah bar Abbuha to heaven and then Rabbah picks the leaves on his own initiative, we have a story in which the mortal person takes his reward (quite literally) in his own hands. If, on the other hand, Elijah picks the leaves for Rabbah, he manifests an unselfconscious desire to help that is all the more human for being slightly misapplied. All things being equal, this second possibility is more likely, for it is hard to see how Rabbah would decide alone to pick the leaves of the trees without Elijah's advice.

Whether taking the leaves from the paradisial trees was first Elijah's idea or Rabbah's, there is a problem inherent in it. It involves breaking a heavenly rule, one that can be inferred from the story of Rabbi Hanina ben Dosa and his wife: people may not borrow from their expected heavenly reward to improve their life on earth because to do so "uses up their eternity." In our story, however, everything turns out for the best. The heavenly rule cannot be broken, but with Elijah's help it can be bent enough to allow Rabbah bar Abbuha to become wealthy and help his family. Elijah and Rabbah have worked together for a happy outcome in which poverty, in many stories an ineradicable evil, is overcome.

As I have discussed, most of the stories in this generic group encourage the appropriate exercise of human freedom—and particularly rabbinic freedom. If the Sages sought to learn, interpret, legislate, even advise God on which traditions he should recite, Elijah could help. Conversely, several stories in which rabbis act on Elijah's advice help to define the *limits* of appropriate freedom. In one sense, these rabbinic heroes act appropriately—the stories show they are worthy to receive advice from Elijah and they do not incur God's punishment for their requests. However, only one of the stories contains a fully successful exercise of human freedom: only Rabbah bar Abbuha can change his life for the better with Elijah's mediation. The unnamed rabbi who asks to see Rabbi Hanina's "heavenly chariot" has the vision he requests, but is temporarily blinded. Elijah can mediate personal success; but he cannot guarantee safety in mystical experience. Rabbi Joshua ben Levi can only learn that he will enter the world to come. He cannot get a firm date for the Messiah's coming or any assurance it will be soon. Both he and the story's audience remain in painful suspense about the date of the Messianic era. Rabbi Judah cannot change the world by bringing the Messiah before his time, and, though he is not punished, Elijah is. One cannot ask Elijah for individual rescue from danger or poverty, but Elijah may come to the rescue. One cannot safely—or at least successfully—ask for anything else.

For the Bavli, it seems that before the messianic era Elijah cannot help the community, even upon the request of extraordinary mortals. Elijah's inability to help the whole community—or, to put it positively, his coming to the aid of individuals—is one of his characteristic features. While there are stories in which the presence of rabbis alive and dead helps their city or locality, Elijah's seems to represent an individual experience of God's blessing.

5

ELIJAH FROM RABBINIC TIMES TO THE TWENTY-FIRST CENTURY

As we saw in chapter 3, Elijah differed from all other mediators of God's power in rabbinic times. He stepped into the roles that earlier Judaism reserved for angels, becoming helper, teacher, and companion of the righteous. Though Jewish storytellers may have borrowed miraculous powers for Elijah from both Christian saints and the Greco-Roman god Hermes, Elijah remains a uniquely Jewish figure. He provides a sense of greater connection to God, as ideal teacher, benefactor, and savior of Jews threatened by Gentiles, yet he still does not intrude on God's authority by ruling on individuals' worth or directly helping them "inherit the world to come." Despite his formidable powers, the rabbinic Elijah was not venerated as the Christian saints were, and, because of his unpredictability, he could not be compelled. While we can learn much by comparing the rabbinic Elijah's roles to those of other supernatural mediators, it is mostly negative knowledge: It tells us what Elijah was *not* like.

Considered broadly, the mere existence of Elijah as a supernatural mediator who is as much or more a teacher and ethical guide than a supernatural rescuer conveys the values of rabbinic society. Elijah's activities reinforce its emphasis on learning and ethics and its relative deemphasis of earthly miracles. As mentioned in earlier chapters, the three generic groups among the Elijah stories can tell us more about the character of Elijah as a whole. Because they were the common property of rabbinic Judaism rather than of any single author or storyteller, they provide a window onto rabbinic perceptions of Elijah, illuminating the commonly held beliefs that served as raw material for the crafting of individual stories. The themes of each generic group are distinct, but one can combine them into a more unified picture of Elijah as the Rabbis believed in him, especially when one also considers the related themes of many stories outside the three groups. Before moving to a higher level of generalization, however, it makes sense to review the messages of each generic group.

The first generic group, that in which Elijah ceases or refuses to visit someone, emphasizes ethical behavior and human responsibility. These stories in the Bavli— together with one in the Yerushalmi—are part of the wider form-critical category of precedent stories, stories that recount a Sage's behavior in order to record its legal significance. In these stories, Elijah makes clear, by leaving, that certain actions are unacceptable to him. The erring parties, as rabbis or pious Jews, are often aware of Elijah's absence because they had a connection with him before Elijah's temporary or permanent severing of the relationship. Even the shortest story of this group includes its essential components. There was "a certain God-fearing man with whom Elijah was accustomed to converse—he built a gatehouse and Elijah did not converse with him again."[1] The theme of this simple story also exemplifies the entire generic group. The story's wider context makes it clear that Elijah abandoned the God-fearing man because his new gatehouse prevented the poor from entering his courtyard to ask for help. Although he did nothing against the letter of the law, his construction project was incompatible with true fear of God.

In the story in Yerushalmi Terumot 46b, Rabbi Joshua defends the action that caused Elijah to desert him for a time, saying, "I acted according to the law" and Elijah retorts, "is this the law of the truly devout?" This question echoes throughout this generic group, in which Elijah silently advocates a higher ethical standard, beyond halakhah. Here, as is usually the case, Elijah interacts with individuals rather than with a community, mediating or representing the individual's experience of the supernatural. These stories portray Elijah as a unique and supernatural figure, but also as one with human motives and freedom. He too is an individual, removing himself when he disapproves of someone's behavior, and sometimes returning to them to tell them what they did wrong.

The stories in the first generic group are related to those in the third, in which Elijah appears and answers a rabbi's question. In both, Elijah is a teacher. In the story of Rav Anan—whom Elijah temporarily abandons when he partly succumbs to the temptation of a bribe—Elijah explicitly teaches the rabbi the Order of Elijah (B. Ketubot 105b). Given the importance of learning in rabbinic culture, as well as Elijah's numerous appearances as teacher in both legal material and legends, it is likely that Elijah's was "accustomed" to converse with or visit someone in order to teach him. If so, there is a possible real-world source for these stories in human experience. If Elijah in some stories represents the kind of intellectual inspiration that seems to be a gift rather than purely a product of one's own insight, then Elijah's absence is the self-doubt or troubled conscience that makes inspiration impossible.

In any case, the shared folkloric motif behind these stories is that only the truly devout and righteous can be visited by Elijah. This reinforced the rabbinic sense that scrupulously ethical behavior — even beyond the law — was necessary for deep intellectual and spiritual insight, two forms of knowing that in late antiquity went hand in hand. It also at times implied a certain rabbinic noblesse oblige. In some stories, the rabbinic need to be scrupulously just and kind seems founded as much on a sense of rabbinic spiritual and social superiority as on the sense the Rabbis were humanly equal to others. After all, Elijah usually deserts people for not being good or helpful to their social inferiors, rather than for failures in humility toward them. Thus many of these morally admirable stories nevertheless imply a hierarchical society with rabbis at its apex — at least in rabbinic eyes.

In contrast, the next generic group, that in which Elijah appears in disguise, finds its characteristic theme in celebrating freedom rather than in emphasizing ethical responsibility and proper social relations. Stories in this group have an especially clear possibility of being inspired by concrete events: times when help arose from an unexpected source, often a Gentile expected to be hostile. Rabbis experienced such occasions as the intervention of Elijah in disguise or at least appreciated stories in which Elijah turned out to be the real savior. Six of the seven stories in this group concern Tannaim; in three of them Elijah rescues a Tanna from a hostile Roman court, and in one from Roman persecution. The setting of these four stories suggests that the genre arose during Roman persecutions after the destruction of the Temple or the Bar Kokhba revolt, although it may have been created later and retrojected into the legendary past. In any case, the stories in the Bavli were told and retold for generations before they reached the written form we possess. Their continuing popularity may in part come from continuing Gentile persecution of Jews, but probably also arises from how vividly they portray Elijah bringing unexpected divine help to the righteous.

When Elijah comes to the rescue in disguise he comes as trickster as well as savior, sometimes impugning the otherwise unassailable dignity of a Sage. In Avodah Zarah 18a–b, for example, Rabbi Meir is threatened by Roman soldiers, and the Talmud includes several alternate versions of his escape. In one of them, "Elijah came and appeared to them as a prostitute and embraced him." We know from other stories that Elijah could have spirited Rabbi Meir away by some miracle.

Instead, he embraces the saintly Rabbi Meir in the form of a woman he would prefer not to know.

In short, several of these stories have a playful quality. And, for an oppressed and colonized people, Elijah the trickster breaks the rules of the rulers' game, introducing unforeseen possibilities and unpredictable freedoms. These stories also illustrate how Elijah's particular mission is to help Jews threatened by other people rather than by forces of nature. The human dangers from which Elijah saves people emphasize the prophet's own humanity. Just as one expects a human patron to help with social rather than natural disaster, Elijah generally rescues people threatened or troubled by other human beings. For the redactors of the Bavli, Elijah in many ways appears as a supernaturally powerful political patron as well as a supernaturally powerful teacher.

The Talmud has a number of stories of Sages praying for help in times of drought or other community disasters, but it very seldom tells of rabbis miraculously helping or healing individuals. Furthermore, it holds that rabbis and other pious folk automatically protect their communities from harm by their good deeds, as when a woman who heated her oven and let others cook in it prevented a fire from burning down her neighbors' houses.[2] In this story people at first think that a certain rabbi's protective power saved the woman's neighborhood, but a dream reveals that this was too minor a miracle to stem from a Sage's special power. For similar reasons, perhaps, the Bavli regards the rescue of individuals as beneath God's majestic power, in that it might make God anthropomorphic, as discussed in chapter 3—overly swayed by personal preference.

Elijah's appearance in disguise tells us several things about the general rabbinic view of Elijah. He conceals his identity to help individual Jews—all of them Sages in the Bavli's stories. In coming in disguise, Elijah also comes as a benign trickster, making fools of Gentile oppressors and sometimes of those he saves. Elijah is a free agent and a force for freedom, embodying the liberating power of divine mercy for individuals within the Jewish community. The folkloric motifs underlying these stories present Elijah coming in disguise as patron and trickster, the champion of Jews in a risky world ruled by Gentiles.

The treatment of this generic group in the Bavli, however, also implies a society that saw miraculous intervention in human troubles as rare and not to be depended on. All but one of the Bavli's stories of Elijah's disguises are set in Tannaitic times, implying that such rescues are more part of the glorious past than the mundane amoraic present. Whereas in the twenty-first century it may seem odd to describe a society that believes in miracles *at all* as pragmatic and human centered, rabbinic society saw supernatural intervention for good as a rare event in a physical world mostly controlled by natural forces and human actions.

The third generic group of stories, those in which a rabbi meets Elijah and asks a question that Elijah answers, is less clearly defined than the first two. The first two groups each have a characteristic plot structure in which Elijah acts. The third group, in contrast, presents Elijah as teaching or imparting secret knowledge on a wide variety of subjects, sometimes leading to different responses. His appearance to instruct, like his appearance in disguise to rescue, comes unexpectedly, welcome but unpredictable. Some of the stories are barely narratives at all, only exchanges of information; others have more developed plots of various kinds. While one can propose a consistent set of folkloric plot motifs—a clear metonymic context, if you will—that informs the stories of first two generic groups, the third group's folkloric antecedents are less distinct.

Nevertheless, it is significant that this group uses a verbal formula used to describe interactions between rabbis. It clearly presents Elijah as a teacher, an immortal Sage who is friend to the Sages. This is also the dominant portrayal of the legendary Elijah in the Yerushalmi, redacted about two centuries before the Bavli. Furthermore, as in the previous two generic groups, Elijah interacts with individuals rather than communities; he is a personal instructor whose teaching should transmitted like other rabbinic teaching rather than prophetically proclaimed to the community as a whole. Finally, Elijah usually comes to teach and encourage and does not, as other supernatural mediators do, actively punish sin, reprove human arrogance, or discourage human initiative. However, despite these common threads within the third generic group, this group has no single distinctive plot motif that might plausibly have come from popular Jewish folklore.

Instead, I believe these stories derive their raw material from the folklore of the rabbinic circles that produced the Bavli. One motif found in a number of stories in this group, enough to suggest it is the product of Babylonian amoraic culture as a whole, is Elijah's support of human power, particularly rabbinic power and freedom to study, legislate, and interpret Scripture as they thought best. Several stories in this group dramatically support rabbinic freedom to interpret Scripture, one affirming that all interpretations are "the words of the living God" (B. Gittin 6b). In these tales, Elijah's approval serves to defuse the pervasive competition for rank within rabbinic society, bringing word that God, like a good teacher, affirms all his disciples.

This is the largest of the three generic groups. Its popularity, together with that of other stories in which Elijah functions as a teacher, shows us the paramount

importance of the rabbi-teacher and the bond of discipleship in amoraic Babylonia. Elijah is the only being of his kind in the Bavli, a supernatural mediator who
interacts freely with humankind as angels and the saintly dead do not. And yet, in
the Bavli, Elijah most often comes simply to teach, rather than to rescue someone
or bring about miracles. Elijah's role as teacher reinforces rabbinic Judaism's deep
conviction that Torah study under a rabbinic Sage is the best and surest path to
connection with God and God's kingdom.

As we have seen, not every Elijah story carries intense theological weight or
directly addresses existential issues faced by the Rabbis. However, the cumulative meaning of the generic groups and similar stories has theological implications. Overall, Elijah comes to support the power of the individual—especially
an individual rabbi—but only in right relationship with others. In the first generic
group, Elijah refuses to visit, teach, and guide those who do not use their power
well, who are not considerate masters, generous almsgivers, and scrupulously
impartial judges. In the second group, Elijah supports people in the most basic
way possible—by helping them remain alive—and also helps clever individuals
to triumph over dehumanizing persecution. In the third group, Elijah is an ideal
teacher, one who presents God as the same, modeling a generous relationship to
students, an ideal that in some other stories the Rabbis themselves conspicuously
fail to embody.

Probably Elijah's most important function is to support and nourish right relationship between individuals and God. In the third generic group Elijah provides
a channel for communication with God, answering the questions of several rabbis about "what is the Holy One blessed be He doing?" and relaying the rabbis' responses back to God. In the famous coda to the oven of Akhnai story in
Bava Meẓia 59b, Elijah brings word that God calls the Sages "sons" at precisely
the moments in which they assert their intellectual freedom most strongly, even
against a bat kol. In a few stories Elijah expresses God's care for the entire Jewish
people. When Elijah meets Rabbi Yossi in the ruins of Jerusalem, the last thing
he tells the rabbi is that, when God hears the congregation of Israel praise him in
synagogues and houses of study, he says "Happy the King whom they praise thus
in his house," regretting his destruction of the Temple and the exile (B. Berakhot
3a). In the second generic group the prophet represents or personifies God's unpredictable mercy when Elijah arrives in disguise to rescue those in danger. Thus
Elijah strengthens the relationship between human beings and God by moderating
one current in rabbinic thought that represents God and the angels who do his will
as faster to judge or punish than to save in this premessianic time.[3]

Without oversimplifying excessively, one can find four characteristic themes among the Elijah stories in the Bavli, some more unique to Elijah and some less. They might be summarized: 1. Elijah as teacher of rabbinic wisdom, most of his instruction resembling what mortal Sages would teach; 2. Elijah as ethical model, mostly in the stories in which he abandons someone for bad behavior; 3. Elijah as rescuer in times of trouble, the only supernatural mediator to appear in disguise to rescue people and also to provide wealth; and 4. Elijah as supernatural teacher of heavenly wisdom.

The first theme finds expression mostly in brief stories, many in the third generic group, in which the content is often more important than the reason Elijah in particular conveys it. Taken as a whole, these stories contribute to the image of Elijah as humanlike Sage and teacher. The second theme is ethical. In most stories reflecting this theme the ethical point hangs on proper consideration for the powerless or respect for nonrabbis. These points are in harmony with Elijah's support for the proper use of power and his encouragement of being in right relationship with others. However, the same points are also made in many other stories. The Sages, as inheritors of the prophetic tradition, were sensitive to their need for the difficult virtue of humility and their need to uphold the rights of the poor and the powerless.

The third theme, Elijah the rescuer, more fully expresses Elijah's uniqueness as a supernatural mediator. This is the theme of the second generic group, in which Elijah assumes a disguise to rescue people, as well as of several additional stories. Here, Elijah comes bringing unforeseen help, including the financial help he gives Rabbah bar Abbuha by taking him to the heavenly garden of Eden to pluck the leaves from the heavenly trees (B. Bava Meẓia 114a–b). In this theme two important characteristics of Elijah intersect. As a supernatural being he represents God's unexpected help, but, as a *human* supernatural being with free will, he mediates God's help so that God's impartial justice is not impaired.

In stories with the fourth theme Elijah appears as a mediator of heavenly wisdom. This function is shared by angels, demons, and accomplished Sages, but Elijah's perspective and much of the knowledge he conveys is unique. Only he can answer the question "What is the Holy Blessed One doing?" at a particular moment. These stories, as we have seen, encourage rabbinic power, particularly in legislation and scriptural interpretation. In these stories Elijah does far more than instruct: He supports human assertion that in other religious traditions might be considered hubris—and that even rabbinic tradition sometimes describes as risky. In stories not including Elijah, for example, rabbis undergo risk or become crippled because they demand rain from God or speak to God reproachfully when no rain falls.[4]

Human assertion that aims only to change God's mind, rather than God's plans for the world, is even more possible. When Elijah tells Rabbah bar Shila that God is not reciting the traditions of Rabbi Meir because he learned from Aḥer the apostate, Rabbah bar Shila defends Rabbi Meir, and God concedes the point and begins to recite Meir's teaching (B. Ḥagigah 15b). It is hard to know today what to make of such far-reaching human authority. We may recognize the loud self-assertion of the rabbis in these stories, but we do not necessarily comprehend how their confidence in their own power goes together with their confidence in their relationship with God. Of course, the rabbis of the stories express an *ideal* of faith and confidence, but, while the ideal of faith is common among monotheistic religions, the Rabbis' ideal of challenging God is most uncommon.

If we return to the idea that Elijah is in many ways a Sage writ large, we gain a little more understanding. The Bavli's Elijah has full individual free choice combined with deep knowledge of God's will, with which he is usually, but not always, completely in harmony. Elijah as supernatural mediator expresses (and produces) a different relationship with God than that found, for example, in Second Temple texts such as 1 and 2 Enoch. In these texts angels were the supernatural mediators, acting as fingers of the divine hand, sustaining the natural order, rewarding and punishing humankind according the strictest justice. Angels thus understood as supernatural mediators produce (and express) an image of God as highly transcendent, awesome, and implacably just. The Rabbis of the Bavli had a more complex image of God, one that could encompass God mourning his own destruction of the Temple, and they were no longer especially interested in angels as mediators in rabbinic (as opposed to biblical) times. They turned instead to traditions of the eternally living prophet Elijah, using them to envision a supernatural mediator more in line with their own spiritual aspirations, one who could dare to be God's colleague in redemption.

What else can the Elijah legends of the Bavli offer the study of rabbinic thought? The methodology employed in my analysis of the three generic groups of Elijah stories provides a template for future examination of generic groups as a way of exploring shared ideas within the rabbinic subculture. The Elijah stories are also a useful group for study because they are preselected. Choosing to focus on the preexisting category of all Elijah legends in the Bavli avoided the risks of choosing only those stories that support a particular agenda. Because the Elijah stories form a relatively diverse group not chosen to support one or another view of rabbinic narrative, they resist overgeneralizing schemes of classification or analysis.

At the same time, common themes among the stories provide a window into Babylonian amoraic thought, including but going far beyond their support for values such as Torah study and kindness. There is no other beneficent supernatural mediator of comparable importance in the Bavli. Although the thirty-odd stories of Elijah's appearance are relatively few, the generic groups and other oral traditional elements found within them indicate that stories of Elijah were widely distributed and passed down over generations. The specific character of Elijah as a supernatural mediator created in the image of the Sages illuminates their understanding of themselves and of the nature of the world.

As we saw in chapter 3, the role of rabbis in supernatural mediation is far more limited than that of the holy men and women who were their Byzantine Christian counterparts. By the fourth and fifth centuries ordinary Christians relied on holy men and women who had won free access to God to serve as mediators of healing and blessing and of salvation. In contrast, the Rabbis had a relatively sporadic and insignificant role as healers or mediators of God's blessing. Most crucially, the Rabbis never served as mediators of salvation. Elijah too, although he knows exactly what God is doing and relays the Rabbis' comments to the Holy Blessed One, never serves as a spiritual mediator in the late antique Christian sense, much less a mediator of salvation. Elijah's role emphasizes that within the rabbinic tradition there are no mediators of salvation: God alone designates the righteous person and the penitent sinner for the world to come.

Compared to biblical narrative, the Elijah stories have an individualist quality. Their heroes act in relation to God and to other individuals rather than in relation to the Jewish community as a whole.[5] From Moses on, most of the protagonists of Scripture, even Ezra and Nehemiah under Persian domination, are either portrayed as leaders of the community or as entrusted with messages for the community. In rabbinic narrative about the Sages, in contrast, the heroes are more often seen interacting with God, with a figure such as Elijah, or with a single fellow person. Even when, for example, a rabbi prays for rain for his region, the story generally hinges on the rabbi's relationship to God or to another individual rather than his leadership of the community. This is probably in part because of the Rabbis' unique position as spiritual leaders. While they did not represent the majority of the Jewish community until the very end of the Talmudic era, if then, they refrained from making their own subgroup a exclusive sect that denied Jewish identity or salvation to nonrabbinic Jews. Not surprisingly, their stories emphasize individual relationships rather than community leadership. The stories that do portray rabbis as leaders tend to focus on the rabbinic community, rather than all Jewish believers.

This is not to say, however, that rabbinic thought sees human beings as fully alone and autonomous in their relationship with God and the universe. In stories where Elijah appears in disguise to rescue someone, for example, the rabbinic hero steers his own individual course only so far. While the rabbi's actions and motives are important, the whole point of these stories is that without Elijah's help the stories would have ended in tragedy. In other stories Elijah is necessary to inform the rabbinic protagonist about some of God's activities that would otherwise be humanly unknowable. Thus Elijah, as a liminal figure, affirms and deepens human contact with God and with supernatural reality in general.[6] Nor was this contact with the supernatural an entirely one-way street. In certain stories God appears akin to the Sages themselves and open to influence from mortal rabbis, an openness Elijah's mediation makes possible or reveals.

In fact, one might say that the stories of Elijah, and Elijah's very existence, tend to blur the boundary between heaven and earth, human and supernatural. Elijah, although a quasi-angelic being with more than mortal knowledge of God's will, appears as an individual endowed with free choice. Elijah stories present a world in which a rabbi-hero, Elijah, and God, when God appears, are all in their respective ways free agents whose decisions determine the course of the plot.[7] Elijah does not impair the free will of the rabbis he helps (in many ways he enhances it), but he does lessen their lonely need to depend on themselves alone in a world from which God appears to have withdrawn into heaven, at least in comparison to God's close involvement with the Israelites of biblical times.[8]

The Rabbis' power to explain and legislate does not actually resemble modern assertions of human power to define the world and decree what is right here on earth. Today both philosophers and ordinary people often either deny God's existence or imagine God as largely beyond human understanding. However, the Rabbis' power to theorize and even to legislate and thus define (and, in defining, change) the nature of the human universe is more closely related to the power of the Christian holy man or woman to successfully ask God for a miracle. As the saint's power comes from his or her being chosen by God and in return choosing a holy God-driven life, the Sage's power is a power bestowed on him by his expertise in law and Scripture, the fruit of his day-to-day spiritual immersion in God's Torah. The power of the Rabbis is in part inherent in the nature of creation (which is by and through Torah) and in part via the direct gift of God to those who study his Torah and seek to do his will. In rabbinic thought Elijah functions as an example and symbol of God's gift of power to the Sages as well as of God's unpredictable grace to those in need.

ELIJAH FROM THE MIDDLE AGES TO THE PRESENT

One could easily write an entire book on Elijah stories after rabbinic times. They cross or even transcend conventional genres. Elijah appears in folktales set "once upon a time," in legends based on real people and events, in sober historical accounts, and in kabbalistic lore. Weinreich observes that Yiddish Elijah tales collected around a century ago vary in truth claim, in setting (real-world or a fairy-tale land), and in narrative purpose. Moreover, some of the Yiddish stories told about Elijah have variant versions in which figures such as famous rabbis take his place.[9] This is true for earlier Elijah stories as well. Thus, though Elijah is a named and in some sense historical figure, a study of Elijah stories is better off not attempting to distinguish between the conventional categories of historical "legend" and fictional "folktale." Still, Elijah differs from a generic fairy-tale helper, even when he fulfills a similar role. A Jewish audience enjoying a folktale would not have found religious significance in the anonymous wise women or similar figures who also appear in Jewish folklore, but the presence of Elijah as helper recalls God's choice of the prophet as mediator of divine blessing to the whole Jewish people and as future herald of the messianic era. Today Elijah is probably the most popular hero of Jewish folklore. Among the first fifteen hundred stories recorded in the Israel Folktale Archives, fifty feature Elijah; Maimonides is the second most-mentioned character, with thirty stories; and all others appear in less than twenty, including Solomon and David.[10]

This section, continuing from our analysis of rabbinic Elijah stories as orally derived legends with roots in rabbinic and popular folklore, will focus mostly on Elijah stories with clear oral-traditional roots. As many have noted, medieval and later tales about Elijah differ significantly from those in the Bavli and other rabbinic sources. Most of the key differences arise either from the growth of popular Elijah traditions or from popular traditions beginning to enter Jewish texts in the Middle Ages. Many medieval stories have anonymous protagonists, often common people rather than religious leaders, and a greater proportion portray Elijah as material benefactor. In still later oral sources, there are stories in which Elijah appears to anyone in need, not just the learned or extremely pious. Some of these stories use Elijah as an all-purpose "fairy godmother" figure, but many contain plot motifs and themes first found in rabbinic sources. To my knowledge, no one has systematically analyzed the structure and content of later Elijah folktales in relation to those in rabbinic sources. This section will begin this process, focusing on stories whose themes, motifs, and often entire plots first appeared in the Middle Ages, remaining popular for centuries. These are much more likely to reflect Elijah's distinctive character than folktales that include Elijah in only a few versions.

In discussing later Elijah stories, one must also consider Elijah's role in liturgy from the Middle Ages to the present. Anyone who has ever attended a Passover Seder knows Elijah's role in it, and anyone familiar with traditional Jewish practice knows that he attends ritual circumcisions and is invoked on Motzei Shabbat, the close of the Sabbath. The Elijah of the Sages was characterized by his unpredictability, always welcome but never expected, controlled, or even requested. Regular attendance at various rituals seems at first sight a complete reversal of the prophet's character. While this is a significant change, we will see that Elijah's ritual role develops from his role in folktales and from rabbinic teaching about the prophet, including its midrashic and messianic themes. In turn, Elijah's presence at various rituals, especially Passover, has generated folktales, many reflecting his traditional characteristics.

Earlier in this chapter I proposed that the legendary Elijah has four major roles in the Bavli: as teacher of rabbinic wisdom, as ethical model, as rescuer in times of trouble, and as mediator of heavenly wisdom. The last three roles are most common in later stories, although they undergo various changes. We find some rabbinic themes expressed by different plot motifs as well as some new morals and themes. Elijah's rabbinic role as savior from danger—and mediator of God's unpredictable mercy—carries forward in later Judaism, but usually with different plot formulas. In later tales Elijah comes in dreams, often helping the entire Jewish community rather than individuals. A number of medieval stories in which Elijah bestows wealth are moral tales in which someone must prove worthy of the prophet's gift. They combine themes of Elijah as ethical model and as rescuer, echoing the theme of kindness found in the Bavli's second generic group and transposing it to the material plane.

Elijah's role of teacher is less common than other rabbinic roles among orally derived stories from the Middle Ages to the present. Folktales and orally derived stories rarely portray Elijah as teacher of halakhah or even proverbial wisdom. Stories in which Elijah serves as mediator of heavenly wisdom appear, but they tend to express different themes than such stories in the Bavli, where the prophet generally comes to support human assertion or even the power to challenge God's will. The medieval and later Elijah tends, in contrast, to affirm faith in God's mysterious justice.[11] While the theme of Jewish leaders challenging God's judgment returns forcefully in Hasidic tales, these do not, to my knowledge, include stories featuring Elijah.

The medieval period includes another source of Elijah stories, Kabbalah. In literary and orally derived kabbalistic lore, Elijah's teaching comes as a reward for deep learning and ascetic piety.[12] In legends based on kabbalistic material, Elijah may support human power, but only by confirming the God-given superiority of great rabbis. This work will not focus on either kabbalistic tales or stories in which Elijah affirms God's justice: Their morals are so different from rabbinic Elijah tales that treating them in depth would distract from the main point of this section, which is examination of how rabbinic themes developed in later eras.

Messianic traditions, many including Elijah's role as herald, are important in medieval Jewish teaching, but, as in the rabbinic texts, they are rarely expressed in narrative. Postrabbinic messianic stories featuring Elijah are relatively recent and seem to be of Hasidic inspiration. In them Elijah can play either of his two roles in the story of Rabbi Judah the Patriarch's effort to bring the Messiah, sometimes providing inspiration for the attempt, sometimes preventing its fruition. In a Polish story from the Israel Folktale Archives, for example, two yeshiva students journey to Jerusalem, longing to see King David's tomb. Elijah tells them how to find the tomb, filled with gold and jewels beyond compare, with the great king lying asleep, a jug of water by his head. Elijah continues that David will stretch out his hands when they enter, and they need only pour water over his hands for him to arise and again go forth as God's Messiah. The students, dazzled by the treasure, fail to help David with his ablutions in time, and his coming is delayed. This story combines the Jewish motif of biblical hero alive in his tomb with the European motif of the king sleeping in the mountain, waiting to arise, to poignant effect.[13]

Elijah blocks the Messiah's coming in an account of the Maid of Ludmir, the one woman Hasidic master. Her public career ended when she was pressured to marry, but this story provides a messianic coda to her life. A recent nonscholarly book recounts how, widowed and living in Jerusalem, she and an elderly kabbalist realized that they could bring the Messiah if they went together and performed certain rituals (apparently at a specific time). Just as the former Maid of Ludmir, Chana Rachel, was leaving to meet the kabbalist, "a poor wayfarer came to the door, asking for food and comfort." By the time she was done caring for him, it was too late to for the meeting. The story concludes that "Chasidic lore" identifies the wayfarer with Elijah.[14] Here Elijah's connection to the Messiah meets the Jewish woman's traditional role as provider for the needy. Like other Hasidic masters, but also distinctively as a woman, Chana Rachel fails to bring the Messiah through no fault of her own.

As we see from this example, Elijah stories continue to be important today. Old stories are retold, in popular books and by individual narrators, and new ones develop. The last few pages of this book include two more modern appearances of Elijah, one from an academic essay analyzing contemporary oral tales and one from a more popular source, the Chabad-Lubavitch Web site. As we will see, they both recall themes found in earlier Elijah tales and explore new ones.

Elijah Provides Wealth

One of the commonest motifs of stories from medieval times to the twentieth century is Elijah's coming to provide wealth. These stories are usually exempla, tales whose plot hinges on a moral value: Elijah gives to people marked by righteous generosity to the poor, piety, or both. The dramatic tension in the story usually hangs on the theme of Elijah's gift as a test. Sometimes there is a contrast between worthy and unworthy recipients of wealth, and sometimes the story tells how one person or family passes or fails the test by remaining or ceasing to be generous or pious. These stories thus generally combine two motifs found in Talmudic Elijah stories: first, Elijah as material benefactor and, second, the contrast between those who are worthy of Elijah's presence and those who are not, now transposed to the issue of who is worthy of Elijah's gifts.

One of the oldest and most perennially popular of these stories is that of "The Seven Good Years." It first appears in a tenth-century midrash from the land of Israel, Midrash Ruth Zuta.[15] A man with a worthy wife loses his property. As he toils plowing his employer's farm, Elijah appears in the form of an Arab and tells him that he can have seven good years, now or at the end of his days. What does he want? At first, thinking Elijah is a magician or fortune-teller, he puts him off, but on Elijah's third visit he tells Elijah to wait while he consults his wife. She says, "Tell him to bring them now." As soon as he relays her message, he returns home to find that his children have discovered a treasure in the dust. He thanks God, and his wife tells him that since the Holy Blessed One has extended grace to them, providing for them for seven years, they should occupy themselves with charity in the hope that God will continue to provide for them after the seven years are over. She enlists their young son to write down all their gifts to others. At the end of seven years, when Elijah appears to her husband asking for the gift's return, the man asks again to consult his wife, and she says, "Go and tell him that if you find people more faithful than we are, I will return what you deposited with us." God sees their faith and rewards them with wealth for the rest of their lives.

This story has over thirty written versions among traditional Jewish texts and transcribed folktales, including seven from the Israel Folktale Archives. In a few of them, the man who offers seven years of wealth is not explicitly Elijah, and others include varying details. The stable elements are the choice of good years now, rather in the future, giving to the poor, and God's response of blessing the righteous family with more wealth.[16] The first known version, in Ruth Zuta, also expresses the motif of human power often found among Talmudic Elijah stories. The question that the righteous woman relays through her husband is close to a demand: "Go and tell him that if you find people more faithful than we are, I will return what you deposited with us." Strikingly, in Rabbi Nissim's more literary retelling a century later, the woman reacts in a much more conventionally pious way, probably in part because Elijah is not named as the one who offers seven good years. In this later version the woman responds with humility to the loss of their wealth—here actual rather than threatened. She "fasted for three days, and then stood up humbling herself before her Lord," before reminding God that Scripture states a loan to the poor is a loan to him.[17] In the first version the woman conveys her question to Elijah and is as bold as any Talmudic Sage in doing so. In Rabbi Nissim's version she directly petitions God and hence must speak more humbly.

Another popular story with many versions is that of three brothers (sometimes three beggars or simply three men) who receive from Elijah a book that imparts great learning, a coin that gives great wealth, or a beautiful and righteous wife. It was first published in the sixteenth-century Yiddish *Ma'aseh Book*, but has older antecedents as well as many later versions. In a Hebrew manuscript, Elijah later visits each of the sons in the guise of a poor beggar and is turned away from the households of the learned and wealthy men, but welcomed by the third brother and his wife. He responds be taking the book and the coin from the two selfish brothers and giving them to the youngest son with his righteous wife.[18] Most later versions feature this conclusion. A twentieth-century Iraqi story has the now learned man refusing to teach a poor widow's son and the rich man turning away charity collectors, while the third man and his pious wife welcome Elijah in beggar's guise and feed him at their table.[19]

The motif of a charity test with ensuing reward or punishment is common in world folklore as well as many Elijah stories,[20] but the details of this story seem distinctively Jewish. The gift of learning was more popularly prized in Jewish society than in other medieval Western cultures, and Elijah's gift of the magic book recalls his earlier role as teacher of the Sages. Women's connection to charity, though not exclusively Jewish, has deep roots in the Jewish tradition, from "The Seven Good Years" all the way back to Talmudic stories.[21]

The longer version of the story, in which Elijah takes back his gifts, resonates with accepted Jewish teaching on charity, but it also has a populist slant. Both the rich man and the learned man become haughty and callous, while the humble man who wanted a beautiful wife passes Elijah's test. Indeed, asking for a lovely wife was foolish and even morally suspect in the context of official Jewish values, which stressed that "Grace is a lie, vain is beauty—a woman who fears the LORD is worthy to be praised" (Prov. 30:30). The ordinary Jewish man or woman who transmitted the story must have enjoyed its slight but definite countercultural hint of romance helped along by Elijah.

The third story discussed in this section is generally called either "Elijah the Slave," or "Elijah the Builder." It first appears in Rabbi Nissim's *Elegant Composition*, written in Judeo-Arabic in the eleventh century, which is often referred to by the title of its Hebrew translation, *Ḥibbur Yafeh*. A pious and learned man is so poor that he must borrow clothing in order to go to market to try to feed his hungry family. He puts his trust in God and meets Elijah, who insists that the pious man sell him as a slave. The prophet's purchaser promises him his freedom if he constructs a palace for the king well and quickly, and Elijah prays to God for miraculous help. The palace is completed overnight, and Elijah disappears, explaining later to the poor man that he has given the king more than his money's worth.[22] In Rabbi Nissim's version, the story has no strictly narrative tension once Elijah appears. It finds its religious drama in the exalted prophet submitting even to slavery to help a pious man and then strictly fulfilling his promise, even to a Gentile. Elijah in a sense represents the whole Jewish people, enslaved to the Gentiles, but with God's help retaining their dignity and achieving success.

A verse version of the story by Ishai bar Mordecai, named after its first line, "There Was a Pious Man" ("Ish ḥasid haya"), implies more narrative tension in Elijah's prayer to God, "Please answer, Awesome One on high / I planned to be sold and become a slave / For your glory, this man to save. /. . . . Mercifully answer my earnest request / Because I meant this for the best."[23] This version seems to imply that Elijah was so moved by the pious man's poverty that he insisted on being sold as a slave without thinking through the consequences, displaying a hastiness in God's cause found in both his biblical and rabbinic incarnations.

Elijah as Provider and the Close of the Sabbath

Ishai bar Mordecai's lively but not especially elegant poem became one of the two songs about Elijah that medieval Judaism introduced after the Havdalah ceremony, the ritual for ending the Sabbath on Saturday evening. These songs insert two new themes into the ritual: praise for God as provider of material sustenance and also anticipation of the Messiah and prayer for his coming. "There Was a Pious Man" was a natural choice to call to mind God's benefits because it contains no moral test, only a generous gift. The other hymn added on Saturday evening is "Elijah the Prophet" ("Eliahu Hanavi"), which has both messianic and material themes. The medieval addition of recalling God's material help, channeled through Elijah, strongly suggest the growing influence of popular piety and folklore in medieval ritual. As we will see, Elijah's medieval entry into the circumcision ceremony and the Passover Seder both also seem to have arisen through the practice of ordinary Jews and later been justified by learned explanations.

Hoffman writes that welcoming Elijah on "Motzei Shabbat, the 'Departure of the Sabbath,' is a folk tradition whose origins are lost to us."[24] We find a hint of its origin from Isaac ben Moses, writing about the middle of the thirteenth century, who says that he read a rabbinic responsum from before 1000 CE approving of the popular practice of singing songs of Elijah on Motzei Shabbat.[25] All subsequent reasons for this custom, although they add richness to practice for those that know them, appear to have arisen as explanations and justifications after the fact. The source cited by Rabbi Isaac responds to the question whether songs about Elijah are appropriate by simply saying that it is right to sing hymns to honor the departure of the Sabbath Queen. Later medieval sources give numerous reasons for invoking Elijah. A twelfth- or thirteenth-century legal text cites the tradition in Bavli Eruvin 43b that Elijah will not come on Shabbat as herald of the Messiah and thus will arrive immediately afterward when the time is right for redemption. A few centuries later, we find the tradition that Elijah sits under the Tree of Life in Eden, recording those who keep the Sabbath, and that the merit of keeping the Sabbath will bring about redemption for Israel.[26]

"There Was a Pious Man" and "Elijah the Prophet" first appear in writing about 1100 in the Maḥzor Vitry and both until recently remained popular zemirot (religious songs) for Motzei Shabbat, though "There Was a Pious Man" is much less common today. "Elijah the Prophet" in its current form emphasizes Elijah's role as messianic herald. As it appears in the Maḥzor Vitry, however, it includes a detailed description of Elijah's sacrifice on Mount Carmel and concludes:

> Elijah the Prophet, a man who runs to return the hearts of fathers to their sons. . . .
> Elijah the Prophet, a man who has the covenant of life.
> Elijah the Prophet, happy whoever has a coin from his hand.
> Elijah the Prophet, swiftly may he come to us, swiftly.

In these last lines Elijah appears as much as God's messenger in the present as he does as messianic herald. At some point a more spiritual conception of Elijah's presence led to a change in the line. Current prayerbooks read, "Happy whoever sees his face in a dream."

Elijah is uniquely suited to the "between time" of Motzei Shabbat, after the Sabbath ends and before the work week really starts, because he is a living symbol of liminality in his travels between heaven and earth and in his partly human, partly angelic nature. Havdalah, the home-based ritual for ending the Sabbath, is a weekly ceremony of liminality, expressing the transition from sacred to secular time. The liturgy of Havdalah, substantially unchanged since rabbinic times, praises God for creating distinctions and divisions: between day and night, between sacred and secular time, and between Israel, the chosen nation, and the nations of the world. Havdalah can be understood as a weekly spiritual and practical transition for the individual and family. The moment of lighting the Havdalah candle shifts the participants between modes of time and experience. For Jews in premodern times, it marked the end of the one day when even poor families had leisure and enough to eat and thus was a time when it made sense to invoke the assistance of Elijah and the angelic powers.[27]

Responding to the tension that comes from leaving sacred time and returning to the secular struggle to feed a family, the first song, "Elijah the Prophet," creates a bridge between sacred, biblical, time and Elijah as legendary benefactor, ending with "happy the man who has a coin from his hand." "There Was a Pious Man" vividly describes a family even more miserably poor than most Jewish families who would be singing the song and tells how Elijah, God's messenger, came to help them. Dr. S. Z. Kahana, introducing a 1961 Israeli folklore conference on Elijah, lays out Elijah's role on Motzei Shabbat at the start of the twentieth century in Eastern Europe. In Dr. Kahana's memories of his childhood, we see an explicit connection between Elijah's role in liturgy and his roles in folklore. For Kahana, Elijah mediates between ways of seeing the world: he connects sacred and secular realities because he oversees the passage from Sabbath to weekday and also because he connects the hope for future redemption with the need for present sustenance.[28] According to Dr. Kahana, Reb Zanwill, a twentieth-century mystic, recounts the tradition that Elijah can appear in the form of water carrier at the close of Shabbat, bring the healing waters of Miriam's well (now hidden within the Sea of Galilee) to those in need.[29] All this may seem like too much weight to bear for one figure invoked in a few songs following one short ceremony, but, to quote Victor Turner, the renowned anthropologist: "The essence of ritual is its multidimensionality, of its symbols, their multivocality."[30] Rituals, like folktales or even more so, are rich in traditional connotations for those who practice them, some of them conscious and some of them not. For medieval Jews, and anyone steeped in Jewish tradition, the very name Elijah calls forth innumerable associations, often beginning with memories of singing "Elijah the Prophet" or hearing folktales like "The Seven Good Years."

Elijah Rescues from Danger

While I have suggested that Elijah's role as mediator of God's material help was probably the main reason he was first invoked on Motzei Shabbat, Hoffman notes that the close of the Sabbath was also seen as a risky time. He calls attention to protective rituals (some involving angel magic) found in early medieval ceremonies marking the transition between Sabbath and weekday. This leaves open the possibility that Elijah was first invoked on Motzei Shabbat as protector, for folk belief also emphasizes Elijah's role as protector and rescuer. Needless to say, these two motivations for including Elijah do not exclude one another—and nor do they cancel Elijah's explicit invocation as messianic herald in "Elijah the Prophet."

In the Middle Ages Elijah also acquires a explicit role of protector against demons, especially those attacking newborn infants and their mothers. Several ancient Jewish traditions have holy men facing off against demons. A first-century work has King Solomon vanquishing a female demon who attacks women in childbirth as well as newborns; he defeats her by learning her name and using its power against her.[31] In a comparable story in the Bavli, the holy man Ḥanina ben Dosa encounters Igrat, queen of demons, attempting to banish her. When she begs for mercy, he forbids her to attack except on certain nights (B. Pesaḥim 112b).

This story underwent many permutations. On a Babylonian magic bowl, Elijah encounters Lilith and forbids her to trouble the household under his protection.[32] In many later versions, which are found in folktales, in manuals of practical kabbalistic magic, and on amulets, the demon is called Lilith, and her target is again a mother and a newborn. By the late Middle Ages, and perhaps earlier, Elijah had become the standard hero of amulets made to ensure the safety of new mothers and infants. The amulets generally have elements of both the first-century story of Solomon and the Talmudic story of Ḥanina ben Dosa. Elijah, going on his way, meets Lilith going to harm a woman who has given birth, and he curses her "by the blessed Name." She begs for mercy, renouncing any intention of harming that particular woman and child and telling Elijah her names, by which she may be bound.[33] Given the frighteningly high mortality of both mothers and newborns before modern medicine, the use of amulets seems reasonable. At least they would have helped control the mother's and father's fear. It also makes sense that Elijah, protector of the Jewish people in so many ways, steps into this particular role, especially since the ancient form of this narrative incantation seems almost designed for him. Jewish tradition and folklore knows Elijah through stories, and he is often encountered traveling, "going on his way," just as he encounters Lilith.

The Talmudic theme of Elijah coming to rescue Jews from despotic Gentile powers continues into the Middle Ages, but takes new forms. Instead of saving individuals, Elijah usually comes to rescue whole communities. This in part simply reflects changed circumstances. The individual persecutions after the Bar Kokhba revolt had become ancient history by the Middle Ages. At the same time, Christian and Muslim rulers often threatened entire Jewish communities with unjust laws and extortion—sometimes with exile or death. This theme appears so often in Jewish folklore that it begins to grate on one as depressing and paranoid—until one reads Jewish history and recognizes that it is realistic and tragic. In folklore the danger is always averted, sometimes by Elijah, while in reality the communities often ended up suffering harm. The concept of Elijah coming to the rescue in disguise remained part of Jewish thought, no doubt in part because of the stories in the Talmud. A fascinating little legend, collected from an anonymous narrator in 1909 Poland, recounts how Czar Nicholas decreed that the whole Talmud was to be burned. "The chief rabbi then disguised himself as the czar" and "tore up and burned the papers on which the edict was printed." The czar could not sign his decree, and when told that he himself had destroyed it, said, "'When Elijah the Prophet meddles in the matter, there's nothing I can do.'"[34] The editor has no comment on this story, but I suspect it is a half-humorous modernization and rationalization of an Elijah tale. Here the chief rabbi takes advantage of the tradition—known even by Czar Nicholas!—to act as Elijah was said to do.

In medieval tales, however, Elijah usually saves the community by appearing in dreams. Sometimes Elijah appears in a dream to a Jewish leader, telling him how to neutralize a threat. Obediah Pervi, originally from Yemen, contributed a tale of thwarted accusation to the Israel Folktale Archives. In it the evil counselors of a good king are jealous of his love for the Jews; they murder the king's young son and hide his body in the synagogue. With the king threatening to kill the whole Jewish community, Elijah appears to the rabbi in a dream and explains to him how to make the little boy's corpse revive and accuse his murderers. The folklore of many lands has the motif of a corpse miraculously woken to accuse his killers.[35] It may be particularly common in Judaism, where it is usually the means of refuting a "blood libel," the horrible medieval Christian fantasy that the Jews thirst to ritually kill a Christian child or use Christian blood in making Passover matzah. In fact, in Judaism the connection between false accusation of murder and blood libel is so strong that such stories are generally referred to as blood libel stories,[36] even tales such as this one from Muslim lands that may have no accusation of *ritual* murder and no connection to Passover.

Such stories often, but do not always, feature Elijah: Sometimes a wonder-working rabbi knows independently how to revive the murder victim. The medieval Elijah, however, has a method of rescue all his own: he can appear in a ruler's dreams to save a Jewish community. Elijah's visiting the dreams of a Gentile ruler has a rabbinic pedigree: As we saw, in Genesis Rabbah, Elijah comes to reprove a Roman emperor for squandering his wealth, a story told in the context of the tradition that the rulers of Rome are destined to store up treasure for the future King Messiah.[37] It seems probable that change from legends of Elijah appearing in disguise to legends and histories of his appearing in dreams is a consequence of the rationalist trend in medieval Judaism that also produced philosophy and plain-sense interpretation of Scripture. Earlier, I proposed that the stories of Elijah appearing in disguise to rescue individuals had roots in actual occurrences, times when a Gentile unexpectedly came forward on the Jewish side. The real-world background of the medieval stories lies in incidents in which rulers threatened and then withdrew decrees against the Jews or ended up being satisfied with a bribe. Historic accounts show that even the educated might conclude that Elijah had appeared in the ruler's dream to make him withdraw his decree.

We find a wonderful example of Elijah's role as dream defender in a document retrieved by Goitein from the Cairo Geniza, a copy of a 1121 letter from Baghdad recounting averted persecution. The story begins when a visionary woman announced that she had seen Elijah in a dream proclaiming that "the redemption of Israel was at hand." The messianic hopes arising from her dream became a pretext for the rulers to round up most of the Jews and threaten them with death. The highest Muslim religious authority tried to protect the Jews, but he did not succeed. When a leader of the Jewish community still at liberty gained an audience to plead with the Caliph, "The latter ridiculed the story [of Elijah's appearance] and said that the Jews were obviously of very low intelligence if they believed such a tale by a woman; he gave orders that she be burned the next day, and that the Jews be outlawed. The same night, however, Elijah appeared to the Caliph himself, who was struck with awe," and the community was delivered.[38] As Goitein writes, "the letter generally gives the impression of a matter-of-fact eye-witness account," and its dates are corroborated by Muslim histories.[39]

The letter convinces us of its accuracy in carefully recording names and dates. It also ignores the folktale convention that Gentile officials are always evil by recounting how a Muslim cleric tried to help the Jews. Here story, history, and faith meet. Elijah, the hero of folktales, is also a savior in recent history, hero of a story circulating among the literate as a factual example of God's continuing grace and favor to the Jewish people. This story hints at the universal Jewish trust in Elijah that allowed him to enter Jewish liturgy on three separate occasions: Motzei Shabbat, circumcision, and Passover. If the common people began to call upon Elijah as protector or benefactor, the custom would have made sense to the learned elite who also believed Elijah appeared to save. If the learned developed new prayers or rituals involving the prophet, they would quickly spread throughout Jewish society because of Elijah's universal popularity.

Elijah Affirms Faith

One category of Elijah stories centers particularly on religious themes. All Elijah stories affirm faith in some respect, faith that God has not forgotten humanity and the Jewish people in particular, faith that the good will be rewarded and perhaps the wicked punished. This set of stories, however, are exempla in which Elijah rewards the protagonists specifically for piety rather than for their help to others. Sometimes Elijah helps people perform a commandment; sometimes he rewards a pious deed. One common theme is Elijah completing a minyan, the quorum of ten Jews—traditionally men—required for public prayer. Several mysterious visitors come to complete a minyan in Jewish folklore, but "Elijah is the most popular figure to perform this function in many Jewish ethnic groups."[40] A twentieth-century oral legend from Jerusalem is also an etiological tale, a story that recounts the origins of something or how it got its name. In "The Tenth for the Minyan," a small synagogue in the Old City, then called the Talmud Torah Synagogue, lacked a tenth man to make the minyan for Yom Kippur, the holiest day of the year. "At the last minute they saw an old Jew, his white beard down to his chest, leaning on his cane and coming down the stairs." After the evening service, the ten men stayed all night in the synagogue, studying the ancient observances of Yom Kippur in the Jerusalem Temple. They prayed fervently all the next day and felt the burden of their sins lifted as the shofar blew at the close of the service. When they turned to thank and bless their visitor, they found he had disappeared. Clearly he had been Elijah, and from that time on the synagogue became the "Eliahu Ha-navi" synagogue, named after Elijah the Prophet.[41] Stories in which Elijah participates in worship may have their origins in recollections of the prophet's presence at circumcisions and Motzei Shabbat. The inspiration may also have gone the other way, although we do have earlier evidence for rituals invoking Elijah than for stories about him participating in a minyan. I suspect, however, that these ritual and narrative roles for Elijah—and their expression in song, liturgy, and story—grew up alongside one another in the Middle Ages, reinforcing one another and adding richness to the developing complex of beliefs about the prophet.

Elijah at Circumcisions and at Passover

While Elijah's role in Passover is better known, he seems to have entered the circumcision ritual earlier and is a more integral part of that ritual. The practice of having Elijah's chair at circumcisions appears to date from the eighth or ninth century,[42] whereas Elijah's cup is first recorded as part of the Passover Seder in fifteenth-century Europe.[43] In today's traditional circumcision ceremony, the guests rise and say, "Blessed be he that comes" (barukh haba), which, as Birnbaum states in his 1949 commentary, is a greeting for both the infant and Elijah, "'angel of the covenant' and protector of children." Then, when the boy is placed on the knees of the sandek, the child's godfather, the mohel who performs the circumcision says, "This is the chair of Elijah, remembered for good."[44] In contrast, Elijah's cup has no place in the traditional printed Passover Haggadah; he appears only in custom and commentary.[45] Only in the nineteenth century do legal authorities even note that some were accustomed to say *barukh haba*, "Welcome," when opening the door to Elijah.[46] Many modern Haggadot do include Elijah in the ritual, so he may be said to have explicitly entered the text of the Passover Seder in the twentieth century.

In both cases, I argue, Elijah entered the rituals through the practice of ordinary Jews, and his presence was then explained and justified in various ways by the learned elite of the Middle Ages. This is particularly true of Elijah's presence at circumcision, which, as we will see, may even have arisen from the Judaizing of non-Jewish magical practices.

ELIJAH AT CIRCUMCISIONS   During circumcisions Elijah stands on different thresholds, recalling his role in the dangerous passage of birth and overseeing the baby boy's passage between mere physical existence and life in the Jewish community. As we have seen, Jews in the Middle Ages increasingly identified Elijah as the defender against Lilith, the demon who preyed on newborns and their mothers. As such, Elijah would be a welcome guest at a circumcision. Even early modern Jewish practice saw Elijah's role at the circumcision to be protective, leaving his chair in place for three days to see the newborn through a time believed to be especially dangerous to his health.[47]

Klein, in *A Time to Be Born*, writes that the practice of setting aside a chair for Elijah may be "an adaptation of a local non-Jewish custom of setting aside a chair or table in the house for a god of fortune who was thought to bring luck." The practice is forbidden in the Talmud, but may have been "legitimized" by connecting the chair to Elijah as "angel of the covenant" and protector of the helpless newborn.[48] Although there is no proof for this theory, Jewish communities often developed customs to protect newborns and held to them with devotion. Sixteenth-century European sources say that the centuries-old custom of having a party in the newborn's house on the night before circumcision was at least in part to protect against demonic attack.[49] Similar practices were found in Eastern and North African Jewish communities, and these often explicitly invoked Elijah. They included dancing by both women and men to ward off evil spirits, especially on the crucial "night of watching" (ליל שימורים) before the circumcision. On that night Kurdish Jews used to bring Elijah's chair from the synagogue and perform dances around it.[50]

This theory of the origins of Elijah's chair is strictly modern. All premodern texts have midrashic explanations for Elijah's presence. Almost all early medieval sources hold that Elijah is present because after he complained at Horeb that Israel had neglected the covenant—the *brit*, which is identified with *brit milah*, the covenant of circumcision—God appointed him "the angel of the covenant" and required him to attend all circumcisions. This midrash first appears in the pseudepigraphical Pirkei de Rabbi Eliezer,[51] a work dating from the eighth or ninth century that draws on rabbinic literature and other ancient traditions, including apocryphal works of the Second Temple. It also shows clear traces of Muslim influence,[52] indicating that the author was influenced by his environment and could have been affected by contemporary customs. Pirkei de Rabbi Eliezer continues the rabbinic tradition that God punishes Elijah for his repeated complaints and harsh judgment of Israel. It also satisfyingly connects the first verse of Malachi, chapter 3, in which God says "*Behold, I am sending* my angel and he will clear the way before me" (הנני שלח מלאכי ופנה דרך לפני), with the last verse, in which God says "*Behold, I myself am sending* Elijah the prophet to you" (הנה אנכי שלח לכם את אליה הנביא; Mal. 3:1, 23).

Pirkei de Rabbi Eliezer's midrash seems, however, rather elaborate to have been accepted as instituting a new liturgical practice. In fact, legal works clearly imply that it was used to justify a preexisting custom that required a prooftext. The thirteenth-century Rabbi Abraham writes, "within every Jewish region they are accustomed to make a chair for Elijah, and I have a support for the matter" (יש לי סמך לדבר) in Pirkei de Rabbi Eliezer.[53] This recalls the Talmudic phrase "there is no proof for the matter, but there is support for the matter," which speaks of biblical verses that seem related to a particular law, but do not really prove it. A fourteenth-century legal work, *Kol Bo*, before quoting the same midrash, says that "they are accustomed to make a chair for Elijah, and this is not a vain thing."[54] These sources suggest that at some point, perhaps during the early second millennium, people began placing a chair for Elijah at circumcisions, probably so he could protect the infant, and rabbis then had to explain the practice.

From what I can gather from earlier medieval sources, while Elijah's chair was universal, Elijah's name was not explicitly part of the official circumcision ritual until the sixteenth century. Then R. Joseph Karo, the great systematizer of rabbinic law, takes care to state explicitly in the *Shulḥan Arukh* that the one placing the infant in the chair "should say out loud that this is the chair of Elijah."[55] While the spoken liturgy found its current form at that time, the exact form taken by Elijah's chair has remained fluid. We find that practices concerning the chair vary from community to community, as one would expect with a folk custom. Some early sources speak of two special chairs, one for Elijah and the other for the sandek who holds the child being circumcised. Today many communities still follow this practice; in others the sandek sits on the chair of Elijah, whereas in others Elijah's chair is a "small, fancy, symbolic" chair installed on the wall of the synagogue. Until recently, Jewish women in many Muslim countries prepared Elijah's chair with silk, brocade, or embroidered hangings on the night before a circumcision performed at home, thus indirectly putting their mark on the ritual in which they did not directly participate.[56]

Why does Elijah in particular have this role at circumcisions as well as the role of protecting mother and child at birth? Once again Elijah's liminal role is key. Because Elijah has both human and angelic attributes, moving freely between this life and and the spiritual realm, and also, as Pirkei de Rabbi Eliezer expresses, because the biblical Elijah is particularly connected to the covenant, Elijah is a most fit guardian of the baby boy at circumcision. He witnesses the liminal moment of transition as the male infant moves from being merely a living person to becoming part of God's covenant with Abraham by receiving the *brit milah*, the "covenant of circumcision." In so doing, Elijah mediates between two ways of looking at the world: the religious one, in which the mitzvah of circumcision is paramount, and what might loosely be called the magical or superstitious worldview in which Elijah's main function is warding off danger from demons or disease in cultures with premodern rates of infant mortality.

Once Elijah's presence at circumcisions was well established, stories based on it arose. A sixteenth-century legend of the thirteenth-century Rabbi Judah the Pious records that he once attended a circumcision at which he refused to stand with the congregation or say "blessed be he who comes" to welcome Elijah and the infant. When they asked about his disrespect for the child, he answered that it was "because I did not see Elijah come in with the child, nor did he sit in the chair which had been prepared for him. He must have believed that no good would come of the child." When they asked him why Elijah was absent, Rabbi Judah said that it must be because in the future the child "will have a desire to apostatize from Judaism," And, indeed, the child grew up and did have such a desire.[57]

A seventeenth-century story from kabbalistic circles is a mirror image or converse of the first. Rabbi Solomon, father of the great Rabbi Isaac Luria, receives an awesome visitation of Elijah who tells him that he will have a son of great power and holiness. "Therefore," Elijah tells him, "be very careful not to have him circumcised until I come and take him on my knees to be his sandek." When the time for his son's circumcision had come, his father did not see Elijah, though he "gazed through all four corners of the synagogue." People urged him to let the ceremony start, but he refused and refused until finally he was overcome with bitter weeping, certain that his own sins blocked the fulfillment of the prophecy. Finally, Elijah came and said, "Take your place upon my seat and I shall circumcise the boy. Indeed, I delayed in order to know whether you would do what I told you or not."[58]

These are very different stories, the first a simple story with clear oral roots, the second literarily complex and reflecting an intense mystical piety. Nevertheless, it may be significant that they were both created in the centuries during which the spoken liturgy of the circumcision ceremony began to invoke Elijah. In their very different ways, each grapples with the questions whether Elijah is "really" present at circumcisions and whether he might be more present at some than at others. Even when the medieval Elijah behaves in some sense as the rabbinic Sages had believed angels behaved, automatically blessing the performance of a commandment, he still has free will to do more, or less, than expected.

ELIJAH AT PASSOVER The custom of having "Elijah's cup" at the Passover Seder may have begun with the prophet's messianic role, but goes far beyond it. Most Ashkenazi Jewish families—today most Jewish families the world over—prepare a cup of wine for Elijah, usually in a special goblet. They pour Elijah's cup either at the start of the Seder or near the end, when they open the door for the prophet. As we have seen with other liturgical customs involving Elijah, there are numerous reasons and beliefs associated with this practice, suggesting a popular origin for it.

Most people knowledgeable about Jewish ritual today believe that Elijah's cup was instituted because of an ancient rabbinic dispute about whether one should drink four or five cups of wine at the Seder (B. Pesaḥim 188a). Since the Talmud states Elijah will come in the future to resolve legal disputes,[59] we pour an extra cup for him. This explanation, however, came after the fact, in the seventeenth century at the earliest, and cannot explain the origins of the practice.[60] The earliest reference to Elijah's cup comes from the fifteenth century. Rabbi Zelikman Bingo wrote that he had "seen people on Passover night who mix a special cup . . . saying this is the cup of Elijah the prophet, and I did not know where the practice came from. It seems likely that the custom came about because if Elijah the prophet should come on Passover night, when we hope for and expect him to come, he will need a cup. . . . and if the cup were not ready we would have to fix it for him, and this might delay us from the Passover Seder."[61]

No one explanation became dominant quickly. In the sixteenth century Rabbi Ḥaim Benvenisti noted that "a few Ashkenazim" connected Elijah's cup to the practice of not leaving any wine left over after drinking each of the four cups. They would pour any leftover wine into an empty cup and call it "the cup of Elijah the prophet." A century later, Rabbi Yospe Shammes has yet another explanation, relating Elijah's cup to the announcement near the start of the Seder, "All who are hungry, let them come and eat," because "he prepares one cup for a guest who will come, and they call this the cup of Elijah the prophet, because we hope for this guest."[62] Perhaps this last theory, coming centuries after the custom of pouring Elijah's cup began, was influenced by stories of Elijah visiting at Passover, as he does, for example, in a story in the late sixteenth-century *Ma'aseh Book*.[63]

In the traditional Seder of the last three centuries, participants open the door for Elijah when they recite the biblical verses beginning "Pour out your wrath" near the end of the Seder.[64] "Pour out your wrath" is an invocation of Judgment Day that first entered the Haggadah in eleventh-century Europe during years of murderous persecution by Christians. The first verses read, "Pour out your fury upon those peoples who do not know You, upon the kingdoms that do not invoke Your name, for they have devoured Jacob and desolated his home" (Ps. 79:6–7 JPS). Pouring Elijah's cup became connected to pouring the fourth cup, opening the door, and reciting "Pour out your wrath."

Invoking Elijah at this point may have come from a desire to emphasize his role as herald of the Messiah in the redemption that many medieval Jews believed would come at Passover. Elijah is visually connected to the messianic redemption in manuscripts from the same time that Elijah's cup is first mentioned: "In Ashkenazi haggadot from the fifteenth century there sometimes appears beside the passage 'Pour out your wrath' a drawing of the householder opening the door with a cup in his hand alongside the King Messiah riding on his donkey, while Elijah the prophet blows a shofar and walks at his side."[65] This suggests that Elijah's cup first entered the Seder because of his role as messianic herald, which accords with the first recorded mention of the custom.

In the picture from the fifteenth-century Haggadah, and in later Passover lore, Elijah connects the great miracles of the Exodus, the small but no less important miracles of the present, and God's final redemption, the great miracle to come. He appears at the opening of the door, the *limen*, or threshold, mediating between the private and familial and the experience of the whole Jewish people. Because Elijah also comes with the prayer asking God to "pour out your wrath," he participates in linking the joy of the domestic holiday with the present or remembered dangers of living in a hostile world. Moreover, as herald of the messianic age, Elijah recalls and mediates the tension between this unredeemed world and the Day of Judgment that will punish all who do evil.

Not long after Elijah's cup became part of the Passover Seder, stories about Elijah at Passover began to be created. Today they are common all over the Jewish world, among people of Sephardic and Middle Eastern origins as well as those of Ashkenazi Central and Eastern European backgrounds. In many stories of European origin, the prophet rescues a Jewish family or the community from blood libel at Passover.[66] These stories often resemble the story from Yemen in which Elijah, or someone advised by him, temporarily brings a murder victim back to life to reveal his killers. Ben-Amos lists forty-one stories from the Israel Folktale Archives in which Jews are falsely accused of murder and the real murderer is miraculously revealed, many but far from all occurring at Passover. In at least five of the forty-one, Elijah is one who rescues the community, while in the rest a saintly rabbi or wonder-worker usually does so. The Archives also have dozens of related stories in which enemies threaten the Jewish community with accusations of violence, several of these including Elijah as well. Sometimes Elijah rescues the community from false accusation at Passover by appearing as an "old man,"[67] his frequent disguise from the Middle Ages up until today. Elijah, as a liminal figure who appears at Passover and is known to rescue Jews from Gentile accusation, is easily integrated into stories of this kind.

In the blood libel stories Elijah is not the sole savior, but, to my knowledge, he is the only supernatural guest at the Passover Seder—certainly he is the most popular. In many of these tales Elijah tests the faith or hospitality of his hosts, occasionally in dramatic ways, but more often simply by showing up unexpectedly. A charming story recounted by Abraham Barzani from Baghdad tells of a worthy and pious young couple who were childless after several years of marriage. The wife was sad and worried as they sat down to their Seder, and her husband encouraged her to have faith. When an elderly traveler knocked on the door, they put aside their concerns and welcomed him, doing him great honor. Rising to go, "he turned to them and instead of thanking them said, 'I have asked God . . . that I will visit you next Passover, and your table will be without a Seder.'" The young couple are surprised and hurt at receiving a curse instead of a blessing, but hold their tongues out of respect for the aged and for a guest. Now in Hebrew, "Seder," means order, and the pun hangs on Hebrew's lack of an indefinite pronoun. The old man might have said "without order," but that seems an unkind wish as well.

Still, when the wife discovers she is pregnant soon after the Seder, they forget all about the strangely rude old man. She gives birth to a beautiful baby boy, and at their next Passover Seder she joyfully holds the baby on her lap. The baby is just learning to grab, so he knocks over the wine bottle, breaks a dish, and yanks at the tablecloth. At that moment, the "old man" knocks on the door. When they see him, the couple realizes that he must have been Elijah the prophet and that his apparent curse was a blessing.[68] This story combines the motif of a riddle tale with that of Elijah's blessing. As in some rabbinic stories, Elijah here brings aid while playing a trick on the people he helps.

At the start of this section, I promised to explain how the unpredictable rabbinic Elijah could regularly appear at various rituals. The stories about Elijah at circumcision and Passover show us how. Elijah may automatically appear at rituals in some indefinable spiritual sense, but his effective appearance to address a danger or lack in the material world is much rarer and always unpredictable. And perhaps, as the creator of the story about the circumcision where Elijah was absent imagines, Elijah may not be fully predictably present at the rituals in which he is invoked. The prophet remains free, and thus his blessing is all the more precious.

Elijah Today

Elijah stories remain popular today. Three books retelling traditional Elijah stories were published in America in the 1990s: Penninah Schram's *Tales of Elijah the Prophet*, Barbara Diamond Goldin's *Journeys with Elijah: Eight Tales of the Prophet*, and Nina Jaffe's *The Mysterious Visitor: Stories of the Prophet Elijah*. All of them retell the stories for reading by or to children, but they also include notes for adults that discuss the roots of the tales in written or oral sources. As we have seen, the Israel Folktale Archives testify that many traditional Elijah stories circulated orally in different versions into the twentieth century, both in Eastern Europe and the Middle East. Coming into the late twentieth and early twenty-first centuries, Ariela Krasney's 2004 article, "Stories of Elijah the Prophet from Contemporary Story Tellers," transcribes and analyzes oral Elijah tales from Israeli women of different ages, including several stories also found in traditional sources.

Clearly, the Jewish world is still charmed and fascinated by the figure of Elijah the prophet, but do Jewish people today still experience a world in which Elijah appears? Some do. A story from Israel recounts Elijah as protector, shielding Jews from imminent disaster. Yehudit Kahalani, an older woman and recent graduate of Shaanan, an Orthodox teacher's college, recounts an Elijah story from her family's history. In 1929 her parents set out to "escape from Syria." They left for the land of Israel with a large number of other Jews. Once in Lebanon, they stayed at the Elijah the Prophet Synagogue in the city of Sidon, on the Mediterranean coast. The Syrian Jews, working through a local man, hired a fisherman to sail them to what was then British Mandate Palestine. While they were discussing their plans, "an aged man approached, clothed in a white *jalbia*, his beard pure white as snow." The old man asked them where they were going, and, when they told him Israel, he asked if he might come along. Then he asked if they had any food, and they gave him some, telling him when the boat would leave. He told them not to go by sea, but rather by land.

However, as they later prepared to leave, her father looked for the old man, but could not find him. Her father told their companions, "that Jew made a strong impression on me. I advise that we listen to him and escape [to the land of Israel] by land." The group paid a guide to take them over the mountains, and when they arrived in Haifa they heard that the boat they would have sailed on sank, drowning all aboard. "That very night, my father dreamed of an old man with a white beard, dressed in a white *jalbia*, dressed like a local Arab. The old man in the dream said, I warned you against this trouble."[69]

Krasney, who transcribed the story, writes that Elijah appears "as a twentieth-century person, immersed in a realistic world," to fulfill his traditional function of saving "Jewish soul[s] in his mysterious ways." She also notes that the quest to immigrate to the land of Israel acquires a "Messianic character" with the appearance of Elijah.[70] While this may be true, one can also see Elijah here as more generally supporting religious Zionism, just as he supports other expressions of Jewish faith. The story includes several traditional motifs found in other Elijah tales, combining them skillfully. The key event of the plot is Elijah's appearance in disguise to save Jews from danger and his subsequent disappearance. The role of food may at first seem odd, but metonymically recalls many traditional Elijah tales. When the prophet asks for and receives something to eat before giving his crucial advice, he plays out an abbreviated version of the hospitality test so common in medieval and later Elijah stories.

Later, when Elijah appears in the dream, the story employs a traditional motif in a new way. Elijah does not appear with useful council, but to assure the narrator's father—and her audience—that he had indeed come to save. Perhaps the modern narrator feels the need to make this clear. On the other hand, she never explicitly says "Elijah appeared" when describing the distinguished old man in an Arab jalbia, either in Sidon or in the dream. Perhaps she wanted to leave an element of mystery as to whether the old man was really Elijah or perhaps she thought it would be immodest to assert that Elijah definitely appeared to her own family. The story's openness to interpretation is distinctively modern, whatever its cause. It subtly expresses a tension between how its events *could* be explained rationally, but *should* be seen through the eyes of faith. Thus the narrative both supports faith and expresses a challenge faced by those today who want to uphold traditional teachings on providence. How does a believer see life's blessings as gifts and its troubles as divine lessons or chastisements, rather than framing her experience as purely the result of individual talent and psychology, heredity, random chance, social support or oppression, or any of the myriad possible secular explanations?

Yaakov Brawer, a science professor and Lubavitch Hasid, addresses this question more directly in his personal story, "The Three Visits of Elijah the Prophet," on the Chabad Web site. In these visits Elijah comes on Passover night to affirm and strengthen faith rather than rescue anyone. Brawer writes with the precision of a scientist and the fervor of a preacher, and so clearly presents his story as nonfiction testimony to Elijah's invisible but authentic presence that it is difficult analyze the story's homiletic technique without appearing either credulous or disrespectful of the author's belief. This awkwardness itself reveals that Elijah is still a force to be reckoned with. Though Elijah's miraculous coins are only old world fairy tales for most North Americans, stories of Elijah's appearance remain attractive to Jews (and anyone else) wanting to hear about personal encounters with a messenger of God.

In Brawer's story, the prophet confirms his faith and also performs a task particularly dear to the Lubavitch movement, bringing an unaffiliated Jew to a life of Orthodox Judaism. The first visit of Elijah is a small but real miracle at the first Seder after the family became Hasidic. When his young son went to open the door for Elijah,

> before my son could take a step, the door unlatched and swung wide open. No one, or at least no one visible, was there. My son dropped the candle and ran to his mother. I hesitantly got up and went to the open doorway. The night was clear and there was not so much as a breeze.
>
> With us that Passover was my parents' housekeeper, a simple, devout, G-d fearing Catholic woman. . . . During the Seder, she stayed in her room . . . on the second floor. . . . She told us that during the night, she had heard the front door open and that she was suddenly and inexplicably overcome by an intense, awesome feeling of fear.[71]

The addition of a devout Gentile witness is particularly convincing to the reader, included to suggest an objective confirmation that Elijah appeared at the threshold in some special way. Like Yehudit Kahalani, the Israeli woman, Brawer does not add "this proves it was Elijah," leaving his readers to draw the obvious conclusion.

The next year the family celebrates Passover in a second-floor apartment. When his children go downstairs to open the front door for Elijah, they run right back up, jabbering incoherently in terror. Brawer disarmingly confesses to an attack of spiritual pride at this point. He wonders whether his children's fear means that "perhaps I had reached the state of personal perfection necessary for a full revelation of Elijah." On the contrary, when he goes downstairs he finds that his children have been unhinged by the appearance of two monstrous, ugly dogs sitting calmly on the porch. Puzzled and disappointed, he climbs back upstairs. The next day, a yeshiva administrator asks him to host a young man interested in deepening his Jewish observance. The man is utterly amazed to discover that Brawer's porch is precisely where he had found his missing dogs, many blocks from where he was staying, after looking for hours the night before. "Providence had guided those monsters, his 'pets,' to my house. The experience left a deep impression on all of us and I felt particularly uplifted. If Elijah did not exactly come in person, at least he sent his dogs." Brawer implies that this providential coincidence was a tipping point, for the men became friends, and in time the young man became a devout Hasid.[72] I particularly enjoyed this episode in Brawer's story because of Elijah's legendary association with dogs (first found in B. Bava Kamma 60b), which the author gives no indication that he knows. The traditional motif of Elijah as trickster is also in the ascendant in this story: he frightens the children, more gently confounds the narrator, and dumbfounds the young man invited to their home.

Brawer describes Elijah's third visit as what happens every year. The family opens the door to Elijah, as do all Jewish families who observe Passover: "Although it would be improper and incorrect to refer to it as a 'no show,' it is a very low key visit." This subtle presence is a visit too, as Brawer explains by recounting a story about the Kotsker Rebbe. The Rebbe promised his disciples a revelation of Elijah at Passover. Nothing special seemed to happen: the Rebbe rejoiced; the disciples were crushed with disappointment. "'Fools,' he thundered. 'Do you think that Elijah the Prophet comes in through the door? Elijah comes in through the heart.'" Then Brawer, like the good preacher he is, brings the moral home to his audience. Elijah comes through the heart, and every act of faith and devotion opens the heart wider. "Every small, private, inner step on the path to spirituality and goodness is a step toward the Redemption."[73]

This message, linking personal faith and effort to the messianic era that Elijah will herald, is a distinctive part of American Jewish faith. Its most explicit manifestations are found in Hasidic and Reform Judaism. The Chabad-Lubavitch Hasidim expect that faithful Jews striving to live "Torah true" lives will bring the personal Messiah of traditional teachings. Reform Jewish messianism envisions a universal Jewish and finally human struggle for peace and justice in the world, inspired and supported by God, which will finally result in a messianic era. Rabbi Sue Levi Elwell, author of *The Open Door*, a 2002 Reform Passover Haggadah, describes how she decided to keep the difficult words "Pour out Your wrath upon those peoples who do not know You . . . for they have devoured Jacob and desolated his home," but also resolved to add to them. Combining and modifying scriptural verses, she inserted a call for peace and justice and for *tzedakah*, justice in the form of charity, to enemies as well as neighbors. She concludes, "When we stand at our doors and declaim these words, we become empowered as agents of change and messengers of peace. By dreaming a better world, we become partners with Elijah and with the Holy One in hastening a messianic time." Thus Elijah's spiritual presence connects present reality with messianic hope for both the Hasid and the Reform rabbi.[74]

In these contemporary stories and Elwell's invocation of Elijah we see manifestations of the prophet particularly suited to today, just as earlier Elijah folktales were suited to their premodern world. In the Middle Ages the popularization of rabbinic Elijah traditions resulted in stories where Elijah provides material rewards for the virtues of simple Jews—hospitality, charity, and piety—as well as the learning of the Jewish elite. The poverty of ordinary people called forth tales in which Elijah helps the hungry, and the popular appetite for wonders introduced more folktale elements into the Elijah tradition.

Today, in a world influenced by both scientific rationalism and renewed yearning for wonders, Elijah stories take both old and new forms. Jews are still threatened by physical danger, so Elijah appears in disguise to help them. In today's North America, however, spiritual hunger is more common than physical hunger, and Elijah comes to feed it. People long for spiritual connection, but most today live in a more skeptical world. They find it easier to believe in wonders that speak directly to the heart, rather than their ancestors' stories in which material gifts provide evidence of Elijah's help. For Jews, Elijah, a historical figure who reappears in later histories and legends, folktales and mysticism, who is invoked during Passover and other rituals, fills today's need for wonder. Because of his deep roots in tradition and his liminal nature, Elijah can function as a modern divine mediator, appearing on the boundaries of what the Jewish people dare to believe. I suspect that until the Messiah, or the messianic era, arrives, Jewish communities will read and tell stories of Elijah. Elijah, always on the road, always with a plan to help someone, is both a supernatural representative of the Jewish people and a concrete and homely symbol of the omnipresence of God. Elijah, standing at the threshold of heaven, holds open the door between God and humanity.

APPENDIX: THE ELIJAH STORIES OF THE BAVLI IN TRANSLATIONS WITH SIGNIFICANT VARIANT READINGS

I am placing the translations in alphabetical order by tractate of the Talmud rather than in the traditional order to make them easier for all readers to find.

1. AVODAH ZARAH 17B

[Earlier on the same page, Rabbi Ḥanina ben Teradion meets Rabbi Eleazar ben Perata in prison during the Roman persecutions of the 100s and predicts that Rabbi Eleazar will be saved, despite five charges against him, because he has both studied Torah done and good deeds. Rabbi Ḥanina also predicts that he himself will die because he has occupied himself with Torah alone.]

They brought Rabbi Eleazar ben Perata [to trial]. They said, "Why have you taught and why have you stolen?"

He said to them, "If one is a robber one is not a scholar and if one is a scholar one is not a robber, and since I am not one I am not the other either."

"Why do they call you 'Rabbi' [master]?"

"I am a master of the weavers."

They brought him two coils of thread and asked, "Which is for the warp and which is for the woof?"

A miracle occurred for him, and a female bee came and sat on the warp and a male bee came and sat on the woof.

He told them, "This is the warp and this is the woof."

They asked him, "Why don't you go to the meeting place?"

He said to them, "I am an old man and I am afraid that I might be trampled underfoot."

They asked, "And, up until now, how many old men have been trampled?"

A miracle occurred, and that very day an old man was trampled.

"Why did you free your slave?"

He replied to them, "These things never happened."

One of them got up to testify against him.

Elijah came [and] appeared to him as one of the great men of the empire.

He said to him, "Since a miracle occurred for him in all [the rest], in this one too a miracle will occur for him, and you [lit. that man] will show your bad nature."

He did not heed him [Elijah] and rose to speak to them [to denounce Rabbi Eleazar].

[At that moment] there was a letter, which was written by important men of the kingdom to send to Caesar's court, and they sent it by that man [who wanted to accuse Rabbi Eleazar].

Elijah came and tossed him four hundred leagues.

He went and did not come [back].

They brought Rabbi Ḥanina ben Teradion [to trial.] They said to him, "Why are you occupying yourself with Torah?"

He said, "[I do] as the Lord my God commanded me."

Immediately, they sentenced him to burning, his wife to death, and his daughter to life in a brothel.

2. AVODAH ZARAH 18A–B

[Rabbi Meir was married to the other daughter of Rabbi Ḥanina, Beruria. She asks him to get her sister out of the brothel. Rabbi Meir convinces the brothel keeper to release her by showing him that calling out "God of Meir, answer me" will save him. The government finds out and is about to punish the brothel keeper when he calls out "God of Meir, answer me."]

They said to him, "What is this?"

He said to them, "This is what happened."

They came and engraved Rabbi Meir's picture on the gate of Rome.

They said, "Anyone who sees this face should bring him [in]."

One day they saw him and ran after him.

He ran from them into a house of prostitution.

There are those who say he saw a dish of food belonging idol worshipers; he dipped with this [finger] and licked with that [finger].

There are those who say that Elijah came and appeared to them as a prostitute and embraced him.

They said "Spare us! If it were Rabbi Meir, he wouldn't have done that!"

MS JTSA is rather different:

When Meir happened to be there they wanted to seize him.

Elijah came and appeared to him as a prostitute and embraced him.

There are those who say there was a dish of food belonging to idol worshipers; he dipped this [finger in] and licked that. They said, "If it were Meir, he wouldn't have acted in that way!"

3. BAVA BATRA 7B

[The Mishnah appears] to say that a gatehouse is an improvement.

But what about a certain God-fearing man whom Elijah was accustomed to converse with—

he built a gatehouse and Elijah did not converse with him again. [Rashi's commentary: because it prevented the poor from calling out, and their voice was not heard.]

This is not a problem, this [gatehouse that *is* an improvement] is inside [the courtyard], and that outside.

4. BABA KAMMA 60B

The Rabbis teach, "Dogs howling—the angel of death has come to town; dogs frolicking—Elijah has come to town."

(But this holds only when there's no female among them.)

5. BAVA MEZIA 59B

The Rabbis teach: On that day Rabbi Eliezer answered [them] with all the arguments in the world, and they did not accept them from him.

He said to them, "If the halakhah is according to me, let this carob tree prove it."

The carob tree was uprooted a hundred cubits from its place, and some say four hundred cubits.

They said to him, "One cannot bring evidence from the carob tree."

Again he said to them, If the halakhah is according to me, let this canal prove it."

The canal flowed back[ward] behind them.

They said to him, "One cannot bring evidence from the canal."

Again he said to them, "If the halakhah is according to me, let the walls of the house of study prove it." The walls of the house of study inclined [and began] to fall.

Rabbi Joshua rebuked them . . . [And in the end the walls remained standing but still bent, out of respect for both Rabbi Eliezer and Rabbi Joshua.]

Again he said to them, "If the halakhah is according to me, let it be proved from the heavens."

A heavenly voice went forth and said, "What do you have to do with Rabbi Eliezer, since the halakhah is according to him in every case?"

Rabbi Joshua stood on his feet and said, "[For this commandment which I command you this day . . .] It is not in heaven" [Deut. 30:12].

What does "It is not in heaven" mean?

Rabbi Yermi'ah said, "That Torah has already been given from Mount Sinai—

we pay no attention to a heavenly voice because You have already written at Mount Sinai in the Torah, 'One should incline after the majority' [Exod. 23:2]."

Rabbi Natan met Elijah and said to him, "What was the Holy One blessed be He doing at that time?"

He said to him, "He was laughing and saying, 'My sons have prevailed over me, my sons have prevailed over me.'"

6. BAVA MEZIA 83B–84A

[The story just preceding this one is that of Rabbi Eleazar ben Shimon who became a thief catcher or informer for the Romans. Even though he was called "vinegar, son of wine," unrighteous son of a righteous father, he was proved to be righteous.]

And Rabbi Ishmael son of Rabbi Yossi—an event like this one happened to him.

Elijah met him; he said to him, "How long will you hand over the people of our God to be killed?"

He said to him, "What can I do? It is the king's decree."

He said to him, "Your father fled to Asia Minor—you must flee to Laodicea."

7. BAVA MEZIA 85B

Rav Ḥaviva said, Rav Ḥaviva of Surmaki told me:

I saw one of the rabbis with whom Elijah was often found.

In the morning his eyes were well, and in the evening they appeared as if scorched with fire.

I said to him, "What is this?"

And he said to me, "I said to Elijah, 'Show me the rabbis as they ascend to the heavenly court.'

He said to me, 'You can look at all of them, except for the chariot of Rabbi Ḥiyya, which you should not look at.'

'What are their distinguishing marks?'

'With all of them go angels when they ascend and descend, except for the chariot of Rabbi Ḥiyya, which ascends and descends by itself.'

I could not control my desire [lit. settle myself]—I looked at it.

Two sparks of fire came forth and struck 'that man' [me] and blinded his eyes.

The next day I went and prostrated myself on his [Rabbi Ḥiyya's] grave. I said 'I repeat your teachings, sir.'"

And I was healed."

8. BAVA MEZIA 85B

Elijah was often found at the court of Rabbi [Judah the Patriarch].

One day it was the New Moon. It became dark, and he did not come.

He [Rabbi Judah] said to him, "Why were you delayed [lit. why did it become dark], sir?"

He said to him, "[I waited] until I had gotten Abraham up and washed his hands, and he prayed, and I laid him [back] down, and the same for Isaac and the same for Jacob."

"And [why not] wake them up at the same time?"

"I thought that they might become strong in prayer and bring the Messiah before his time."

He said to him, "And does their likeness exist in this world?"

He said to him, "There are Rabbi Ḥiyya and his sons."

Rabbi decreed a public fast. He had Rabbi Ḥiyya and his sons go down [to the ark to lead the prayers for rain].

He said, "He causes the wind to blow," and a strong wind blew; he said, "He causes the rain to fall," and rain came.

When he reached, "He causes the dead to live," the world shook.

They said in heaven, "Who has revealed secrets on earth?"

They said, "Elijah."

They brought Elijah; they struck him with sixty fiery lashes.

He came and appeared as a fiery bear. He came among them and scattered them.

Most early MSS, including Munich, Hamburg 165, Vatican 115, and Florence, have Elijah appearing simply as "a bear" not as a "fiery bear."

MS Florence has a significant variant at the end:

They brought him and struck him with sixty fiery lashes.

Permission was given to him. He came like a bear among them and scattered them.

9. BAVA MEẐIA 114A–B

[The background is a sugya on assessment of debtors. If a someone owes more than he can pay, does one assess what he pays his creditor so that some possessions remain to him? One of the arguments given for leaving the debtor some of his possessions is an analogy to the ritual law concerning "valuations" of a vow to God: "But if he is poorer than your valuation . . . the priest shall assess him; the priest shall assess him according to what the vower can afford" (Lev. 27:2–8, JPS with changes toward the literal translation).]

Rabbah bar Abbuha met Elijah standing in a graveyard of the Gentiles.

He said to him, "What is the law concerning whether they assess a debtor?"

He said to him, "Learn it from the use of the root 'poor' in the laws of valuation [and debtors]. Concerning valuation it is written, 'But if he is *poorer* (מך) than your valuation,' [Lev. 27:8]; concerning the debtor it is written, 'And if your brother becomes *poor* (ימוך)' [Lev. 25:35]."

"What is the scriptural source for the law that a naked person should not separate *terumah*?"

As it is written, "So that He should not see in you any improper thing" [Deut. 23:15].

He said to him, "Aren't you a priest, sir? Why are you standing, sir, in a graveyard?"

He said to him, "Haven't you studied 'Purities,' sir?

"As it is taught in a tradition, Rabbi Shimon ben Yoḥai says, the graves of the Gentiles do not make one impure. As it is said, 'But you are my flock, the sheep of my pasture; you are human beings' [Ezek. 34:31]. You are called human; Gentiles are not called human."

He said to him, "I cannot manage four [orders of Mishnah], how can I manage [all] six?"

He said to him, "And why [not]?"

He said to him, "I am poor" [lit. affair(s) are narrow for me].

He led him and brought him into the Garden of Eden. He said to him, "Spread out your cloak—pick and take some of these leaves."

He picked and took.

As he was going out he heard that which said, "Who uses up his eternity as Rabbah bar Abbuha does?" He shook out [his cloak], threw them away.

Even so, he took his cloak—his cloak absorbed the scent.

He sold it for twelve thousand denars [which] he divided among his sons-in-law.

All early MSS have a graveyard of "Gentiles" (גוים) rather than "star worshipers" (עובדי כוכבים), and it is Gentiles rather than "star worshipers" later on who "are not human beings" in the midrash on Ezekiel. The translation reflects this.

10. BERAKHOT 3A

A tradition teaches Rabbi Yossi said:

Once I was walking on the road and I entered one ruin among the ruins of Jerusalem to pray. Elijah, remembered for blessing, came and waited for me at the entrance until I had finished my prayer.

When I had finished my prayer, he said, "Peace be with you, Rabbi."

And I said, "Peace be with you, my Rabbi and teacher."

And he said to me, "My son, why did you enter that ruin?"

I said to him, "To pray."

And he said to me, "You should have prayed along the way."

And I said to him, "I was afraid that passersby would interrupt me."

And he said to me, "You should have prayed a short prayer."

At that moment I learned from him three things.

I learned that one should not enter a ruin, and I learned that one should pray along the way, and I learned that one who prays along the way says a short prayer.

And he said to me, "My son, what voice did you hear in this ruin?"

And I said to him, "I heard a divine voice which coos like a dove and says,

'Alas for the children for whose sins I destroyed my house and burnt my sanctuary and banished them among the nations.'"

And he said to me, "By your life and the life of your head, not in this hour alone does it speak so, but it speaks so three times every day, and not this alone but at the hour when Israel enters synagogues and houses of study and responds, 'May His great name be blessed!' the Holy One blessed be He shakes his head and says, 'Happy the king whom they acclaim so in his house. What is the matter with the father who exiled his children? And alas for the children who were exiled from their father's table/altar.'"

In line 15 two MSS lack "Alas for the children"; MS Paris 671 has "Alas *for me* that I destroyed my house" and MS Oxford has "Alas that I destroyed my house."

11. BERAKHOT 4B

A tradition teaches, Michael in one [flight], Gabriel in two, Elijah in four, and the Angel of Death in eight, and, in time of plague, in one.

12. BERAKHOT 29B

Elijah said to Rav Judah, brother of Rav Sala the pious,

"Do not get boiling hot [angry] and you will not sin; do not get soggy [drunk] and you will not sin, and when you depart on a journey, take council of your Creator and depart."

13. BERAKHOT 58A

Rav Shila flogged a man who had sex with an Egyptian woman.

The man went and informed on him [lit. ate food] at the king's palace. He said, "There is a certain man among the Jews who passes judgment without authorization by the king."

An officer was sent to him [to summon him]. When he came, they said to him, "Why did you have this man flogged?"

He [Rav Shila] said to them, "He had intercourse with a donkey."

They said to him, "Do you have witnesses?"

He said to them, "Yes."

Elijah came, appeared to him as a man, and testified.

They said to him, "If so, he deserves to be killed!"

He said to them, "From the time we were exiled from our land we have had no authority to execute. You do whatever you want with him."

While they were considering his case, Rav Shila started to recite and said [in Hebrew] "Yours, Lord, is the greatness and the power" [and the glory, and the victory and the majesty: for all that is in heaven and earth is Yours, Yours is the kingdom and You rule as head of all. (1 Chron. 29:11)]. They said to him, "What did you say?"

He said, "This is what I was saying, blessed is the Merciful who has given kingship on earth [attributes] similar to the kingship of heaven, and gives you rule and mercy in judgment."

They said, "Is the honor of the monarchy so dear to him?"

They gave him a staff, and told him "You may pass judgment."

As he was going out, that man [whom he has sentenced] said to him, "Does God do miracles like this for liars?"

He said to him, "You scoundrel, are not they called asses? For it is written, "[For she (Jerusalem) doted upon her paramours in Egypt] whose members [lit. flesh] were like the members of asses' (Ezek. 23:20)."

And he saw that he was going to go tell them that he had called them asses.

He said [to himself] "This man is a 'pursuer,' and the Torah says if someone comes to kill you, hasten to kill him."

He struck him with his staff and killed him.

He said, "Since a miracle was done for me through this verse, I will expound it:

'Yours, Lord, is the greatness,' this is the work of creation, and thus it says 'Who does great things past finding out' (Job 9:10). . . . .

'And the victory [nezah],' this is the fall of Rome, as it says, '[I have trodden the wine press alone. . . . I have trodden them in my wrath and trampled them in my fury,] and their life blood [nizham] was sprinkled on my garments' (Isa. 63:3) . . . ." etc.

Unusually, the early MSS differ as to whether Elijah appears or not. It is impossible to say whether this is because some scribes were uncomfortable with Elijah's doing even indirect harm and eliminated him or because other scribes were uncomfortable with the rabbi-hero lying and brought Elijah in to endorse his actions. The MSS are united in making the Rabbi "Rabbi," as opposed to "Rav" Shila, and making the Gentile government Roman.

14. ERUVIN 43A

[In a discussion about whether the Sabbath limit applies over ten handsbreadths above the ground] Come and hear: Those seven traditions that were recited on the Sabbath morning before Rav Ḥisda in Sura [and] the same evening before Rava in Pumbedita—who recited them, wasn't it Elijah? Thus there are no Sabbath limits above ten [handsbreadths].

No—perhaps the demon Yosef recited them.

15. GITTIN 6B

And, furthermore, wasn't Rabbi Aviatar someone whose master approved his decision?

As it is written, "And his concubine offended him" [Judg. 19:2];

Rabbi Aviatar said that he found a fly with her;

Rabbi Yonatan said that he found a hair on her.

And Rabbi Aviatar met Elijah. He said to him, "What is the Holy One blessed be He doing?"

He said to him, "He is occupied with 'the concubine in Gibeah'"

"And what is he saying?"

He said to him, "My son Aviatar, he speaks this way; my son Yonatan, he speaks that way."

He said to him, "Spare us! Is there doubt before Heaven?"

He said to him, "[Both] these and those are the words of the Living God. He found a fly and did not object; he found a hair and objected."

Rav Judah said, "The fly was in his dish, and the hair was in 'that place'; the fly was a disgusting thing, but the hair was a danger."

16. GITTIN 70A

Elijah said to Rabbi Natan,

"Eat a third, and drink a third, and leave a third for when you get angry [and then] you will have had your fill" [lit. you will rest in your fullness].

17. ḤAGIGAH 9B

Elijah said to Bar Hei Hei, and others say to Rabbi Eleazar,

"What is [the meaning of] that which is written, 'Behold, I have refined you and not as silver; I have tried you in the furnace of *affliction*' (Isa. 48:10);

"This teaches that the Holy One blessed be He went over all good qualities to give to Israel and found nothing but *poverty*."

[The same word, *oni*, appears twice; it means both poverty and affliction].

18. ḤAGIGAH 15B

Rabbah bar Shila met Elijah. He asked him, "What is the Holy One blessed be He doing?"

He said to him, "He is reciting traditions from the mouths of all the Rabbis, but from the mouth of Rabbi Meir he is not reciting [traditions]."

He said to him, "Why?"

"Because he learned traditions from the mouth of Aḥer [the Other]."

He said to him, "Why? R. Meir found a pomegranate, ate its flesh, and threw away its skin."

He said to him, "Now He says, 'Meir my son says, When a human being suffers [the penalty of death] what does the Shekhinah say? My head is heavy, my arm is heavy.

If the Holy One blessed be He suffers thus over the blood of the wicked, how much the more so [does He suffer] over the blood of the righteous which is poured out?'" (M. Sanh. 6.5).

19. KETUBOT 61A

[The previous lines state that it is unhealthy to see and crave and strong-flavored food without being able to taste it.]

Abbuha bar Ihi and Minyamin bar Ihi: one fed [his waiter] some of every kind [of food], and one fed [him] one kind. Elijah conversed with one, but Elijah did not converse with the other.

Two God-fearing men—and some say [they were] Rav Mari and Rav Pinḥas sons of Rav Ḥisda—one fed [his waiter] first, and the other fed him afterward.

The one who fed him first, Elijah conversed with him; the one who fed him afterward, Elijah did not converse with him.

20. KETUBOT 77B

[The prior context of this story is a discussion of a frightful and contagious disease called *ra'atan*. Several eminent rabbis took care not to come into even remote contact with people who had the disease.]

Rabbi Joshua ben Levi [however] came close to them and studied Torah. He said, "'A lovely hind and a gracious doe' [Prov. 5:19]—if she gives grace to those who study her, won't she certainly protect [them]?"

When he was lying [on his death bed,] they said to the angel of death, "Go do what he wants."

He [the angel] went and appeared to him.

He [Rabbi Yehoshua] said to him, "Show me my place."

He said to him, "By my life."

He said to him, "Give me your knife so as not to frighten me on the way."

He gave it to him.

When he arrived there, he raised him up, showing [his place] to him. He leapt and fell on the other side.

He held him by the corner of his cloak.

He said, "By [my] oath, I will not come."

The Holy One blessed be He said, "If he has petitioned [to annul his own misguided] oath he shall return, and if not he shall not return."

He said to him, "Give me my knife."

He would not give it to him.

A divine voice went forth and said, "Give it to him—it is needed for created beings."

Elijah proclaimed before him, "Make way for the son of Levi, make way for the son of Levi."

He went along and met Rabbi Shimon ben Yohai, who was sitting on thirteen stools of fine gold.

He [Rabbi Shimon] said to him, "Are you *the* son of Levi?"

He said to him, "Yes."

"Did the rainbow appear in your days?"

He said to him, "Yes."

"If so, you are not [the] son of Levi."

But this is not so. There wasn't a thing [in the way of a rainbow], but he thought,

"I will not claim goodness for myself."

21. KETUBOT 105B

Rav Anan: a certain man brought him a bale of small fish from Bei Gilei.

He said to him, "What is your business?"

He said, "I have a case to try."

[Rav Anan] did not take [the gift]. He said, "I am unfit to try your case."

He said to him, "I'm not asking for your judgment, sir, [but] do, sir, take them and do not prevent me, sir, from offering first fruits.

"For they teach, 'And a man came from Baal-shalisha and brought the man of God bread of the first fruits, twenty loaves of barley and fresh ears of grain in his sack' (2 Kings 4:42), and was Elisha one who [ought to] eat first fruits? Rather, this teaches you that whoever brings a gift to a disciple of the wise, it is as if he offered first fruits."

He said, "I did not want to accept, but now that you have told me a reason I will accept."

He sent him before Rav Naḥman, and sent off [a message] to him: "Judge this man's case, for I, Anan am unfit to judge him."

[Rav Naḥman] said, Since he sent me this message, one should conclude that he [the man] is a relative of his.

A case brought by some orphans was before him. He said, "This is a positive precept and this [too] is a positive precept. The precept of honoring Torah is superior." He put aside the orphans' case and brought in that man's case.

When that man's opponent saw the honor that they did him, his claim was silenced [because he was intimidated by the judge's favor to his opponent].

Rav Anan: Elijah was accustomed to come to him, for he was teaching him the Order of Elijah. Since he [Rav Anan] had done this, he went away.

He [Rav Anan] sat in fasting and asked for mercy [from God].

And he came, [but] when he came he really frightened him.

He [Rav Anan] made a box, and sat [in it] before him until he had expounded his Order to him.

This is why people speak of the Greater Order of Elijah, the Lesser Order of Elijah (Seder Eliahu Rabbah, Seder Eliahu Zuta).

There are several distinctly different versions of the part about Elijah. MS Munich has a much shorter one, and MS Leningrad a longer.

MS Munich 95: Rav Anan was accustomed that Elijah would come to Anan and teach him the Order of Elijah.

This is why we speak of the Greater Order of Elijah, the Lesser Order of Elijah

MS Leningrad: He [Rav Anan] afflicted himself and sat in fasting and asked for mercy [from God].

And he came.

When he came, he said to him, "Why haven't you come, sir?"

He said to him, "Because of this [that you did]."

He said to him, "What about our Order? What [. . . *smudged*] that is begun for us in it—let us finish it."

He said to him, "By my life [let's do it]."

Until that day whenever [anyone] asked anything of him he would explain it, from that time on, he [Elijah] really frightened him.

He made a box and was placed in it.

One gentleman sat in the box, and the other gentleman outside, and he completed it.

And this is why they call it the Greater Order of Elijah and the Lesser Order of Elijah.

22. KIDDUSHIN 40A

[In context, this story serves a prooftext for the dictum that whoever is tempted to sexual immorality and resists has a miracle done for him.]

Rav Kahana was selling reed baskets. A certain matron propositioned him.

He said to her, "I will go get myself ready."

He went up and threw himself from the rooftop to the earth.

Elijah came and caught him. He said to him, "You have troubled me [by making me come] four hundred leagues."

He said to him, "What made me [do it]—wasn't it poverty?"

He gave him a bushel of dinars.

23. KIDDUSHIN 70A

Rabbah bar Rav Ada said (and some say Rabbi Sala said in the name of Rav Hamnuna),

"Anyone who marries a wife who is not fit for him, Elijah binds him and the Holy One blessed be He flogs him."

And it teaches, "Elijah writes concerning them all and the Holy One blessed be He signs:

'Alas for him who makes his seed unfit and blemishes his family and marries a wife who is not fit for him. Elijah binds him and the Holy One blessed be He flogs him.'"

24. MAKKOT 11A

[The question is why the mothers of the High Priests supplied food and clothing to people in the cities of refuge. Why did the High Priests need these people not to curse them (or to pray for them) if they had done no wrong?]

An elder said "I heard in a *pirka* [public lecture] of Rava, that they [the High Priests] should have prayed for mercy on their generation and they did not pray."

This is like what happened with a man who was eaten by a lion three leagues from Rabbi Joshua ben Levi, and Elijah did not converse with him for three days.

25. MEGILLAH 15B

"Let the King and Haman come to the feast" [the words of Esther in 5:4].

The Rabbis teach, What did Esther consider when she invited Haman?

Rabbi Eleazar says, "She prepared a trap for him, as it says, 'Let their table before them become a snare' [Ps. 69:32]."

Rabbi Joshua says, "From her father's house she learned, 'If your enemy hungers, give him bread,' etc." [For you heap coals of fire on his head; Prov. 25:21–22].

Rabbi Meir says, "So that he would not take counsel and rebel."

Rabbi Judah says, "So that he would not come to know that she was Jewish."

Rabbi Nehemiah says, "So that Israel would not say, 'We have a sister in the king's palace,' and dismiss [God's] mercy from their minds."

Rabbi Yossi says, "So that he should be accessible all the time."

Rabbi Shimon ben Menasia says, "[She thought] maybe God will feel [compassion at my situation] and do a miracle for us."

Rabbi Joshua ben Korha says, "[She thought] I will encourage him [i.e., seduce Haman] so that he will be killed, he and she [Esther herself]."

Rabban Gamaliel says, "[She thought] the king is a fickle man."

Rabbi Gamaliel said, "We still need the Modean, as it is taught, 'Rabbi Eliezer the Modean says, she made the king jealous of him and she made the princes jealous of him.'"

Rabbah said, "[She thought] 'Pride goes before a fall' [Prov. 16:18]."

Abaye and Rava both said, "[She thought] 'In their heat I will make feasts for them,' etc. [I will make them drunk . . . and sleep an eternal sleep and not wake; Jer. 51:39].

Rabbah bar Abbuha met Elijah and said to him, "In accord with whose opinion did Esther decide and act as she did?"

He said to him, "[She thought] like all the Tannaim and like all the Amoraim."

26. NEDARIM 50A

Rabbi Akiva—the daughter of Kalba Savua's son betrothed herself to him.

The son of Kalba Savua heard and vowed she should not benefit from any of his property.

She went and married herself to him in winter.

They used to sleep in straw, and he would be picking the straw out of her hair.

He said to her, "If I could, I would give you a Jerusalem of gold [a coronet]."

Elijah came and appeared to them as a man, and he was begging at the door.

He said to them, "Give me a little straw, because my wife has given birth and I don't have anything to let her lie down on."

Rabbi Akiva said to his wife, "See this man, who doesn't even have straw!"

She said to him, "Go to a rabbi's [to study Torah]."

He went for twelve years . . .

[The rest of this story recounts how Rabbi Akiva returned after twelve years. Before meeting his wife he overheard her say he could stay away even another twelve to study Torah. So he left again, and finally returned after twenty-four years, showing his wife great honor.]

27. SANHEDRIN 63B–64A

Come and hear, "And I will throw your carcasses on the carcasses of your idols" (Lev. 26:30, part of the curses on the unfaithful Israel).

They said: Elijah the righteous was searching for those who were sick with hunger in Jerusalem.

Once he found a child sick [with hunger] and lying on a dung heap.

He said to him, "What family are you from?"

He said to him, "I'm from such-and-such family."

He said to him, "Is anyone left from that family?"

He said to him, "No, except for me."

He said to him, "If I teach you something that you will live by, will you learn?"

He said to him, "Yes."

He said to him, "Say every day, 'The Lord is our God, the Lord is One.'"

He said to him, "Quiet! Do not speak the name of the Lord" (Amos 6:10). His father and his mother had not taught him. Immediately he took what he worshipped from near his heart and embraced it and kissed it, and his belly split open, and what he worshipped fell to earth and he fell on it, to confirm what is said, "And I will throw your carcasses on the carcasses of your idols" (Lev. 26:30).

28. SANHEDRIN 97B

Elijah said to Rav Judah the brother of Rav Sala the Pious, "The world will not exist less than eighty-five jubilees, and in the last jubilee the son of David will come."

He asked him, "At its beginning or its end?"

He said to him, "I do not know."

"Will it be completed [the last jubilee] or won't it be completed?"

He said to him, "I do not know."

29. SANHEDRIN 98A

Rabbi Joshua ben Levi met Elijah who was standing at the entrance to Rabbi Shimon ben Yoḥai's tomb.

He asked him, "Will I enter the world to come?"

He said to him, "If this lord wishes."

Rabbi Joshua ben Levi said, "I saw two and heard three." He asked him, "When will Messiah come?"

He said to him, "Go ask him."

"And where [is he]?"

"He sits at the gate of the city."

"And how will I know him? [lit. what are his distinguishing marks?]"

He sits among the poor who suffer from diseases, and all of them loosen [their bandages] and tie up [their bandages] all at once; [but] he loosens one and ties one [at a time]."

He says, "Perhaps I will be needed [at any moment] so I should not be delayed."

[Rabbi Joshua] went to him. He said to him, "Peace be with you, my master and teacher."

He said to him, "Peace be with you, son of Levi."

He said to him, "When are you coming, sir?"

He said to him, "Today."

[Rabbi Joshua] came to Elijah.

He said to him, "What did he say to you?"

He said to him, "'Peace be with you, son of Levi.'"

He said to him, "He promised you and your father the world to come."

He said to him, "He surely lied to me! For he said he would come today, and he did not come."

He said to him, "This [is what] he said to you, '[For He is our God, and we are the people of his pasture, the flock he tends.] Today, if you will hear his voice' [Ps. 95:7]."

MS Florence, Munich and Karlsrühe all have Rabbi Joshua meeting and speaking to both Elijah and Rabbi Shimon ben Yoḥai. This makes more sense of "I saw two and heard three." He saw Elijah and Rabbi Shimon and the third, perhaps, was a bat kol, speaking on a matter concerning salvation (see chapter 3).

In the MS Florence, Rabbi Joshua meets the two at Shimon ben Yoḥai's tomb as in the Vilna text, whereas in Munich and Karlsrühe it is the gate of Paradise.

In all three MSS the Messiah is found "at the gate of Rome," an originally universal reading eliminated by censorship.

The third substantial difference between the Vilna text and the three manuscripts lies in the order of the last section. To quote MS Florence:

He said to him, "When are you coming, sir?"

He said to him, "Today."

He went to Elijah; he said to him, "Surely he lied to me, for he told me, 'Today.'"

He said to him, "'Today if you will hear my voice.'" He said to him, "What did he say to you?"

"'Peace be with you son of Levi.'"

He said to him, "He promised you and your father the world to come."

30. SANHEDRIN 113A–B

Rabbi Yossi expounded in Sepphoris, "Father Elijah was a hot-tempered man."

He [Elijah] was accustomed to come to him; he withdrew himself from him for three days and did not come.

When he came, he [Rabbi Yossi] said to him, "Why didn't you come?"

He said, "You called me hot-tempered."

31. SHABBAT 13A–B

It is taught by the House of Elijah: the story of a certain scholar who learned a great deal of Mishnah and read a great deal of Bible and served the disciples of the Sages a great deal and died when half his days had passed.

And his wife used to take his tefillin and bring them around the synagogues and study houses.

She said to them, "It is written in the Torah, 'For it is your life, and the length of your days.' My husband who learned a great deal of Mishnah and read a great deal of Bible and served the disciples of the Sages a great deal. Why did he die when half his days had passed?"

And no one answered her a word.

Once I lodged at her house, and she told me the whole story.

I said to her, "My daughter, in the days of your menstruation, how was he with you?"

She said to me, "God forbid! He did not touch me with even his little finger."

"In the days of your white [clothing, before you purified yourself], how was he with you?"

"He ate with me, and he drank with me, and he slept with me in bodily contact, but nothing else ever occurred to him."

And I said to her, "Blessed be God who killed him for he did not show favoritism to Torah [study], for surely the Torah says, 'Do not approach a woman in her menstrual impurity'" (Lev. 18:19).

32. SHABBAT 33B

[Rabbi Shimon ben Yoḥai criticizes the Roman government and is sentenced to death. He and his son hide in the house of study while his wife brings them food and water.]

When the decree became more harsh, he said to his son, "Women's minds are light. Perhaps they will torture her and she will reveal us."

They went and hid in a cave.

A miracle was brought about for them; a carob tree and spring of water was created for them.

The used to undress and sit up to their necks in sand. All day they studied; at the time for prayer they dressed, covered themselves and prayed, then undressed again so their clothes would not wear out. They stayed twelve years in the cave.

Elijah came and stood at the mouth of the cave.

He said, "Who will tell the son of Yoḥai that the emperor is dead and his decree is annulled?"

They went out and saw people who were planting and sowing.

He said, "They leave eternal life and busy themselves with the life of the moment."

Everywhere they directed their eyes was immediately burned up.

A divine voice went forth and said to them, "Have you come out to destroy my world? Return to your cave!"

[They returned to the cave for a year, when another bat kol told them to go out. This time what the father wounded, the son healed. They saw a man honoring the Sabbath, and their minds were set at ease.]

33. SHABBAT 109B

One who swallows a snake should be made to eat a gourd with salt and made to run three miles. Rav Shimi bar Ashi saw a man who swallowed a snake and appeared to him as a horseman,
made him eat a gourd with salt and run before him three miles, and the snake came out of him chunk by chunk.

There are those who say that Rav Shimi bar Ashi swallowed a snake; Elijah came and appeared to him as a horseman, made him eat a gourd with salt and run before him three miles, and the snake came out of him chunk by chunk.

34. TA'ANIT 21A

This story has two versions, one in Ta'anit, the other in Sanhedrin.

Ta'anit 21a	Sanhedrin 108b–109a
Why did they call him Naḥum of Gamzu? Because, everything that happened to him, he said, this too (*gam zu*) is for good.	Naḥum of Gamzu used to say about everything that happened to him, "This too (*gam zu*) is for good."
One time Israel wanted to send a gift to Caesar.	One day Israel wanted to send a gift to the Emperor.
They said, "Who will go? Let Naḥum of Gamzu go, because he has experience in miracles."	They said, "By whom shall we send it? We will send it by Naḥum Gamzu because he has experience in miracles."
They sent, by his hand, a bag full of precious stones and pearls. He went and spent the night in a certain inn.	When he came to a certain inn he wanted to spend the night. They asked him, "What do you have with you?" He said, "I am bringing tribute to Caesar."
At night those innkeepers got up and took his bags and filled them with dust. The next day when he saw them he said, "This too is for good."	They got up at night, unfastened his bags, removed everything that was in them, and filled them with dust.
When he got there [before the emperor], they unfastened his bags, and they were full of dust.	When he got there [before the emperor] they found dust.
The king wanted to kill all of them. He said, "The Jews mock me!"	He [the emperor] said, "The Jews are mocking me!" They took him out to be executed.
He said, "This too is for good." Elijah came and appeared to him as one of them. He said to them, "Perhaps this is some of the earth of Abraham their father.	He said, "This too is for good." Elijah came and appeared to them as one of them. He said to them, "Perhaps this is some of the dust of Abraham our [*sic*] father.

"For he would throw dust, and there were swords, chaff, and there were arrows.

"As it is written, 'His sword makes them as dust, his bow as driven stubble' [Isa. 41:2]."

There was a country which they could not conquer; they tried some of it [the dust] and conquered it.

They took him to the treasury.

And he filled his bags with precious stones and pearls. And they sent him [on his way] with great honor.

When he returned, he stayed at that inn.

They said to him, "What did you bring there that they did you such great honor?"

He said to them, "What I took from here, I brought there."

They tore down their inn and brought it to the court. They said to him, "That dust he brought here was ours.

They tried and did not find it [so], and they killed those innkeepers.

"He would throw dust, and there were swords, chaff, and there were arrows."

They tested and found it was so.

There was a city that they could not conquer; they threw some of that dust on it and they conquered it.

They took him to the treasury and said, "Take what pleases you!"

He filled his bags with gold.

When he returned, he came [to the same inn].

Those innkeepers said to him, "What did you bring to the court?"

He said to them, "What I took from here I brought there."

They took [some dust] and brought it there,

and they killed those innkeepers.

Rabbi Beroka Ḥoza'a was often found in the marketplace of Bei Lapat;

Elijah was often found with him.

He said to him, "Is there a son of the world to come in this marketplace?"

He said to him, "No."

At that moment he saw a man who had black shoes and did not wear a blue thread on his cloak.

He said, "This one is a child of the world to come."

He [Rabbi Beroka] ran after him and said to him, "What do you do?"

He said to him, "Go away now and come back tomorrow."

The next day he said to him, "What do you do?"

He said to him, "I am a jailer, and I lock up the men alone and the women alone and put my bed between these and those so that they do not fall into the hands of sin. When I see a Jewish woman whom the Gentiles fix their eyes on, I risk my life to save her. One day there was a betrothed girl among us whom the Gentiles fixed their eyes on, and I took wine lees and threw them on her hem and said that she was unclean" [the Zoroastrian Persians also had a strong belief in menstrual impurity].

He said to him, "Why don't you have a [blue] thread and why do you wear black shoes?"

He said to him, "I come and go among Gentiles—[it is] so that they do not know I am a Jew. When they decree a decree [against the Jews] I tell the Rabbis, and they pray for mercy and the decree is annulled."

"And why, when I said to you, 'What do you do,' did you say 'Go away now and come back tomorrow.'"

He said to him, "At that hour they decreed a decree, and I said, I will go and tell the Rabbis so that they pray for mercy about this thing."

At that moment these two [men] came.

He [Elijah] came [and] said to him, "These too are sons of the world to come."

He went to them and said to them, "What do you do?"

They said to him, "We are funny fellows, and we make sad people laugh. Then too, if we see two people who have strife between them, we take pains and make peace between them.

36. TA'ANIT 24B

Rav Judah saw two men who were playing recklessly with a loaf.

He said, "Conclude from this that there is plenty in the world."

He set his eye [on them] and there was famine.

The Rabbis said to Rav Kahana son of Rav Nehunya, his attendant,

"Sir, you are always with him, get him to go out by the gate near the market."

He got him to go out to the market—he [Rav Judah] saw a crowd.

He said to them, "What is this?"

They said to him, "They are standing by some date pulp that people are selling."

He said, "Conclude from this that there is famine in the world."

He said to his attendant, "Take off my shoes." He took off one shoe and rain fell.

When he reached out to take off the other, Elijah came and said to him,

"The Holy One blessed be He says, 'If you take off the other, I will destroy the world.'"

37. YEBAMOT 63A

Rabbi Yossi met Elijah.

He said to him, "It is written, 'I will make a helper for him.'

In what [way] is woman a helper for man?"

He said to him, "A man brings wheat—does he chew on wheat [rather than bread]? Flax—does he wear flax [rather than linen cloth]? Isn't she found to brighten his eyes and stand him on his feet?"

38. YOMA 19B–20B

[On the eve of Yom Kippur, the leading men of Jerusalem would watch all night. An early tradition teaches that they would do this outside Jerusalem, but they would sin.]

Abaye—or others say Rav Naḥman bar Yiẓhak—said, "This means Nehardea."

For Elijah said to Rav Judah brother of Rav Sala the Pious, "You have said, 'Why doesn't the Messiah come?' And this very day is Yom Kippur, and how many virgins were debauched in Nehardea?"

He said to him, "What does The Holy One blessed be He say?"

He said to him, "'Sin crouches at the door'" (Gen. 4:7: "its desire is for you, but you must rule it).

"And Satan, what does he say?"

He said to him, "On Yom Kippur Satan has no authority to accuse."

[There is a pun on Satan in Aramaic: "Satan, which means 'The Accuser,' has no authority to accuse."]

NOTES

1. THE STUDY OF RABBINIC NARRATIVE

1.   See Ayali, "From Where Does Elijah Come." He explores the prehistory of the rab-
     binic conceptions of the biblical Elijah, but does not cover the legendary Elijah.
2.   E.g., Mark 8:27–28: "he asked his disciples, 'Who do people say that I am?' And they
     answered him, 'John the Baptist; and others, Elijah; and still others, one of the proph-
     ets'" (NRSV).
3.   This critique of Elijah is found in both early and later rabbinic midrash. See the Mekh-
     ilta de Rabbi Ishmael, p. 4; Pesikta Rabbati, p. 42b, says that Elijah was punished by
     the command to go anoint his replacement, Elisha (1 Kings 19:16), because he said
     that the people had forsaken God's covenant (1 Kings 19:10, and 14).
4.   The standard Vilna edition has thirty-nine references to Elijah, including a story in
     B. Berakhot 6b in which Elijah appears in the form of an Arab (*tayaye*) and kills a man
     who is behaving disrespectfully toward God by praying with his back to a synagogue.
     Rabbinovicz's *Dikdukei Soferim*, however, shows that no MS readings of this story
     contain the prophet Elijah; instead an ordinary Arab kills the impious man. This fits
     with the legendary Elijah's refusal to punish. See Margaliot, *Elijah the Prophet*, p. 53
     where he notes that Rashi and the Rif lack Elijah here. Also, the positive view of the
     tayaye as stern defender of God's honor accords with other Amoraic sources on the
     tayaye. See Kalmin, *Sages, Stories,* pp. 266–67.
5.   Friedmann, *Seder Eliahu Rabbah and Seder Eliahu Zuta*; see also Strack and Stem-
     berger, *Introduction to the Talmud and Midrash*, pp. 369–70.
6.   Friedmann's approach is much like nineteenth-century Christian historians who tried
     to sift through the miraculous events of the Gospels in search of an objective historical
     core: see Kee, *Miracle in the Early Christian World*, pp. 12–14.
7.   *Tanna Devei Eliahu*, pp. 40–42.
8.   Fraenkel, *Techniques and Principles*, 1:238; Hasan-Rokem, *Tales of the Neighbor-
     hood*, p. 4.

9. Kee, *Miracle in the Early Christian World*, pp. 14–16, 42.

10. Segal, *Elijah*; Segal's work is echoed by Eliezer Margaliot's later collection in Hebrew.

11. Ibid., pp. 5, 6.

12. Wiener, *The Prophet Elijah*, pp. 54–55, 59.

13. Ibid., p. x.

14. Fraenkel, *Techniques and Principles*, 1:253.

15. Ibid., 1:255–56.

16. Peli, "Elijah in the Beit Midrash," p. 144. In a partial exception to this rule, Rav Anan in B. Ketubot 106a fasts in order to see Elijah, but that is *after* Elijah stopped appearing to him because of something he did.

17. Ibid., p. 145.

18. Brown-Gutoff notes that irony is often easier to identify than humor in "That's Not Funny."

19. Peli, "Elijah in the Beit Midrash," p. 168.

20. Ibid., pp. 154, 156, and 157.

21. Foley, "Word-Power," pp. 291–92.

22. For various contemporary schools of folklore studies and their relevance to the study of ancient texts see Niditch, *Folklore and the Hebrew Bible*, pp. 3–31. See also Foley's introduction in his *Oral Tradition in Literature*.

23. For some other factors in the imperfect acceptance of folklore studies in Judaic studies, some stemming from the historical bias of "scientific" Jewish studies toward philosophy and halakhah and against narrative, some from shortcomings of Jewish folklore studies itself, see Ben-Amos, "Jewish Studies and Jewish Folklore," 2:1–20.

24. Ben-Amos, "The Idea of Folklore," pp. 11–12. See also Dundes, "Who Are the Folk?" p. 4.

25. See Brunvand, *The Vanishing Hitchhiker*, pp. 15–17.

26. Niditch, *Folklore and and the Hebrew Bible*, p. 3.

27. Ibid., p. 4. See also Ben-Amos, "Folklore in the Ancient Near East."

28. Ben-Amos, "Narrative Forms," pp. 26–28.

29. E.g., Jason, *Studies in Jewish Ethnopoetry*.

30. Yassif, *The Hebrew Folktale*, p. 9.

31. Foley, "Word-Power," p. 217.

32. Niditch, *Folklore and the Hebrew Bible*, p. 9.

33. For more a more comprehensive treatment of this literature, see Yassif, "Folklore Research"; Ben-Amos, "Jewish Folklore Studies" and "Jewish Folk Literature."

34. Ginzberg, "Jewish Folklore East and West," p. 63.

35. Patai, *On Jewish Folklore*, p. 38.

36. E.g., the learned collection of essays by Sperber, *Magic and Folklore in Rabbinic Literature*.

37. Fraenkel, *Techniques and Principles*, 1:280–85.

38. Ben-Amos, "Folklore in the Ancient Near East," pp. 818–19.

39. Ben-Amos, "Generic Distinctions in the Aggadah," p. 47.

40. Yassif, "The Cycle of Tales," pp. 103–13.

41. Mac Eoin, "Orality and Literacy," p. 182.

42. Yassif, "The Cycle of Tales," p. 107, on B. Sanhedrin 109a. Many rabbinic sources had minimal editing: Neusner, *The Development of a Legend*, pp. 187–88, argues that stories of Rabbi Yoḥanan had no comprehensive editing, and thus "we already have the Yoḥanan-tradition in, if not in oral, at least in pre-literary form."

43. Richard Kalmin pointed out in conversation a possible example of editing for paralellism in B. Ketubot 61a: "Abbuha bar Ihi and Minyamin bar Ihi: one fed [his waiter] some of every kind, and one fed one kind. Elijah conversed with one, but Elijah did not converse with the other. Two God fearing men . . . one fed [his waiter] first, and the other fed him afterwards. The one who fed him first, Elijah conversed with him; the one who fed him afterwards, Elijah did not converse with him."

44. See chapter 2, n. 68.

45. E.g., Yassif, *The Hebrew Folktale*; Jason, *Studies in Jewish Ethnopoetry*; Ben-Amos, "Narrative Forms."

46. See Saldarini, "Form Criticism"; for both summaries and examples of form criticism, see Bokser, "Talmudic Form Criticism"; and Hezser, *Form, Function, and Historical Significance*.

47. Yassif, "The Cycle of Tales"; Neusner, *Judaism and Story*; Hezser, *Form, Function, and Historical Significance*; Ben-Amos, "Narrative Forms."

48. Kalmin, *Sages, Stories*, p. 17.

49. Compare a completely non-narrative description of Elijah's activities, e.g., B. Berakhot 4b: "A beraita teaches, Michael [arrives] in one [flight], Gabriel in two, Elijah in four . . . " to B. Berakhot 29b in which the prophet comes to teach someone: "Elijah said to Rav Yehudah . . . 'Do not get boiling hot [angry] and you will not sin.'"

50. Hock and O'Neil, *The Chreia in Ancient Rhetoric*, p. 23; for possible influences (or similar theories of pedagogy) see Jaffee, "The Oral-Cultural Context."

51. Kalmin, *Sages, Stories,* p. 17.

52. Yassif, "The Cycle of Tales," pp. 111–13, and see my earlier discussion of Yassif in "Folklore Studies, Biblical Studies, and Rabbinics."

53. Saldarini, "Last Words and Deathbed Scenes." Saldarini notes similarities in the stories' introductory phrases, and many common motifs, pp. 42–43.

54. B. Ta'anit 22a, in which Elijah points out dubious-looking characters who are "sons of the world to come," and B. Nedarim 50a, which narrates the rise of Rabbi Akiva.

55. Neusner, *Judaism and Story*, pp. 46, 49–50. Neusner also discusses the more complex tales, "sage stories" on pp. 50–53, 59–60, but his findings for "The Fathers According to Rabbi Natan" do not transfer well to Elijah stories in the Talmud.

56. Hezser, *Form, Function, and Historical Significance*, p. 291.

57. Ibid., pp. 303–4.

.58. Ibid., pp. 312, 314.

59. Saldarini discusses it in "Form Criticism," pp. 269–72; Niditch as well notes that approaches such as his are comparable to form criticism, see *Folklore and the Hebrew Bible*, 20.

60. Ben-Amos, "Narrative Forms," pp. 59, 74.

61. Ibid., pp. 86, 87.

62. Ibid., pp. 89–90, 94–95.

63. Ibid., p. 98; Bava Meẓia 114a–b.

64. Ben-Amos, "Narrative Forms," p. 99. There are also stories featuring negative or neutral supernatural forces not relevant to rabbinic Elijah material.

65. Ben-Amos, "Narrative Forms," pp. 163, 165, 172–73.

66. B. Nedarim 50a, B. Ta'anit 22a, discussed in chapter 4.

67. B. Berakhot 29b, B. Yoma 19b–20a, B. Megillah 15b, B. Ḥagigah 9b, B. Yebamot 63a, B. Gittin 6b, B. Gittin 70a, B. Sanhedrin 97b.

68. B. Berakhot 3a, B. Shabbat 13a–b, B. Sanhedrin 98a.

69. B. Berakhot 58a, B. Shabbat 33b, B. Shabbat 109b, B. Ta'anit 22a, B. Ketubot 77b, B. Kiddushin 39b–40a, B. Bava Meẓia 83b–84a, B. Bava Meẓia 85b, B. Bava Meẓia 85b, B. Bava Meẓia 114a–b, B. Sanhedrin 108b–109a (the same story appears with variant wording in Ta'anit 21a), B. Avodah Zarah 17a–b, B. Avodah Zarah 18a–b.

70. B. Bava Meẓia 59a, B. Ḥagigah 15b.

71. Bateson, *Mind and Nature a Necessary Unity*, pp. 32–33, citing Alfred Korzybski, inventor of general semantics.

72. One of these stories is an exemplum, one is an extended pronouncement story, three are simple pronouncement stories, three are legends, while the remaining two have characteristics of both legend and pronouncement story.

2. ORAL-FORMULAIC STUDIES AND THE CULTURE OF THE BAVLI

1. Finnegan, "What Is Oral Literature Anyway?" p. 254.

2. Ibid., p. 256.

3. Dundes, "Who Are the Folk?" pp. 16–19. He notes, for example, that Franciscans tell Jesuit jokes.

4. Josephus, *Jewish War*, 6.292.

5. Kee, *Miracle in the Early Christian World*, pp. 180, 181.

6. Neusner, *A History of the Jews of Babylonia*, 3:126–28. Kalmin, *Sages, Stories,* p. 80, contrasts Babylonia and Palestine in this regard, stating that although Babylonian rabbis had institutional roles, the Palestinian sages may have had closer contact with ordinary people. Even so, Babylonian rabbis had an increasing influence on the faith and practice of ordinary Jews as the rabbinic period progressed.

7. For more on this story see Meir, "The Literary Context of the Sages' Aggadic Stories."

8. Yaakov Elman called my attention to B. Ḥagigah 4b–5a, in which the messenger of the angel of death kills the wrong person by mistake, a motif that may be popular and certainly contradicts dominant rabbinic teaching on death.

9. Y. Ketubot 35a.

10. Kelber, *The Oral and Written Gospel*, p. 26.

11. Thomas, *Literacy and Orality in Ancient Greece*, p. 27, writes that the most interesting questions about literacy in the ancient world are about the various ways writing may (or may not) be used and "the specific manifestations of oral communication . . . "

12. Yassif, *The Hebrew Folktale*, p. 89.

13. Ong, *Presence of the Word*, p. 55; Kelber, *The Oral and Written Gospel*. Speaking of classical Greece, Rosalind Thomas writes that most social "activities were carried out without writing . . . when writing was added to these it was usually in a supplementary and subordinate position." *Literacy and Orality in Ancient Greece*, p. 91.

14. Achtemeier, "*Omne Verbum Sonat*," pp. 11, 7, citing an example from Patristic tradition; see also Lieberman, *Hellenism in Jewish Palestine*, pp. 83–99, on the oral publication of the Mishnah; see also the appendix of *Helenism in Jewish Palestine*, "Jewish and Christian Codices," pp. 202–8.

15. Achtemeier, "*Omne Verbum Sonat*," pp. 12, 15, 17, 18.

16. Jaffee, "The Oral-Cultural Context of the Talmud Yerushalmi," pp. 66–67, 152. Rabbinic sources present (at least) two theologies of Oral Torah. In one, Oral Torah constitutes an ongoing line of memorized tradition since its revelation to Moses. In contrast, other sources "focus on Oral Torah as teaching . . . unfolded through intensive analysis, interrogation, and debate." Alexander, "The Orality of Rabbinic Writing," p. 39.

17. Lieberman, *Hellenism in Jewish Palestine*, p. 87; see also Jaffee, "How Much 'Orality' in Oral Torah?" and Strack and Stemberger, *Introduction to the Talmud and Midrash*, pp. 33–47.

18. E.g., B. Temurah 14b.

19. Alexander, "Orality of Rabbinic Writing," pp. 46–47, B. Temurah 14b (translation and italics Alexander's).

20. B. Temurah 14b (with a partial parallel in B. Gittin 60b).

21. This is roughly Lieberman's model for the Mishnah, in his *Hellenism in Jewish Palestine*, pp. 204–5, but the relationship and authority of written and oral versions of rabbinic traditions was probably even more complex. For more on this topic see Fraade, "Literary Composition," pp. 35–36.

22. Alexander, "Orality of Rabbinic Writing," pp. 52–54.

23. Fraade, "Literary Composition," pp. 37–38.

24. Goodblatt, *Rabbinic Instruction in Sasanian Babylonia,* see particularly part 3, "Talmudic Formulae Denoting Academic Activity," pp. 199–259.

25. Ibid., pp. 204, 205 for formulae with "*qammeh* Rabbi X."; p. 238 for formulas containing the root יתב, to sit before a particular master; p. 205 for reading the biblical text.

26. Elman, "Orality and the Redaction of the Babylonian Talmud," p. 65.

27. B. Avodah Zarah, 19a–b (translation Goodblatt, *Rabbinic Instruction in Sasanian Babylonia*).

28. Elman, *Authority and Tradition,* pp. 138–39.

29. Jaffee, *Torah in the Mouth*, pp. 124–25.

30. For an approach to the Targums informed by folklore study, see Shinan, *The Embroidered Targum.*

31. Goodblatt, *Rabbinic Instruction in Sasanian Babylonia*, p. 177; B. Ḥullin 15a, B. Sanhedrin 38b.

32. Ibid., pp. 179, 182, 185; see also p. 184, n. 26.

33. B. Shabbat 30b, B. Gittin 58a.

34. Ben-Amos, "Narrative Forms."

35. Henderson, "Didache and Orality."

36. Ibid., pp. 295, 305.

37. Henderson, "Didache and Orality," p. 305.

38. Foley, *The Singer of Tales in Performance*, pp. 46, 66.

39. Jaffee, "Rabbinic Authorship as a Collective Enterprise," pp. 34–35.

40. Ben-Amos, "Narrative Forms," p. 3.

41. Gerhardsson, *Memory and Manuscript.*

42. Ibid., p. 105, citing B. Ta'anit 7b–8a.

43. Gerhardsson, *Memory and Manuscript*, pp. 96, 97–98.

44. See, e.g., Elman, *Authority and Tradition*, p. 85, "Other types of variants [among the Toseftan *beraitot* in the Bavli] are recasting of the material into different formularies, syntactic changes of various sorts, the transposition of terms and clauses," and so on. "All these are typical of texts transmitted orally . . and are less likely to have been the product of scribal error."

45. Bokser, "Talmudic Form Criticism," pp. 50–52.

46. Vansina, *Oral Tradition as History*, pp. 16, 19–20, 48–51.

47. E.g., B. Ḥagigah 9b, "He who repeats his chapter one hundred times is not to be compared to him who repeats his chapter one hundred and one times." See also B. Eruvin 53b–54b.

48. Smith, "A Comparison," pp. 172–74.

49. B. Sukkah, 28a.

50. Strack and Stemberger, *Introduction to the Talmud and Midrash*, p. 44. Goodblatt agrees that aggadic texts are less exactly transmitted, considering anecdotes an uncertain source of historical data, much less of reliable attribution, *Rabbinic Instruction in Sasanian Babylonia*, p. 6. The distinction between legal and nonlegal passages even carries forward into rabbinic manuscript texts. Collections of variant readings reveal that halakhic passages have fewer and small variations between manuscripts than nonlegal passages, particularly longer narratives.

51. Kalmin, *Sages, Stories,* p. 39.

52. Y. Kilayim 32b, Y. Ketubot 35a, B. Bava Meẓia 85a.

53. For an excellent summary of the history of oral-formulaic studies and its bearing on theories of rabbinic oral transmission see Alexander, *Transmitting Mishnah*, pp. 1–30.

54. Foley, *The Singer of Tales in Performance*, p. 73–79.

55. Ibid., p. 57.

56. Many of these sets fall into Yassif's category of "genre," discussed in chapter 1.

57. Foley, "Word-Power," pp. 275–80; see also Foley, *The Singer of Tales in Performance*, chapter 1.

58. Niditch, *Folklore and the Hebrew Bible*, p. 5.

59. Renoir, "Oral-Formulaic Context," pp. 422–24; Foley, *The Singer of Tales in Performance*, pp. 53–58.

60. Bradbury, "Traditional Referentiality," p.138.

61. E.g., Roberts, "The Middle Welsh Prose Narratives," p. 216; Davies, "Storytelling in Medieval Wales," p. 238. Rubenstein, *Talmudic Stories*, p. 243, also notes the Bavli's stories prefer "interior monologue and dialogue to narration" in addition to other forms of patterned repetition characteristic of "a predominantly oral culture."

62. This observation about dialogue and oral performance is made in both the classic work of Olrick, *Principles for Oral Narrative Research*, pp. 3, 42–43, and in a late twentieth-century work on urban legends, Brunvand's *The Vanishing Hitchhiker*, pp. 29, 34, 35, 37.

63. Propp, *Morphology of the Folktale*, pp. 25–65.

64. Elman, *Authority and Tradition*, p. 83.

65. Tedlock, "On the Translation of Style," pp. 119–120. This is even more true for non-narrative material; see Tannen, "Oral and Literate Strategies," pp. 7–10.

66. Renoir, "Oral-Formulaic Context," pp. 423–24.

67. See, e.g., Boyarin, *Carnal Israel*, pp. 10–14.

68. Fischel, "Story and History," pp. 67–73.

69. Hasan-Rokem, *Tales of the Neighborhood,* pp. 48–51.

70. As when Origin's heavenly academy is portrayed in ways very similar to the Rabbis': see Fischel, "Story and History," p. 465; for cross-cultural comparison as a tool see Niditch, *Folklore and the Hebrew Bible,* p. 11.

71. B. Berakhot 3a.

72. Hasan-Rokem, *Tales of the Neighborhood,* 1.

73. Olrick, *Principles for Oral Narrative Research*, p. 10, cf. Ginzberg, "Jewish Folklore East and West," pp. 61–73.

74. Olrick, *Principles for Oral Narrative Research*, p. 11. Note that the elite folklore of one time may influence the popular folkore of a later era. As we will discuss later, Elijah legends seem to have traveled this route.

75. Kelber, *The Oral and Written Gospel*, p. 24.

76. Jason, "Concerning the 'Historical,'" pp. 143–44.

77. Vansina, *Oral Tradition as Tradition*, p. 7.

78. Boyarin, *Carnal Israel,* pp. 12–13.

79. See also Kalmin, *Sages, Stories,* chapter 1, for his consideration of the ideological basis for stories on the relations between various Sages.

3. ELIJAH IN RABBINIC CULTURE AND THE WIDER CULTURE OF LATE ANTIQUITY

1. Y. Berakhot 12 or 13c, Y. Terumot 40d, Y. Terumot 46b, and Y. Kilayim 32b (parallel Y. Ketubot 35a).

2. The Pesikta de Rav Kahana's possible dates range from 450–700, see Strack and Stemberger, *Introduction to the Talmud and Midrash*, p. 321. Genesis Rabbah also

has three Elijah legends. Two of them are also found in the Yerushalmi, but the third depicts Elijah appearing in a dream to a Roman emperor (83.4, p. 1000). Leviticus Rabbah has only one reference to Elijah in the rabbinic present: he appears with the King Messiah in the angelic role of recording people's good deeds in heaven (34.8, pp. 590–91).

3. Pesikta de Rav Kahana 11.15, pp. 190–91, 11.22, pp. 196–97, 18.5, pp. 296–98.

4. Perhaps the Bavli unifies two strands of tradition about Elijah, or perhaps in Babylonia these strands were not as separate as in the land of Israel, where the Yerushalmi and PRK were redacted.

5. In B. Me'ilah 17b a demon even helps Rabbi Shimon ben Yoḥai get the better of the authorities in Rome by possessing the emperor's daughter and leaving her at the rabbi's command.

6. Among thirty-five passages, most of those in which "angel" (מלאך) and "the ministering angels" (מלאכי השרת) and individual names (Michael, etc) appear in the Bavli, twenty-five are midrashic and only ten take place in the rabbinic present.

7. B. Megillah 15a, and cf. 10b, 12b (two instances), 16a (four instances), and 16b; see also B. Sotah, 12b, 13b on angels helping Moses as a baby.

8. B. Shabbat 119b.

9. See also B. Menaḥot 41 for impersonal angelic reward and punishment. B. Bava Batra 11a is a partial exception in which angels advocate before God for a righteous man. A few such stories, where angels collectively speak to God, show them well-disposed to humanity in the rabbinic present, but only verbally in heaven, not in action on earth.

10. These include B. Shabbat 119b, B. Ta'anit 11a, in which angels condemn one who has separated himself from the community "When Israel is in trouble," and B. Ketubot 104a, in which angels herald the souls of the righteous and condemn the wicked as they enter into reward or punishment. See also Ta'anit 11,with a parallel on Ḥagigah 16a, and B. Shabbat 32a.

11. Most of the Bavli's descriptions of angelic activities in the rabbinic present are general and non-narrative, compared to three general references and thirty-eight stories about Elijah, including unique sayings to individuals.

12. B. Berakhot 4b.

13. B. Kiddushin 70a.

14. B. Bava Meẓia 114a–b.

15. For Elijah as Pinḥas see Ginzberg, *Legends of the Jews*, 6:316–17.

16. B. Bava Kamma 60b; the context is a number of traditions about the angel of death.

17. B. Bava Meẓia 85b. B. Yoma 77a has the Bavli's sole story of an *angel*'s disobedience for the sake of Israel in which an angel identified with Gabriel does not follow God's

commands to the letter, refraining from entirely destroying people of Jerusalem, and is punished with burning lashes. The story of the angel seems created to solve a difficulty in the biblical text, and the angel merely deviates from God's command; Elijah has his own plan, or supports a human plan, to force the coming of the Messiah.

18.   Diamond, "Wrestling the Angel of Death," pp. 87–89, 80.

19.   Bokser, "The Wall Separating God and Israel," pp. 350, 358–59. I refer to the second reading proposed by Bokser of a passage in B. Berakhot 32b, which argues that in context the passage "actually reflects a distancing from the trauma of the Temple's destruction."

20.   B. Berakhot 55a, quoting Prov. 13:12. B. Ta'anit 23b, 25a.

21.   See, e.g., B. Berakhot 5b, for ambivalence about healing: two stories about healing accompany a long discussion of illness as either necessary punishment or as the "chastisements of love." For ambivalence about healers, note B. Berakhot 34b: Ḥanina ben Dosa heals Rabbi Yoḥanan ben Zakkai's son where his own father cannot, and the rabbi says this is because "he resembles a slave before the King, and I resemble a prince before the King."

22.   E.g. Ta'anit 24a–24b.

23.   B. Ta'anit 18b; Ben-Amos, "Narrative Forms," p. 110.

24.   B. Ketubot 8b, B. Shabbat 33a.

25.   R. Eleazar ben Perata, B. Sanhedrin 113a–b; Rabbi Akiva, B. Berakhot 61b.

26.   E.g., Bava Meẓia 85b, B. Ta'anit 23b.

27.   B. Ta'anit 21a.

28.   B. Megillah 29a.

29.   Not including the story on B. Berakhot 6b in which a bedouin warrior, in the Vilna edition Elijah in disguise, kills someone who was praying with his back to a synagogue, because no MS has Elijah. See chapter 1, n. 5.

30.   B. Berakhot 58a. In the Vilna edition, the protagonist of the story is titled "Rav," but in the MSS he is "Rabbi" Shila and the Gentiles are specifically Romans.

31.   For a Sage cursing in defense of God's honor see e.g., B. Ta'anit 24a, where Rabbi Yossi of Yokerit causes the death of his son and his daughter, and B. Bava Batra 75a; for causing harm through wounded feelings, see, e.g., B. Bava Meẓia 59b, and the discussion later in this chapter. See also Kalmin, Sages, Stories, pp. 36–37.

32.   B. Shabbat 67a.

33.   Schaefer, The Hidden and Manifest God, pp. 51–53.

34.   Morgan, Sepher Ha-Raẓim, pp. 7, 94–95.

35.   B. Avodah Zarah 41b.

36.   Morgan, Sepher Ha-Raẓim, 36–39.

37. B. Ḥagigah, 13a; the biblical referent is Ezekiel 1:4. Scholars differ on whether the rabbinic community discouraged mystical practice for noninitiates or for everyone. See Peter Schaefer's discussion in the introduction to *The Hidden and Manifest God*, pp. 2–5. Cf. Scholem, *Jewish Gnosticism, Merkabah Mysticism, and Talmudic Tradition*, pp. 9–13, 56–59; and Gruenwald, *Apocalyptic and Merkavah Mysticism*, pp. 73–98. Gruenwald sees the Amoraim as open to Merkavah mysticism; the other two, however, are more inclined to reserve judgment.

38. B. Shabbat 13a–b and B. Bava Batra 7b.

39. There are a few instances of the overheard bat kol that do not use the actual term, e.g. Y. Shabbat 8c; see Urbach, *The Sages*, p. 579. See also Lieberman, *Hellenism in Jewish Palestine*, pp. 194–99, for the bat kol being at times consulted much as an oracle, as in B. Megillah 32a.

40. Urbach, *The Sages,* pp 579, and n. 32.

41. B. Sotah 33a, stating that a bat kol in Aramaic refutes the contention that the ministering angels do not understand Aramaic.

42. One of the few exceptions is the bat kol in the ruined Temple in Jerusalem in B. Berakhot 3a, expressing God's regret at having destroyed it. Although this is a message for the community at large, it does not come to any particular individual, but rather can be heard by anyone who goes to the right place and listens in the right way.

43. B. Berakhot 12b.

44. B. Berakhot 61b.

45. See B. Ta'anit 29a, in which a Roman officer saves Rabban Gamaliel by committing suicide, thus abrogating the decree against the patriarch, and, for more sinners and martyrs, see B. Ketubot 103a and 104a, B. Gittin 57b, B. Bava Meẓia 86a, B. Avodah Zarah 10b and 18a.

46. One story in B. Sanhedrin 104b has the Great Assembly of Second Temple times trying to list King Solomon among those who have no part in the world to come because of his support of his wives' idolatry. After they ignore one bat kol, a second, unambiguous bat kol tells them humans cannot reject anyone whom God has chosen for eternal life.

47. Elijah in B. Ta'anit 22a. Others in B. Berakhot 4b and 9b, B. Shabbat 153a, B. Bava Batra 10b, B. Sanhedrin 88b. B. Berakhot 9b reads, "Rabbi Yoḥanan said, 'Who is a son of the world to come? Whoever joins the Ge'ulah prayer to the evening Tefillah.'"

48. B. Sanhedrin 98a; this story is discussed in detail in the third section of chapter 4.

49. See B. Berakhot 12b, in which a bat kol goes out from Mount Horeb about Rabbi Ḥanina; B. Sotah 48b, where there are traditions about two Tannaim, Hillel the Elder

and Shemuel the Younger, in which a bat kol says each deserves that the Shekhinah should rest on him, but his generation is not worthy.

50. B. Eruvin 13b.

51. Elijah also behaves like a bat kol in reporting God's words to Rav Yehudah in B. Ta'anit 24b. Note that the prophet's message from God affirms the miracle-working power of Rav Yehudah, even while telling him to use it with care.

52. Cf. the second story on Bava Meẓia 85b, where Elijah provides information on how to force the coming of the Messiah and is punished for doing so.

53. B. Ta'anit 24b, in which the appearance of angels bringing grain portends the end of a famine.

54. E.g., B. Megillah 15b, in which Rabbah b. Abbuha asks Elijah about Esther's motives; B. Gittin 6b, in which Rabbi Aviatar Elijah asks about the concubine in Gibeah; B. Bava Meẓia 59b, in which Elijah tells R. Natan "God was laughing" during the discussion of the oven of Akhnai.

55. Bokser, "Wonder-Working and the Rabbinic Tradition," pp. 84–85. This line of argument from the redaction dates of various sources is convincing, particularly when applied to longer aggadic narratives as opposed to halakhic passages, as discussed in chapter 2. Most of the Elijah stories are in Aramaic and very few are introduced with *tanya*. Both these factors seem to suggest post-tannaitic composition or revision in longer narratives.

56. Ibid.; see also Green, "Palestinian Holy Men," pp. 647–49; for the non-Jewish cultural context, see, e.g., Brown, *Society and the Holy in Late Antiquity*, pp. 142–52.

57. Brown, *The Cult of the Saints*, p. 55.

58. Amat, *Songes et visions*, p. 295.

59. Cohn, "Sainthood on the Periphery," p. 108.

60. Urbach, *The Sages*, p. 107.

61. The word כישוף, "magic" or "sorcery," was not used of rabbinic magic, because *kishuf* is by definition pejorative.

62. B. Ta'anit 20b–21a. The rabbis are the Amora Adda bar Ahavah and the Tanna Naḥum Ish Gamzu.

63. B. Berakhot 5b, with two close parallels on the same page.

64. B. Bava Kama 73b. In context, the two customarily different greetings are proposed as different short measures of time (no second hands in the ancient world!).

65. This form comes up more than fifteen times in short stories and halakhic passages in the Bavli, introduced by "אשכחיה, ל- אמר ליה," He found someone, he said to him/asked him."

66. B. Beẓah 25b, B. Bava Batra 87a, B. Niddah 48a, B. Ḥullin 57b, 110a, 111a, and 111b.

67. B. Yebamot 63a.

68. B. Berakhot 29b.

69. B. Bava Meẓia 114a. This story also has Elijah conveying Rabbah bar Abbuha to Paradise; it will be discussed in more detail in the next chapter.

70. Cf. how, in Y. Terumot 1:6, 40d, Elijah informs a "certain pious man" why it is not pleasing to God to recite the Shema while naked.

71. However, in a text on a Babylonian magic bowl, Elijah parallels a rabbinic holy man/ magician in the Bavli. In B. Pesaḥim 112b the holy man Ḥanina ben Dosa and the later Rabbi Abaye encounter Igrat, queen of demons, and forbid her to enter settled areas. On the magic bowl, Elijah encounters Lilith and forbids her to trouble the household under his protection. See Neusner, *History of the Jews of Babylonia*, 5:212, 226.

72. Ibid., 4:283, 5:163, 159.

73. Ibid., 5:163. Jaffee, "A Rabbinic Ontology," p. 530. For the Christians of the time, see Brown, "The Saint as Exemplar," p. 4.

74. B. Ḥagigah, 15a.

75. Brown, *The Cult of the Saints*, pp. 63, 59.

76. Ginzberg, "Jewish Folklore East and West," p. 68, n. 43, notes more generally that there are often parallels between the stories of Christian saints and Jewish holy men.

77. B. Berakhot 27b. This tradition seeks to prevent something disciples really did, because we find stories of rabbis who did contradict their masters in court, such as Rav Asi in B. Bava Meẓia 96b–97a; see Rubenstein, "Social and Institutional Settings," pp. 69–70.

78. B. Sanhedrin 110a.

79. Kalmin, *Sages, Stories*, pp. 205, 206–7.

80. See Neusner, *History of the Jews of Babylonia*, 5:164.

81. The phrase that literally translates "his heart became sick," חלש לביה, refers to physical weakness. A story on B. Ta'anit 24b shows the difference: "Rav Papa ordained a fast, but no rain came; his heart became weak (חלש ליביה) and he swallowed a plate of cracked grain and prayed, and no rain came. Rav Naḥman bar Ushpazarti said to him, 'Sir, if you swallow another plate of cracked grain, rain will come.' He was ashamed and heartsick (איכסיף וחלש דעתיה) [both before God and at the insult], and rain came."

82. The six are B. Shabbat 51a, B. Ta'anit 9a, B. Bava Kama 117a, B. Bava Meẓia 84a, B. Bava Batra 9b, and B. Sanhedrin 93b, a midrash that portrays Saul as a teacher jealous of his protégé David's excellence.

83. B. Bava Meẓia 84a, Bava Batra 22a.

84. B. Bava Meẓia 59b and Ḥagigah 15b; we will return to these stories in the next chapter.

85. Kalmin, *Sages, Stories,* pp. 28–34; and note also Rava's acrimonious interactions with several contemporary rabbis, reviewed by Kalmin, *Sages, Stories,* pp. 41–42.

86. Ibid., p. 145.

87. See B. Berakhot 45b and Neusner's comments in *History of the Jews of Babylonia,* 5:156–57, about three rabbis of the exactly the same age and rank who said grace separately because they could not figure out who should have the honor of leading.

88. B. Gittin 6b.

89. B. Eruvin 13b.

90. See Peli, "Elijah in the Beit Midrash of the Sages," p. 151.

91. Hedner-Zetterholm, "Elijah's Different Roles," p. 180–82.

92. Price, "Introduction," p. xxvi.

93. Brown, *Society and the Holy,* pp. 124–25 on exorcism, pp. 143 and 147 on healing, p. 146 on "safe conduct."

94. B. Ta'anit 21b.

95. Pesikta Rabbati (a composite collection of sermons containing material from the fourth to ninth centuries), piska 22.5, fol. 111b.

96. Wiener, *The Prophet Elijah,* pp. 179, 177.

97. Segal, *Elijah,* p. 15.

98. Ben-Amos, "Narrative Forms," p. 107, n. 64.

99. See also the comparative essays collected by Fischel in *Essays in Greco-Roman and Related Talmudic Literature.*

100. Brown, *Society and the Holy,* p. 179.

101. Brown, *The Cult of the Saints,* p. 52.

102. Boyarin, "Hellenism in Jewish Babylonia," pp. 336, 344–47.

103. Lieberman, *Greek in Jewish Palestine,* p. 119.

104. Sperber, "Some Rabbinic Themes in Magical Papyri," p. 93. Sperber himself is building on the observations of Scholem, in *Jewish Gnosticism,* and Goodenough, who argues that the way in which pagan and Jewish names are used almost interchangeably in magical texts shows that Jews and pagans were deeply influenced by one another, *Jewish Symbols in the Greco-Roman Period,* 2:155–56.

105. Morgan, *Sepher Ha-Razim,* p. 10.

106. B. Yebamot 121b, Y. Demai 22a.

107. Theodoret of Cyrrhus, *History of the Monks of Syria,* p. 32.

108. Cyril of Scythopolis, *Lives of the Monks of Palestine,* p. 67.

109. Ibid., pp. xiii, xxxiii.

110. B. Bava Kama, 117a, B. Bava Meẓia 84a and 85a (with the bat kol).

111. Schwartz, *Imperialism and Jewish Society,* pp. 142, 176.

112. Miller, "Roman Imperialism," pp. 340–50.

113. Schwartz, *Imperialism and Jewish Society,* 175.

114. See Hasan-Rokem, *Tales of the Neighborhood,* p. 11, who, without claiming that Jews became semipagan, writes, "I hope to demonstrate that the neighboring pagan, Jewish, and Christian dwellers in the Galilee in Late Antiquity shared, rather than influenced, each other's theological and cultural worlds."

115. B. Sanhedrin 109a.

116. Elman, "Middle Persian Culture and the Babylonian Sages," p. 180.

117. Stein, "The Influence of Symposia Literature." Baruch Bokser, taking a different tack, discusses how the authors of the Mishnah systematically distinguished between the comparable rituals of the Seder and the symposium, but nevertheless, like Stein, describes the development of the Seder within the social context of the Greco-Roman formal banquet: *The Origins of the Passover Seder,* pp. 63–66.

118. Patai, *On Jewish Folklore,* p. 43.

119. MacMullen, *Paganism in the Roman Empire,* p. 171, n. 11.

120. See B. Avodah Zarah 49b–51a, B. Berakhot 57b, B. Sanhedrin 64a. See also the discussion on the merkolis in Lieberman, "Palestine in the Third and Fourth Centuries," pp. 53–54.

121. Apollodorus, *The Library,* book 3, chapter 10.2, 2:4–11.

122. Branham, *Unruly Eloquence,* p. 150.

123. Bar-Oz, "An Inscribed Astragalus," p. 215.

124. Raingeard, *Hermes psychagogue,* pp. 272–274.

125. Oppenheimer, *Babylonia Judaica,* p. 313.

126. Lieberman, "Palestine in the Third and Fourth Centuries," pp. 53–54.

127. M. Sanhedrin 7,6.

128. B. Sanhedrin 66b, B. Avodah Zarah 51a.

129. Oppenheimer, *Babylonia Judaica,* pp. 113–14.

130. Montgomery, *Aramaic Incantation Texts from Nippur,* pp. 146–47; cf. Naveh and Shaked, *Amulets and Magic Bowls,* p. 132, n. 8.

131. Hermes averted a plague from a city by carrying a ram around its walls; Morgan, *Sepher Ha-Razim,* p. 18, n. 62 (my citation combines the text and the note on the same page).

132. B. Yebamot 121b.

133. This view was prevalent in the more Hellenized philosophical or alchemical Hermetica, whereas some of the more Egyptian texts see Hermes as a god, and often even a creator god, although it gets more complicated than that. See Fowden, *The Egyptian Hermes,* pp. 25–28.

134. VanderKam, *Enoch and the Growth of an Apocalyptic Tradition*, p. 189. One might also compare it to the way that the Church over the centuries, asserting Jesus's superior fulfillment of the highest current model of human virtue, has found in him echoes of a warrior king, a charismatic teacher, and sometimes a compassionate liberal or heroic revolutionary.

135. Mussies, "The Interpretatio Judaica of Thot-Hermes," pp. 93, 118.

136. Y. Berakhot 5.2, 9b. In this midrash, Elijah has "stolen" the rain and the dew by making a prophecy in the form of an oath to Ahab in 1 Kings 17:2, "As the LORD lives, the God of Israel whom I serve, there shall be no rain or dew, except at my bidding" (JPS).

137. B. Megillah 15b, Ḥagigah 15b, Gittin 6b; Bava Meẓia 59b.

138. B. Ta'anit 24b, Rav Yehudah takes off one shoe (beginning a ritual act in praying for rain), and rain begins to fall. Elijah arrives and says, "The Holy One blessed be He says, 'If you take off the other shoe I will destroy the world.'"

139. B. Bava Meẓia, 114a–b.

140. Raingeard, *Hermes psychagogue*, p. 548.

141. B. Berakhot 3a, B. Berakhot 29b.

142. *Tanna Devei Eliahu;* and see Ben-Amos, "Jewish Folk Literature," pp. 235–36.

143. B. Shabbat 13a–b.

144. B. Yebamot 121b.

145. B. Bava Meẓia 85b; B. Sanhedrin 98a; MS readings for this passage vary significantly, as discussed in chapter 4.

146. B. Bava Kama 60b.

147. Raingeard, *Hermes psychagogue*, pp. 359–60.

148. Libanius, *Autobiography*, p. 129, 1:195.

149. See note on this story in the appendix. The early MSS, unusually, are divided on Elijah's presence in the story, but here I assume it.

150. B. Ta'anit 21a, with a very close parallel (see appendix for wording) in B. Sanhedrin 108b–9a.

151. Propp, *Morphology of the Folktale*, pp. 25–53.

152. See Genesis Rabbah, 83.5, p. 1000.

4. THE THREE GENERIC GROUPS OF ELIJAH STORIES

1. Yassif, "The Cycle of Tales," pp. 111–13.

2. Foley, "Word-Power," pp. 275–301.

3. See Friedman, "On the Development of Variant Readings."

4. Jaffee, "A Rabbinic Ontology," p. 541.

5. B. Pesaḥim 3b; see also B. Yoma 9b, which says Reish Lakish could not have "conversed" with an undistinguished rabbi because he did not converse with the much more distinguished Rabbi Eleazar.

6. B. Makkot 11a; the story is brought to illustrate a statement that the high priests of old were culpable because they should have prayed for the people but did not.

7. B. Sanhedrin 98a; discussed in this chapter, B. Ketubot 77b, in which Elijah heralds Rabbi Joshua in heaven. Pesikta de Rav Kahana 11.15 (p. 190–91), 18.5 (pp. 296–98).

8. Y. Terumot 46b; "And is this the law of the truly devout?" is וזו משנת חסידים.

9. Bereshit Rabbah 94.9 has a version of a phrase found in the Bavli: אליהו בהדי הוון קא משתעי, "Elijah was accustomed to converse with him."

10. Daube, *Appeasement or Resistance*, pp. 80–83.

11. Ibid., pp. 81–84.

12. "Accustomed to come" is רגיל דאתי; the stories discussed above use an *itpe'il* of ש ע י, "converse," such as משתעי בהדיה or אישתעי בהדיה. MSS Munich, Vatican 113, Vatican 130, and Leningrad of this story all lack any form of ש ע י.

13. See chapter 1, n. 3, this volume.

14. B. Sanhedrin 113a–b; the normal phrase הוה רגיל למיתי גביה, "was accustomed to come," is absent from MSS Florence, Karlesruehe, and Munich 95. In fact, the exact phrase here, רגיל למיתי, does not appear anywhere in any MS in the Lieberman Institute manuscript concordance. It may well be that the Vilna text's version inserted this phrase to bring the story into the usual form for our generic group, juxtaposing Elijah's presence and absence.

15. Yaakov Elman suggested to me that the halakhic context of the oven of Akhnai story makes it an inappropriate analogy to this story of midrashic self-assertion. I make this leap from midrashic to halakhic story because the Bavli itself uses Elijah to connect midrashic and halakhic realms. In Gittin 6b Elijah says contradictory aggadic midrashim "are both the words of the Living God," the phrase of the famous bat kol resolving the legal dispute between Beit Shammai and Beit Hillel.

16. Nonhuman forms are found in Kiddushin 29b, where a demon appears as a snake with seven heads, and in Bava Meẓia 85b, where Elijah appears as a bear. The Aramaic *itpe'il* forms *idmei*, "he appeared," and *idmu*, "they appeared" (אידמי, or אדמי/ו), in the Bavli, and the Hebrew *bidemut* (בדמות), "in the form of," in the Yerushalmi, are both highly specialized. Each expression is the only one used by the text for the appearance of a supernatural being in "disguise." Other documents do not have such

linguistic specialization, suggesting a stronger oral background for the Talmuds than for midrashic literature. The specialized function of *idmei* and *bidemut* in the two Talmuds is further underlined by the distinctly different use of two other *itpe'il* verbs, both meaning "he was seen"—*ithazi* (אתחזי) in the Bavli and *ithami* (אתחמי) in the Yerushalmi. Both these terms refer to people (alive or dead) appearing in dreams as well as to supernatural beings "being seen," but not in disguise, e.g., Y. Ta'anit 64b, a living person in a dream; B. Shabbat 152b, a dead person in a dream; and B. Ketubot 77b, the angel of death.

17. All three are on B. Kiddushin 81a.

18. B. Megillah 16a.

19. B. Kiddushin 29b.

20. B. Gittin 66a, in a discussion of whether it is permitted to write a divorce document for a man thrown into a pit, who therefore cannot be seen clearly, states as a matter of fact that demons can appear like men and thus we must take care to see the man's shadow.

21. B. Mo'ed Katan 28b.

22. B. Avodah Zarah 17b, B. Ta'anit 21a and B. Sanhedrin 108b–9a, B. Berakhot 58a.

23. B. Shabbat 109b. The story follows a close parallel: "Rav Shimi bar Ashi saw a man who swallowed a snake and appeared to him [*idmei lei*] as a horseman, made him eat a gourd with salt," etc. The use of *idmei* with Rav Shimi may have come from a version of the story with Elijah, since the word *idmei* is not otherwise used with living men. Alternately, the Rav Shimi version may have been the original, as Elijah almost always rescues people from human, not natural, dangers. However, since all MSS contain both versions, it is impossible to know whether either version is the original and it's possible that the two stories of Elijah and Rav Shimi were revised to increase their parallelism, like the stories of those whom Elijah visited because of their consideration for those who served their meals.

24. Ben-Amos, "Narrative Forms," pp. 89, 98.

25. In the Vilna text, but not in the MSS, it is a "fiery" bear.

26. Foley, "Word-Power," pp. 275–301.

27. The Bavli's one exception is B. Shabbat 109b in which Elijah rescues the rabbi who swallows a snake, certainly a natural crisis, but a problem effecting only one individual. Elijah occasionally rescues from natural disaster in other rabbinic texts: see, e.g., Pesikta de-Rav Kahana, piska 18, 5.

28. Note B. Rosh Hashanah 18a and its treatment in Elman, "Righteousness as Its Own Reward," p. 65.

29. For a link between the Tannaitic traditions about the value of suffering and the mar-tyrdom story told about Rabbi Akiva in the Bavli, see Aderet, *From Destruction to Restoration,* pp. 147–49.

30. Ben-Amos, "Narrative Forms," pp. 109, 111.

31. B. Berakhot 5b; see Kraemer, *Responses to Suffering,* pp. 194–97.

32. Elman "Righteousness as Its Own Reward," 45; Kraemer, *Responses to Suffering,* p. 170.

33. Blidstein, "Rabbis, Romans and Martyrdom," p. 57.

34. Lieberman, "Roman Legal Institutions," pp. 78–79.

35. Blidstein, "Rabbis, Romans and Martyrdom," holds that Rabbi Eleazar really was "a fighter for Jewish independence." This reading supplies a good explanation for the difference between Rabbi Eleazar and Rabbi Ḥanina: the former can lie in order to continue his fight against Rome, but the latter must die in order uphold his nonviolent activism, his fearless witness to Torah. I am skeptical, however, in the context of rab-binic belief that a military profession is irreconcilable with a rabbinic vocation. See B. Bava Meẓia 84a in which Reish Lakish becomes too weak to pick up his armor and weapons after merely resolving to study Torah.

36. A medieval commentator, the Maharsha, here cites B. Sanhedrin 14a: after the Temple was destroyed "the wicked government [Rome] decreed that whoever performed ordi-nation should be killed and whoever received ordination should be killed."

37. See Mishnah Eduyot 1:3, with the commentary of the Bartenura.

38. Richard Kalmin, personal communication.

39. See B. Shabbat 116a.

40. Even if this story was composed in a later Christian empire in which gladitorial com-bat had been ended, there were still violent shows in which men fought wild animals as well as the popular and dangerous chariot races.

41. A possible alternate translation of these lines in the Vilna text has Elijah say "'in this too a miracle will occur for him.' And [then] *that man showed his wickedness*; he did not listen to him and rose to speak to them." MS JTSA unambiguously reads: "'a miracle will occur for him.' That man showed his wickedness; he didn't listen to him [Elijah] and rose to speak to them." The reading reflecting JTSA is smoother in translation and just as logical; "that man," sometimes used in second person address, is more often simple third person. The first reading, however, also possible in other MSS, is more in line with the Bavli's narrative, which rarely states *why* someone does something. It is also funny to imagine Elijah using the third person in order to be polite to the accusing Roman.

42.   B. Berakhot 24a, B. Pesaḥim 62b.

43.   B. Sanhedrin 95a, B. Gittin 68b.

44.   The Bavli uses *four hundred* forty-eight times altogether as a generic large number
      (like *a million* in English today).

45.   See, e.g., the discussion of the classical form of comedy in Levin's "General Introduc-
      tion," pp. 22–23.

46.   Peli, "Elijah in the Beit Midrash of the Sages," p. 143.

47.   There are, for example, forty-seven instances of אשכחיה לרבי/לרב, in which a rabbi
      "meets Rabbi/Rav" So-and-so. In contrast, angels are never encountered with any
      verb of the root שכח, "find," and in the Bavli, they rarely answer questions.

48.   B. Beiẓah 25b, B. Bava Batra 87a, B. Niddah 48a, B. Ḥullin 57b, 110a, 111a, and
      111b.

49.   E.g., B. Ḥagigah 15b, Raba bar Shila meets Elijah and asks him what God is doing,
      and B. Bava Meẓia 59b, R. Natan meets Elijah and asks how what God was doing
      when the Rabbis overrode a bat kol on the subject of the oven of Akhnai.

50.   B. Bava Batra 58a.

51.   See Genesis Rabbah 59, 8, p. 636, for how the "elder of his household," identified
      with Eliezer, was a reflection and counterpart to Abraham and administrator of all
      that was his and thus much more than an ordinary slave; yet he is still called "slave"
      (עבד) and hence is not Jewish. For Eliezer as trickster see Yassif, "The Cycle of Tales,"
      107.

52.   While the formula הוה שכיח גביה\ב- superficially resembles the phrases הוה רגיל or
      משתעי בהדיה ("was accustomed to visit" or accustomed "to converse with") in the sto-
      ries in the second generic group in which Elijah stays away, there is no overlap in their
      use. Wherever שכיח גביה or שכיח ב- are found Elijah answers a question, and wherever
      הוה רגיל or משתעי בהדיה occurs Elijah refuses to visit someone. The adjective שכיח, the
      Aramaic equivalent of the Hebrew מצוי, "often found," or "common," is itself com-
      mon, but the precise formula הוה שכיח, "was often/usually found," appears only fifteen
      times in the Bavli, describing someone often found in a particular place or with a
      particular person.

53.   Elijah appears in B. Ta'anit 22a, with Rabbi Beroka, and twice on B. Bava Meẓia 85b;
      the angel of death on B. Ḥagigah 4b.

54.   Cf. however, Segal's view that Elijah's answer "implies that the Rabbis ascribed
      to Esther remarkable intellectual or—more likely—prophetic gifts that enabled her
      to think of all the considerations and possibilities." Segal, *The Babylonian Esther
      Midrash*, 3:34–35. Segal's view, however, does not take into account the parallel

story, discussed later in this chapter, in which Elijah answers a comparable midrashic question in much the same way as here.

55. The Levite's objection to finding a hair in "that place" recalls a passage in B. Sanhedrin 21a saying female pubic hair is dangerous and that Israelite women customarily removed it.

56. B. Eruvin 13b.

57. Peli, ""Elijah in the Beit Midrash of the Sages," p. 51.

58. Rubenstein, *Talmudic Stories*, p. 42. For more on this story and a summary of secondary sources on it, see Izhak Englard, "Majority Decision vs. Individual Truth: The Interpretations of the 'Oven of Achnai' Aggadah," *Tradition* 15 (Spring-Summer 1975): 137–52; and all of chapter 2 in Rubenstein's *Talmudic Stories*.

59. Literally, "I am lighter (קלני, *kalani*) than my head, lighter than my arm." It is a punning midrash on Deut. 21:23, which reads, "For one who is hanged [after execution] is cursed קללת (*kilelat*) of God.

60. See Peli, "Elijah in the Beit Midrash of the Sages," pp. 156–57.

61. B. Ketubot 77b.

62. All three early manuscripts, MSS Florence, Munich, and Karlsrühe, say that the Messiah is found אפיתחא דרומי "at the gate of Rome," a reading Rabbinovicz, in *Dikdukei Soferim*, 10:292, says was eliminated by censorship. The Vilna text has "at the gate of the city."

63. MacMullen, "The Unromanized in Rome," pp. 53, 56. MacMullan also writes that the largest and oldest Jewish community was in a poor neighborhood on the outskirts of Rome and that Jews and the poor in general clustered in the outlying neighborhoods "at the gate of Rome," that is to say, outside the older city limits and sometimes at the literal gates; see pp. 54, 63.

64. In this brief treatment of a very rich story, I pass over Rabbi Joshua's initial concern with personal salvation. See Fraenkel, "The Image of Rabbi Joshua ben Levi," pp. 403–17, and comments in my thesis "Story and Theology," pp. 316–18.

65. B. Ta'anit 22a. This story lacks the phrase "was often found with him," in important MSS. Because of its exemplum form, unusual among Elijah stories, one cannot know whether this story originally lacked the formula or whether certain scribes deleted it. MSS used by the Vilna edition do contain the formula, and this too is natural because the story has the plot formula in which the questioner acts in response to Elijah's answer. "Children/Sons of the world to come" seems to mean those especially pleasing to God rather than those assured of heaven: "life of the world to come." Five times, for example, the phrase appears in the form "Who is the son of the world to

come? One who" performs a valuable commandment (but not one vital for salvation). See B. Berakhot 4b and 9b, B. Shabbat 153a, B. Bava Batra 10b, B. Sanhedrin 88b.

66. Ben-Amos, "Narrative Forms," pp. 163, 172–73.

67. In its original context, this verse (Deut. 23:14) teaches that when the Israelites go to war they should relieve themselves outside the camp and bury their excrement. The connection between good sanitation and ritual purity provides a parallel to the connection between proper clothing and fitness to perform a ritual act.

68. See Neusner, *A History of the Jews of Babylonia,* 3:60–61.

69. The question is probably connected to a similar exchange in Y. Terumot 1.6, 40d. "A certain God-fearing man asked Elijah of blessed memory, 'May a naked man say the Shema?' He said to him, 'and no improper thing shall be seen in you [Deut. 23:15].'" Both have a question about a naked person and contain the same prooftext in answer.

70. E.g., B. Shabbat 154b, in which Abaye criticizes Rabbah for amusing his little son by sliding him down the back of a donkey on Shabbat. Rabbah retorts that using the sides of the donkey does not constitute making it work in a forbidden way.

71. 1 Kings 18. An early identification of Elijah with Phinehas the son of Aaron may also stand behind our story, though it is not stressed in the Bavli. For the Elijah-Phinehas connection, see Ginzberg, *Legends of the Jews,* 6:316–17, n. 3; and *Midrash Mishlei,* chapter 7, p. 68, n. 20.

72. The midrashic point is that *adam* (אדם), the word best translated "human," is only applied to Jews, and hence a verse written with the term *adam* must not apply to Gentiles. Since Num. 19:14, about the impurity of corpses, rather unusually uses the word *adam,* Shimon bar Yoḥai concludes that impurity from a graveyard, derived from Num. 19:14, applies only to a Jewish graveyard. See a fuller version of this beraita on the top of B. Yebamot 61a.

73. MS Hamburg has explicitly "because of [lack of] sustenance" (מזונות).

74. B. Ta'anit 25a; the text of this last sentence is difficult in both the Vilna edition and the manuscripts, and it is not quite clear whether husband or wife has the dream of the two-legged table and which of them first proposes to pray for the table leg's return.

75. Bokser, "The Wall Separating God and Israel," pp. 358–59.

5. ELIJAH FROM RABBINIC TIMES TO THE TWENTY-FIRST CENTURY

1. B. Bava Batra 7b.

2. B. Ta'anit 21b.

3. Wiener, *The Prophet Elijah,* pp. 54–55, 76, makes some comparable points, but in very different language.

4. B. Ta'anit 24b–25a, though note that other rabbis on the same pages speak almost as demandingly to God and bring rain without ill effect to themselves. See also B. Ḥagigah 11b and 13a for the mortal danger of mystical speculation.

5. In this way, among others, the Elijah stories tend to support much of Fraenkel's conclusion that rabbinic stories as a whole "express the Sages' understanding of the religious reality in which a human being lives and which he creates by his actions," rather than the relationship of the whole Jewish community to God, see Fraenkel, *Techniques and Principles,* p. 242.

6. Fraenkel, in contrast to this view, tends to draw a sharp distinction between the human and supernatural realms, on the one hand the autonomous individual Sage and, on the other hand, the tremendous force supernatural influences, which nevertheless do not overwhelm human conscience, Fraenkel, *Techniques and Principles,* p. 253.

7. Cf. ibid., p. 255, where Fraenkel states that rabbinic narrative is that in which human self-determination is seen in opposition to "influence from above."

8. See Fraenkel, *Techniques and Principles*, p. 243.

9. Weinreich, "Genres and Types of Yiddish Folk Tales," pp. 205, 208.

10. Noy, "Elijah the Prophet at the Seder Night," p. 110.

11. A famous example is the tale of Rabbi Joshua ben Levi and his journey with Elijah in which Elijah confounds the rabbi by harming a generous poor couple, helping a stingy rich man, and apparently blessing an inhospitable and cursing a hospitable town. This story is first found in Nissim ben Jacob, *An Elegant Composition,* pp. 13–16.

12. Jacobs, *The Jewish Mystics,* p. 112, citing the *maggid,* the spiritual guide, of Rabbi Joseph Karo; cf. chapter 1, n. 17, this volume.

13. Noy, *Folktales of Israel,* pp. 5–7.

14. Lisa Stevensen, "Great Jewish Women," in Kornbluth and Kornbluth, *Jewish Women Speak About Jewish Matters,* p. 179.

15. *Midrasch Ruth Zuta,* 4:11.

16. Berlowitz, "Seven Good Years," pp. 317–19.

17. Nissim ben Jacob, *An Elegant Composition,* 162.

18. Gaster, *Ma'aseh Book,* pp. 312–16.

19. Ben-Zvi, *The Bride Who Argued with God,* pp. 163–66, Ben-Zvi notes this is one of fifteen versions in the Israel Folktale Archives.

20. Schwarzbaum, *Studies in Jewish and World Folklore,* p. 8.

21. In B. Ta'anit 23b, for example, when a holy man and his wife pray for rain, the clouds first appear in the direction she is facing because she satisfies the hungry directly with food rather than only giving money.

22. Nissim ben Jacob, *An Elegant Composition,* pp. 99–102.

23. My translation, with help from Herb Basser, based on the medieval Maḥzor Vitry, which differs slightly from the modern version, reading: עניני עניני נורא עלילה. יזמתי ונמכרתי
להעבידי לכבודך ולא לכבודי . . . .רחמיך יכמרו בחנינתי. כי גם לטובה כוונתי . . .

24. Hoffman, *Beyond the Text*, p. 41.

25. Isaac ben Moses, "Hilkhot Motzei Shabbat," siman 95, in *Or Zarua* (Jitomir/Zhyto-myr, Russia, 1862), says the responsum was probably from Rav Joseph Gaon, one of two ninth-century Babylonian Geonim. See "Isaac ben Moses of Vienna," "Joseph ben Abba," and "Joseph bar Ḥiyya," in *The Jewish Encyclopedia* (New York: Funk and Wagnalls, 1901–1906), http://www.jewishencyclopedia.com.

26. Hoffman, *Beyond the Text,* p. 25.

27. Ibid., pp. 39–44.

28. Kahana, "Elijah, the Prophet," pp. 10, 12; see also Hoffman, *Beyond the Text*, p. 44, on Elijah's messianic role in popular Jewish thought after 1000 CE.

29. Kahana, *Tales of the Enlightened*, p. 15.

30. Turner, *Blazing the Trail*, p. 152.

31. Klein, *A Time to Be Born*, p. 146.

32. Neusner, *A History of the Jews of Babylonia*, 5:212, 226.

33. Klein, *A Time to Be Born*, pp. 147–48.

34. Weinreich, *Yiddish Folktales*, pp. 320, 398.

35. Noy, *Folktales of Israel*, pp. 22–24.

36. Ben-Amos, *Folktales of the Jews,* vol. 1: *The Sephardic Dispersion*, pp. 99–101.

37. Genesis Rabbah 83.5.

38. Goitein, "A Report on Messianic Troubles," 58–59. For a comparable story see Bin Gorion and Bin-Gorion, *Mimekor Yisrael,* 1:401–2.

39. Goitein, "A Report on Messianic Troubles," pp. 60, 61–63.

40. Ben-Amos, *The Sephardic Dispersion,* p. 4.

41. Ibid., pp. 2–3.

42. Klein, *A Time to Be Born*, p. 185. Elijah's chair is mentioned clearly by Rabbi Nissim ben Jacob of Kairouan c. 970; see Klien, *A Time to Be Born,* p. 263, n. 46.

43. Safrai and Safrai, *Haggadah of the Sages*, p. 177.

44. Birnbaum, *Daily Prayer Book,* p. 741. In other communities the child is briefly placed on Elijah's chair, which is left empty, and then given to the sandek.

45. Guggenheimer, *The Scholar's Haggadah*, pp. 364–67.

46. Safrai and Safrai, *Haggadah of the Sages,* 177.

47. Solomon Schecter and M. Grunwald, "Elijah's Chair," *The Jewish Encyclopedia.*

48. Klein, *A Time to Be Born,* p. 185.

49. Ibid., pp. 179–82.

50. Friedhaber, "Dances at the Circumcision Ceremonial," p. 65.

51. Pirkei de-Rabbi Eliezer, chapter 28.

52. Ben-Amos, "Jewish Folk Literature," p. 235.

53. Laws of Circumcision, *Sefer Haminhag,* p. 583. R. David ben Yosef Abudraham, writing at about the same time also speaks of a "support," "Circumcision and its Benedictions," in *Sefer Abudraham Hashalem,* beginning "They are accustomed to make."

54. *Kol Bo,* siman 73.

55. "Yoreh Deah," siman 265, par 11–12, *Shulḥan Arukh.*

56. Klein, *A Time to Be Born,* pp. 182–83, 185.

57. Gaster, *Ma'aseh Book,* pp. 391–92.

58. The story is from Shivḥe he-Ari, written in the century after Luria's life in the 1500s; Bin Gorion and Bin Gorion, *Mimekor Yisrael,* 2:852–53, 3:1517.

59. E.g. B. Shabbat 108a, Berakhot 33b.

60. Guggenheimer, *The Scholar's Haggadah,* p. 366; cf. Safrai and Safrai, *Haggadah of the Sages,* p. 177.

61. Cited in Guggenheimer, *The Scholar's Haggadah,* pp. 365–66 (translation mine).

62. Safrai and Safrai, *Haggadah of the Sages,* pp. 177–78.

63. Gaster, *Ma'aseh Book,* pp. 394–95.

64. Guggenhaimer, *The Scholar's Haggadah,* 365–66.

65. Safrai and Safrai, *Haggadah of the Sages,* pp. 174, 177–78.

66. Noy, "Elijah the Prophet at the Seder Night," p. 114–15; Weinreich, "Genres and Types of Yiddish Folktales," p. 221.

67. Ben-Amos, *Tales from the Sephardic Dispersion,* pp. 100–5.

68. Noy, "Elijah the Prophet at the Seder Night," p. 112.

69. Krasney, "Stories of Elijah the Prophet," p. 303.

70. Ibid., p. 304.

71. Brawer, "The Three Visits of Elijah the Prophet."

72. Ibid.

73. Ibid.

74. Elwell, "Opening the Door for Elijah."

BIBLIOGRAPHY

EDITIONS AND TRANSLATIONS OF PRIMARY SOURCES

Abraham ben Nathan of Lunel. *Sefer Haminhag*. Ed. I. Raphael. Jerusalem: Mossad Harav Kook, 1978.

Aharon ben R. Jacob ha-Cohen. *Kol Bo*. Jerusalem: Mekhon Even Yisrael, 1997.

Appollodorus. *The Library*. Trans. Sir James George Frazer. New York: Putnam, 1921.

Cyril of Scythopolis. *Lives of the Monks of Palestine*. Trans. R. M. Price. Intro. John Binns. Kalamazoo: Cistercian, 1991.

David ben Yosef Abudraham. *Sefer Abudraham HaShalem*. Jerusalem, 1993

Flavius Josephus. *The Jewish War*. Ed. and intro. E. Mary. Smallwood. Trans. G. A. Williamson. New York: Penguin, 1981.

Gaster, Moses, ed. and trans. *Ma'aseh Book: Book of Jewish Tales and Legends Translated from the Judeo-German*. Philadelphia: Jewish Publication Society, 1981.

Genesis Rabbah. In J. Theodor and Ch. Albeck, eds., *Midrash Bereshit Rabba: Critical Edition with Notes and Commentary*. Berlin, 1912–36; rpt. Jerusalem: Wahrmann, 1965.

The Holy Bible: Containing the Old and New Testaments with the Apocryphal/Deuterocannonical Books, New Revised Standard Version. New York: Collins, 1989.

JPS Hebrew-English Tanakh: The Traditional Hebrew Text and the New JPS Translation. 2d ed. Philadelphia: Jewish Publication Society, 1999.

Joseph Karo. *Shulḥan Arukh*. Ed. Z. H. Presler and S. Havlin. Jerusalem: Ketuvim, 1993.

Leviticus Rabbah. In Mordecai Margulies [Margaliot], ed., *Midrash Vayikra Raba*. 5 vols. New York: Jewish Theological Seminary of America, 1953–1960.

Libanius. *Autobiography and Selected Letters*. Ed. and trans. A. F. Norman. Cambridge: Harvard University Press, 1992.

Mekhilta de Rabbi Ishmael. Ed. H. S. Horowitz and I. A. Rabin. Frankfurt, 1931; rpt. Jerusalem: Bamberger and Wahrman, 1960.

Midrash Mishlei. Ed. Burton Visotzky. New York: Jewish Theological Seminary of America, 1990.

Midrasch Ruth Zuta. In Solomon Buber, ed., *Midrasch Suta*. Vilna, 1925.

Nissim ben Jacob. *An Elegant Composition Concerning Relief After Adversity*. Trans. William M. Brinner. New Haven: Yale University Press, 1977.

Pesikta de Rav Kahana. In Bernard Mandelbaum, ed., *Pesikta de Rav Kahana According to an Oxford Manuscript*. 2 vols. New York: Jewish Theological Seminary of America, 1962.

Pesikta Rabbati. Ed. Meir Friedmann. Vienna, 1880; rpt. Tel Aviv, 1963.

Pirkei de Rabbi Eliezer. Ed. Michael Higger. "Pirkei de Rabbi Eliezer." *Horev* (1944–46).

Sepher Ha-Razim: The Book of the Mysteries. Ed. and trans. Morgan, Michael A. Atlanta: Scholars Press, 1983.

Tanna Devei Eliahu. In Meir Friedman, ed., *Seder Eliahu Rabba and Seder Eliahu Zuta*. Vienna, 1902; rpt. Jerusalem: Bamberger and Wahrman, 1960.

Theodoret of Cyrrhus. *History of the Monks of Syria*. Trans. R. M. Price. Kalamazoo: Cistercian, 1985.

SECONDARY SOURCES

Achtemeier, Paul J. "*Omne Verbum Sonat*: The New Testament and the Oral Environment of Late Western Antiquity." *Journal of Biblical Literature* 109 (1990): 3–27.

Aderet, Avraham. *From Destruction to Restoration: The Mode of Yavneh in Re-Establishment of the Jewish People* [Hebrew]. Jerusalem: Magnes, 1990.

Alexander, Elizabeth Shanks. "The Orality of Rabbinic Writing." In Martin S. Jaffee and Charlotte Elisheva Fonrobert, eds., *The Cambridge Companion to the Talmud and Rabbinic Literature*, pp. 38–57. New York: Cambridge University Press, 2007.

——— *Transmitting Mishnah: The Shaping Influence of Oral Tradition*. New York: Cambridge University Press, 2006.

Amat, Jacqueline. *Songes et visions: L'au-delà dans la littérature Latine tardive*. Paris: Études Augustiniennes, 1985.

Ayali, Meir. "From Where Does Elijah Come: The Ancestry and Origins of Elijah in the Midrash of the Sages" [Hebrew]. *Tura: Studies in Jewish Thought* 3 (1994): 43–64.

Bar-Oz, Guy. "An Inscribed Astragalus with a Dedication to Hermes." *Near Eastern Archaeology* 64, no. 4D (2001): 215–17.

Bateson, Gregory. *Mind and Nature a Necessary Unity*. New York: Bantam, 1980.

Ben-Amos, Dan. "Folklore in the Ancient Near East." In D. N. Freedman, ed., *Anchor Bible Dictionary*, 2:818–28. New York: Doubleday, 1992.

—— "Generic Distinctions in the Aggadah." In Frank Talmage, ed., *Studies in Jewish Folklore*, pp. 45–72. Cambridge: Association for Jewish Studies, 1980.

—— "Jewish Folk Literature." *Oral Tradition* 14, no. 1 (March 1999): 140–274.

—— "Jewish Folklore Studies." *Modern Judaism* 11 (February 1991): 17–66.

—— "Jewish Studies and Jewish Folklore." In *Proceedings of the Tenth World Congress of Jewish Studies, 1989*, division D, pp. 1–20. Jerusalem: World Union of Jewish Studies, Hebrew University Press, 1990.

—— "Narrative Forms in the Haggadah: Structural Analysis." Ph.D. diss., Indiana University, 1967. University Microfilms, Ann Arbor, Michigan, 1979.

—— "The Idea of Folklore: An Essay." In Issacher Ben-Ami and Joseph Dan, eds., *Studies in Aggadah and Jewish Folklore*, 7:11–18 [Hebrew and English]. Jerusalem: Magnes, 1983.

Ben-Amos, Dan, ed. *Folktales of the Jews*, vol. 1: *The Sephardic Dispersion*. Philadelphia: Jewish Publication Society, 2006.

—— *Folktales of the Jews*, vol. 2: *Tales from Eastern Europe*. Philadelphia: Jewish Publication Society, 2007.

Ben-Zvi, Hava. *The Bride Who Argued with God: Tales from the Treasury of Jewish Folklore*. New York: iUniverse, 2006.

Berlowitz, Yafah. "Seven Good Years." In Yoav Elstein, Avidov Lipsker, and Rella Kushelevsky, eds., *Encyclopedia of Jewish Story*, pp. 307–22 [Hebrew]. Ramat Gan: Bar-Ilan University Press, 2004.

Bin Gorion, Micah Joseph, and Emanuel Bin Gorion, eds. *Mimekor Yisrael: Classical Jewish Folktales*. Introduction by Dan Ben-Amos. Bloomington: Indiana University Press, 1976.

—— *Mimekor Yisrael: Classical Jewish Folktales*. Intro. Dan Ben-Amos. Abridged and annotated ed. Bloomington: Indiana University Press, 1990.

Binns, John. "Introduction." In Cyril of Scythopolis. *Lives of the Monks of Palestine*. Trans. R. M. Price. Kalamazoo: Cistercian, 1991.

Birnbaum, Philip, ed. and trans. *Daily Prayer Book: Ha-Siddur Ha-Shalem*. New York: Hebrew Publishing, 1949.

Blidstein, Gerald J. "Rabbis, Romans and Martyrdom—Three Views." *Tradition* 21 (Fall 1984): 54–64.

Bokser, Baruch. "Talmudic Form Criticism." *Journal of Jewish Studies* 31 (Spring 1980): 46–60.

—— *The Origins of the Passover Seder: The Passover Rite and Early Rabbinic Judaism*. Berkeley: University of California Press, 1984.

——— "The Wall Separating God and Israel." *Jewish Quarterly Review* 73, no. 4 (April 1983): 349–74.

——— "Wonder-Working and the Rabbinic Tradition: The Case of Ḥanina Ben Dosa." *Journal for the Study of Judaism* 16, no. 1 (June 1985): 42–92.

Boyarin, Daniel. *Carnal Israel: Reading Sex in Talmudic Culture*. Berkeley: University of California Press, 1993.

——— "Hellenism in Jewish Babylonia." In Martin S. Jaffee and Charlotte Elisheva Fonrobert, eds., *The Cambridge Companion to the Talmud and Rabbinic Literature*, pp. 336–63. New York: Cambridge University Press, 2007.

Bradbury, Nancy Mason. "Traditional Referentiality: The Aesthetic Power of Oral Traditional Structures." In John Miles Foley, ed., *Teaching Oral Traditions*, pp. 136–45. New York: Modern Language Association, 1998.

Branham, R. Bracht. *Unruly Eloquence: Lucian and the Comedy of Traditions*. Cambridge: Harvard University Press, 1989.

Braude, William G., trans. *Pesikta Rabbati: Discourses for Feasts, Fasts and Special Occasions*. New Haven: Yale University Press, 1968.

Brawer, Yaakov. "The Three Visits of Elijah the Prophet." Chabad.org, a Division of the Chabad-Lubavitch Media Center, http://www.chabad.org/library/article_cdo/aid/1986/jewish/The-Three-Visits-of-Elijah-the-Prophet.htm; accessed September 30, 2008.

Brown, Norman O. *Hermes the Thief: The Evolution of a Myth*. Madison: University of Wisconsin Press, 1947.

Brown, Peter. *Cult of the Saints: Its Rise and Function in Latin Christianity*. Chicago: University of Chicago Press, 1981.

——— *Society and the Holy in Late Antiquity*. Berkeley: University of California Press, 1982.

——— "The Saint as Exemplar in Late Antiquity." In John Stratton Hawley, ed., *Saints and Virtues*, pp. 3–14. Berkeley: University of California Press, 1987.

Brown-Gutoff, Shoshana. "That's Not Funny—Or is It? The Use of Humor in Eycha Rabba." Paper presented at the Twenty-Sixth Annual Conference of the Association for Jewish Studies, Boston, December 18–20, 1994.

Brunvand, Jan Harold. *The Vanishing Hitchhiker*. London: Pan, 1983.

Cohn, Robert L. "Sainthood on the Periphery: The Case of Judaism." In John Stratton Hawley, ed., *Saints and Virtues*, pp. 87–108. Berkeley: University of California Press, 1987.

Daube, David. *Appeasement or Resistance and Other Essays on New Testament Judaism*. Berkeley: University of California Press, 1987.

Davies, Sioned. "Storytelling in Medieval Wales." *Oral Tradition* 7, no. 2 (1992): 231–57.

Delehaye, Hippolyte. *Legends of the Saints.* New York: Fordham University Press, 1962.

Diamond, Eliezer. "Wrestling the Angel of Death: Form and Meaning in Rabbinic Tales of Death and Dying." *Journal for the Study of Judaism* 26, no. 1 (Winter 1995): 76–92.

Dundes, Alan. "Who Are the Folk?" In *Interpreting Folklore*, pp. 1–19. Bloomington: Indiana University Press, 1980.

Eilberg-Schwartz, Howard. *The Savage in Judaism: An Anthropology of Israelite Religion and Ancient Judaism.* Bloomington: Indiana University Press, 1990.

Elman, Yaakov. *Authority and Tradition: Toseftan Beraitot in Talmudic Babylonia.* Hoboken, NJ: Ktav, 1994.

—— "Middle Persian Culture and the Babylonian Sages: Accommodation and Resistance in Shaping of Rabbinic Legal Tradition." In Martin S. Jaffee and Charlotte Elisheva Fonrobert, eds., *The Cambridge Companion to the Talmud and Rabbinic Literature*, pp. 165–97. New York: Cambridge University Press, 2007.

—— "Orality and the Redaction of the Babylonian Talmud." *Oral Tradition* 14, no. 1 (March 1999): 52–99.

—— "Righteousness as Its Own Reward: An Inquiry Into the Theologies of the Stam." *Proceedings of the American Academy for Jewish Research* 57 (1990–91): 35–67.

Elwell, Sue Levi. "Opening the Door for Elijah and Pouring Out Fury? Dealing with Difficult Texts." *Eilu V'Eilu* 14, no. 1 (2007). http://urj.org/torah/ ten/eilu/v14w1/; accessed October 1, 2008.

Englard, Izhak. "Majority Decision vs. Individual Truth: The Interpretations of the 'Oven of Achnai' Aggadah," *Tradition* 15 (Spring-Summer 1975): 137–52.

Finnegan, Ruth H. "What Is Oral Literature Anyway? Comments in the Light of Some African and Other Oral Material." In John Miles Foley, ed., *Oral-Formulaic Theory: A Folklore Casebook*, pp. 243–82. New York: Garland, 1990.

Fischel, Henry A., ed. *Essays in Greco-Roman and Related Talmudic Literature.* New York: Ktav, 1977.

—— "Story and History: Observations on Greco-Roman Rhetoric and Pharisaism." In Henry A. Fischel, ed., *Essays in Greco-Roman and Related Talmudic Literature*, pp. 443–72. New York: Ktav, 1977.

Foley, John Miles, ed. *Oral Tradition in Literature: Interpretation in Context.* Columbia: University of Missouri Press, 1986.

—— "Word-Power, Performance and Tradition." *Journal of American Folklore* 105 (Summer 1992): 275–301.

—— *The Singer of Tales in Performance.* Bloomington and Indianapolis: Indiana University Press, 1995.

Fowden, Garth. *The Egyptian Hermes: A Historical Approach to the Late Pagan Mind.* Cambridge: Cambridge University Press, 1986.

Fraade, Steven. "Literary Composition and Oral Performance in Early Midrashim." *Oral Tradition* 14, no. 1 (March 1999): 33–51.

Fraenkel, Yonah. *Techniques and Principles of Aggadah and Midrash* [Hebrew]. 2 vols. Givataiim: Yad LaTalmud, 1991.

—— "The Image of Rabbi Joshua Ben Levi in the Stories of the Babylonian Talmud" [Hebrew]. In Avigdor Shinan, ed., *Sixth World Congress of Jewish Studies in Jerusalem*, pp. 403–17. Jerusalem: World Union of Jewish Studies, 1981.

Freidhaber, Zvi. "Circumcision Dances Dedicated to Elijah" [Hebrew]. *Yeda-'Am* 7, no. 1 (Autumn 1961): 64–65.

Friedländer, G., ed. and trans. *Pirkei de Rabbi Eliezer.* New York: Hermon, 1965.

Friedman, Shamma. "On the Development of Variant Readings in the Babylonian Talmud" [Hebrew]. *Sidra* 7 (1991): 67–102.

Friedmann, Meir. "Introduction." *Seder Eliahu Rabba and Seder Eliahu Zuta (Tanna Devei Eliahu).* Jerusalem: Bamberger and Wahrman, 1960 [1902].

Gerhardsson, Birger. *Memory and Manuscript: Oral Tradition and Written Transmission in Rabbinic Judaism and Early Christianity.* Trans. Eric J. Sharpe. Denmark: Villadsen og Christensen, Kobenhavn, 1964.

Ginzberg, Louis. "Jewish Folklore East and West." In *On Jewish Law and Lore*, pp. 61–73. Philadelphia: Jewish Publication Society of America, 1955.

—— *Legends of the Jews.* 7 vols. Philadelphia: Jewish Publication Society, 1909–39.

Goitein, S. D. "A Report on Messianic Troubles in Baghdad in 1120–21." *Jewish Quarterly Review* 43, no. 1 (July 1952): 57–76.

Goldin, Barbara Diamond. Illustrations by Jerry Pinkney. *Journeys with Elijah: Eight Tales of the Prophet.* New York: Gulliver, 1999.

Goodblatt, David M. *Rabbinic Instruction in Sasanian Babylonia.* Leiden: Brill, 1975.

Goodenough, Erwin Ramsdell, and Jacob Neusner. *Jewish Symbols in the Greco-Roman Period.* Princeton: Princeton University Press, 1988.

Green, William Scott. "Palestinian Holy Men: Charismatic Leadership and the Rabbinic Tradition." In *Aufstieg und Niedergang der Romischen Welt*, 2:619–47. New York: de Gruyter, 1979.

Gruenwald, I. *Apocalyptic and Merkavah Mysticism.* Leiden: Brill, 1980.

Guggenheimer, Heinrich. *The Scholar's Haggadah: Ashkenazic, Sephardic, and Oriental Versions.* Northvale, NJ: Aronson, 1995.

Halperin, David J. *The Faces of the Chariot: Early Jewish Responses to Ezekiel's Vision.* Tübingen: Mohr, 1988.

Hasan-Rokem, Galit. *Tales of the Neighborhood: Jewish Narrative Dialogues in Late Antiquity*. Berkeley: University of California Press, 2003.

Hedner-Zetterholm, Karin. "Elijah's Different Roles—A Reflection of the Rabbinic Struggle for Authority." *Jewish Studies Quarterly* 16, no. 2 (June 2009): 163–82.

Henderson, Ian. "Didache and Orality in Synoptic Comparison." *Journal of Biblical Literature* 111 (1992): 283–306.

Hezser, Catherine. *Form, Function, and Historical Significance of the Rabbinic Story in Yerushalmi Neziqin*. Tübingen: Mohr, 1993.

Higger, Michael, ed. "Pirkei de Rabbi Eliezer." *Horev* 8:82–119, 9:95–116, 10:185–294 (1944–46).

Hock, Ronald F., and Edward N. O'Neil. *The Chreia in Ancient Rhetoric*. Atlanta: Scholars Press, 1986.

Hoffman, Lawrence A. *Beyond the Text: A Holistic Approach to Liturgy*. Bloomington: Indiana University Press, 1987.

Jacobs, Louis, ed. *The Jewish Mystics*. London: Kyle Cathie, 1990.

Jaffee, Martin S. "A Rabbinic Ontology of the Written and Spoken Word: On Discipleship, Transformative Knowledge, and the Living Texts of Oral Torah." *Journal of the American Academy of Religion* 65, no. 3 (Fall 1997): 525–49.

—— "How Much 'Orality' in Oral Torah? New Perspectives on the Composition and Transmission of Early Rabbinic Tradition." *Shofar* 10, no. 2 (Winter 1992): 53–72.

—— "Rabbinic Authorship as a Collective Enterprise." In Martin S. Jaffee and Charlotte Elisheva Fonrobert, eds., *The Cambridge Companion to the Talmud and Rabbinic Literature*, pp. 17–37. New York: Cambridge University Press, 2007.

—— "The Oral-Cultural Context of the Talmud Yerushalmi: Greco-Roman Paideia, Discipleship, and the Concept of Oral Torah." In Yaakov Elman, ed., *Transmitting Jewish Traditions: Orality, Textuality, and Cultural Diffusion*, pp. 27–73. New Haven: Yale University Press, 2000.

—— *Torah in the Mouth: Writing and Oral Tradition in Palestinian Judaism, 200 BCE–400 CE*. New York: Oxford University Press, 2001.

Jaffee, Martin S., and Charlotte Elisheva Fonrobert, eds. *The Cambridge Companion to the Talmud and Rabbinic Literature*. New York: Cambridge University Press, 2007.

Jaffee, Nina. Illustrated by Elivia Savadier. *The Mysterious Visitor: Stories of the Prophet Elijah*. New York: Scholastic, 1997.

Jason, Heda. "Concerning the 'Historical' and the 'Local' Legend and Their Relatives." In Americo Paredes and Richard Bauman, eds., *Toward New Perspectives in Folklore*, pp. 134–44. Austin: University of Texas Press, 1972.

—— *Studies in Jewish Ethnopoetry*. Asian Folklore and Social Life Monographs, no. 72. Taipei: Orient Cultural Service, 1975.

Kahana, S. Z. "Elijah, the Prophet, on Saturday Evenings" [Hebrew]. *Yeda 'Am* 7, no. 1 (Autumn 1961): 9–13.

—— *Tales of the Enlightened*. New York: Research Center of Kabbalah, 1985.

Kalmin, Richard. *Sages, Stories, Authors, and Editors in Rabbinic Babylonia*. Atlanta: Scholars Press, 1994.

—— *The Sage in Jewish Society of Late Antiquity*. New York: Routledge, 1999.

Kee, Howard Clark. *Miracle in the Early Christian World: A Study in Sociohistorical Method*. New Haven: Yale University Press, 1983.

Kelber, Werner H. *The Oral and Written Gospel*. Philadelphia: Fortress, 1983.

Klein, Michele. *A Time to Be Born: Customs and Folklore of Jewish Birth*. Philadelphia: Jewish Publication Society, 1998.

Kraemer, David. *Responses to Suffering in Classical Rabbinic Literature*. New York: Oxford University Press, 1995.

Krasney, Ariela. "Stories of Elijah the Prophet from Contemporary Story Tellers" [Hebrew]. *Shenaton Sha'anan* 9 (2004): 283–307.

Kurt, Zevulun. "The Staff of Elijah the Prophet" [Hebrew]. *Yeda 'Am* 7, no. 1 (Autumn 1961): 64.

Levin, Howard. "General Introduction." In William Shakespeare, *The Riverside Shakespeare*. Boston: Houghton Mifflin, 1974.

Lieberman, Saul. *Greek in Jewish Palestine: Studies in the Life and Manners of Jewish Palestine in the Second to Fourth Centuries C.E.* New York: Feldheim, 1965 [1942].

—— *Hellenism in Jewish Palestine: Studies in the Literary Transmission, Beliefs, and Manners of Palestine I Century B.C.E.– IV Century C.E.* New York: Jewish Theological Seminary of America, 1962 [1950].

—— "How Much Greek in Jewish Palestine?" In Henry A. Fischel, ed., *Essays in Greco-Roman and Related Talmudic Literature*, pp. 325–43. New York: Ktav, 1977.

—— "Palestine in the Third and Fourth Centuries." *Jewish Quarterly Review* 37 (July 1946): 31–54.

—— "Roman Legal Institutions in Early Rabbinic Literature and in the Acta Martyreum." In *Texts and Studies*. New York: Ktav, 1974.

Lindbeck, Kristen Harriet. "Story and Theology: Elijah's Appearances in the Babylonian Talmud." Ph.D. diss., Jewish Theological Seminary, 1999. UMI, Ann Arbor, Michigan 1999.

Lord, Albert B. "The Merging of Two Worlds: Oral and Written Poetry as Carriers of Ancient Values." In John Miles Foley, ed., *Oral Tradition in Literature: Interpretation in Context*, pp. 19–64. Columbia: University of Missouri Press, 1986.

Mac Eoin, Gearóid. "Orality and Literacy in Some Middle-Irish King-Tales." In Stephen N. Tranter and Hildegard L. C. Tristam, eds., *Early Irish Literature—Media and Communication*, pp. 149–83. Tübingen: Gunter Narr Verlag, 1989.

McKnight, Edgar V. *What Is Form Criticism?* Philadelphia: Fortress, 1969.

MacMullen, Ramsay. *Paganism in the Roman Empire.* New Haven: Yale University Press, 1981.

—— "The Unromanized in Rome." In Shaye J. D. Cohen and Ernest Frerichs, eds., *Diasporas in Antiquity.* Atlanta: Scholars Press, 1993.

Mandelbaum, Bernard, ed. *Pesikta de Rav Kahana According to an Oxford Manuscript.* New York: Jewish Theological Seminary of America, 1962.

Margaliot, Eliezer. *Elijah the Prophet in the Literature, Faith, and Spiritual Life of Israel* [Hebrew]. Jerusalem: Kiryat Sepher, 1960.

Margulies [Margaliot], Mordecai, ed. *Midrash Vayikra Raba.* New York: Jewish Theological Seminary of America, 1953–60.

Meir, Ofra. "The Literary Context of the Sages' Aggadic Stories as Analogous to Changing Storytelling Situations: The Story of the Ḥasid and the Spirits in the Cemetery" [Hebrew]. In Tamar Alexander and Galit Hasan-Rokem, eds., *Jerusalem Studies in Jewish Folklore XII–XIV for Dov Noy*, pp. 81–98. Jerusalem: Magnes, 1992.

Miller, Stuart S. "Roman Imperialism, Jewish Self-Definition, and Rabbinic Society: Belayche's *Iudeae-Palestina*, Schwartz's *Roman Imperialism and Jewish Society*, and Boyarin's *Border Lines*, Reconsidered." *AJS Review* 31, no. 2 (2007): 329–62.

Montgomery, James A. *Aramaic Incantation Texts from Nippur.* Philadelphia: University of Pennsylvania Museum, 1913.

Mussies, Gerard. "The Interpretatio Judaica of Thot-Hermes." In M. Heerma Van Voss, et al., eds., *Studies in Egpytian Religion Dedicated to Professor Jan Zandee,* pp. 89–120. Leiden: Brill, 1982.

Naveh, Joseph, and Shaul Shaked. *Amulets and Magic Bowls: Aramaic Incantations of Late Antiquity.* Jerusalem: Magnes, 1985.

Neusner, Jacob. *A History of the Jews of Babylonia.* 5 vols. Leiden: Brill, 1965–70.

—— *Judaism and Story: The Evidence of the Fathers According to Rabbi Nathan.* Chicago: University of Chicago Press, 1992.

—— *The Development of a Legend: Studies in the Traditions of Yohanan Ben Zakkai.* Leiden: Brill, 1970.

Niditch, Susan. *Folklore and the Hebrew Bible*. Minneapolis: Fortress, 1993.

—— *Oral World and Written Word: Ancient Israelite Literature*. Lousiville: Westminster, 1996.

Noy [Neuman], Dov. *Motif Index of Talmudic and Midrashic Literature*. Ann Arbor: University Microfilms International, 1979 [1954].

Noy, Dov, ed., *Folktales of Israel*. Trans. Gene Baharav. Chicago: University of Chicago Press, 1963.

—— "Elijah the Prophet at the Seder Night" [Hebrew]. *Machnayim* 43 (March 1960).

Olrick, Axel. *Principles for Oral Narrative Research*. Trans. Kirsten Wolf and Jody Jensen. Bloomington: Indiana University Press, 1992.

Ong, Walter J. S. J. "Text as Interpretation: Mark and After." In John Miles Foley, ed., *Oral Tradition in Literature: Interpretation in Context*, 147–69. Columbia: University of Missouri Press, 1986.

Oppenheimer, Aharon. *Babylonia Judaica*. Weisbaden: Reichert, 1983.

Patai, Raphael. *On Jewish Folklore*. Detroit: Wayne State University Press, 1983.

Peli, Pinchas. "Elijah in the Beit Midrash of the Sages." In Zvi Malakhi, ed., *On the Path of Scholarship [באורח מדע]: Studies in the Culture of Israel, Presented to Aaron Mirsky on the Occasion of His Seventieth Birthday*, pp. 140–68. Israel: Haberman Institute of Literary Studies, 1986.

Prasad, Leela. *Poetics of Conduct: Oral Narrative and Moral Being in a South Indian Town*. New York: Columbia University Press, 2007.

Price, R. M. "Introduction." In Theodoret of Cyrrhus, *History of the Monks of Syria*. Kalamazoo: Cistercian, 1985.

Propp, V. *Morphology of the Folktale*. Trans. Laurence Scott. Revised by Louis A. Wagner. Introduction by Alan Dundes. Austin: University of Texas Press, 1994 [1968].

Rabbinovicz, Raphael Nathan, ed. *Dikdukei Soferim*. 16 vols. Jerusalem: Or ha-Hokhmah, 2001–2002.

Raingeard, P. *Hermes psychagogue: Essai sur les origines du culte d'Hermes*. Rennes: Imprimerie Oberthur, 1934.

Renoir, Alain. "Oral-Formulaic Context: Implications for the Comparative Criticism of Medaeval Texts." In John Miles Foley, ed., *Oral Traditonal Literature: A Festschrift for Albert Bates Lord*, pp. 416–39. Columbus: Slavica, 1981.

Roberts, Brynley F. "The Middle Welsh Prose Narratives." In Leigh A Arrathoon, ed., *The Craft of Fiction: Essays in Medieval Poetics*, pp. 211–30. Rochester, MI: Solaris, 1984.

Rubenstein, Jeffrey L. "Social and Institutional Settings of Rabbinic Literature." In Martin S. Jaffee and Charlotte Elisheva Fonrobert, eds., *The Cambridge Companion to the*

Talmud and Rabbinic Literature, pp. 58–74. New York: Cambridge University Press, 2007.

—— *Talmudic Stories, Narrative Art, Composition, and Culture*. Baltimore: Johns Hopkins University Press, 1999.

Sadeh, Pinchas. *Jewish Folktales Selected and Retold by Pinchas Sadeh*. Trans. Hillel Halkin. New York: Doubleday, 1989.

Safrai, Shmuel, and Ze'ev Safrai. *Haggadah of the Sages: The Passover Haggadah* [Hebrew]. Jerusalem: Karta, 1998.

Saldarini, Anthony. "Form Criticism of Rabbinic Literature." *Journal of Biblical Literature* 96 (1973): 257–74.

—— "Last Words and Deathbed Scenes in Rabbinic Literature." *Jewish Quarterly Review* 68 (July 1977): 28–45.

Schaefer, Peter. *The Hidden and Manifest God*. Trans. Aubrey Pomerance. Albany: State University of New York Press, 1992.

Scholem, Gershom. *Jewish Gnosticism, Merkaba Mysticism, and Talmudic Tradition*. New York: Jewish Theological Seminary, 1965.

Schram, Penninah. *Tales of Elijah the Prophet*. Lanham, MD: Aronson, 1997.

Schwartz, Seth. *Imperialism and Jewish Society: 200 B.C.E to 640 C.E.* Princeton: Princeton University Press, 2001.

Schwarzbaum, Haim. "The Jewish and Moslem Versions of Some Theodicy Legends (AaTh 759)." *Fabula* 3, no. 1–2 (1959): 119–69.

—— *Studies in Jewish and World Folklore*. Berlin: de Gruyter, 1968.

Segal, Eliezer. *The Babylonian Esther Midrash: A Critical Commentary*. 3 vols. Atlanta: Scholars Press, 1994.

Segal, Samuel Michael. *Elijah: A Study in Jewish Folklore*. New York: Behrman's, 1935.

Shinan, Avigdor. *The Embroidered Targum* [Hebrew]. Jerusalem: Magnes, 1992.

Smith, Morton. "A Comparison of Early Christian and Early Rabbinic Tradition." *Journal of Biblical Literature* 82 (Spring 1963): 169–76.

Sperber, Daniel. *Magic and Folklore in Rabbinic Literature*. Ramat-Gan: Bar Ilan University Press, 1994.

—— "Some Rabbinic Themes in Magical Papyri." *Journal for the Study of Judaism* 16, no. 1 (June 1985): 93–103.

Stein, S. "The Influence of Symposia Literature on the Literary Form of the Pesaḥ Haggadah." In Henry A. Fischel, ed., *Essays in Greco-Roman and Related Talmudic Literature*, pp. 198–229. New York: Ktav, 1977.

Stevensen, Lisa, "Great Jewish Women." In Sarah Tikvah Kornbluth and Doron Kornbluth, eds., *Jewish Women Speak About Jewish Matters*. Southfield, MI: Feldheim, 2000.

Strack, H. L., and G. Stemberger. *Introduction to the Talmud and Midrash.* Trans. Markus Bockmuel. Minneapolis: Fortress, 1992.

Street, Brian. *Literacy in Theory and Practice.* Cambridge: Cambridge University Press, 1984.

Tannen, Deborah. "Oral and Literate Strategies in Spoken and Written Narratives." *Language* 58 (March 1982): 1–21.

Tedlock, Dennis. "On the Translation of Style in Oral Narrative." In Americo Paredes and Richard Bauman, eds., *Toward New Perspectives in Folklore*, pp. 114–33. Austin: University of Texas Press, 1972.

Thomas, Rosalind. *Literacy and Orality in Ancient Greece.* Cambridge: Cambridge University Press, 1992.

Towner, Wayne Sibley. "Form-Criticism of Rabbinic Literature." *Journal of Jewish Studies* 24 (Autumn 1973): 101–18.

Turner, Victor. *Blazing the Trail.* Tucson: University of Arizona Press, 1992.

Urbach, Ephraim E. *The Sages: Their Concepts and Beliefs.* Trans. Israel Abrahams. Cambridge: Harvard University Press, 1987.

VanderKam, James C. *Enoch and the Growth of an Apocalyptic Tradition.* Washington, DC: Catholic Biblical Association of America, 1984.

Vansina, Jan. *Oral Tradition as History.* Madison: University of Wisconsin Press, 1985.

Veyne, Paul. *Did the Greeks Believe in Their Myths? An Essay in the Constitutive Imagination.* Trans. Paula Wissing. Chicago: University of Chicago Press, 1988.

Visotzky, Burton. "Most Tender and Fairest of Women." *Harvard Theological Review* 76 (October 1983): 403–18.

Weinreich, Beatrice Silverman. "Genres and Types of Yiddish Folk Tales About the Prophet Elijah." In Uriel Weinreich, ed., *The Field of Yiddish: Studies in Language, Folklore, and Literature*, pp. 202–31. The Hague: Mouton, 1965.

Weinreich, Beatrice Silverman, ed. *Yiddish Folktales.* Trans. Leonard Wolf. New York: Pantheon, 1988.

Wiener, Aharon. *The Prophet Elijah in the Development of Judaism: A Depth-Psychological Study.* Boston: Routledge and Kegan Paul, 1978.

Yassif, Eli. "Folklore Research and Jewish Studies (A)" [Hebrew]. *World Union of Jewish Studies Newsletter* 27 (1987): 3–26.

—— "The Cycle of Tales in Rabbinic Literature" [Hebrew]. *Jerusalem Studies in Hebrew Literature,* pp. 103–43. Jerusalem: Hebrew University, 1990.

—— *The Hebrew Folktale: History, Genre, Meaning* [Hebrew]. Jerusalem: Bialik Institute, 1994.

INDEX

and the angels, 46–47, 51–52, 54, 58–62, 70, 105; answers questions, 65–66, 116–35, 140–41, 150, 189, 215*n*65; appears in disguise, 88–90, 104–15, 186, 191, 212*n*23; appears in dreams, 74–75, 89–90, 153, 156–57, 166; and the bat kol, 54–59, 62, 71, 120, 188; biblical and midrashic, xi–xii, 84–86, 92–93, 103, 131, 153, 159–60, 195*n*1–3; brings wealth or financial help, 74–75, 86, 129–34, 149–54, 167, 184; brings word from or about God, 69, 119–23; at childbirth and as protector of newborn babies, 154–55, 159, 164; at circumcisions, and chair of, 158–62, 218*n*42; as colleague of the rabbis, 64–66, 74, 103, 117–118, 132; cup of, 162–63; as herald of the Messiah, 1, 91, 123–26, 148, 152–53, 163, 187; and Hermes, 74–76, 79, 84–93; and hospitality or charity test, 149–51, 164, 166; as liminal figure, 76, 118, 127, 154, 161, 163, 170; on Motzei Shabbat, 152–54, 218*nn*23–25; at Passover, 158–59, 160–65, 167–69; refuses to visit the unworthy or erring, 16, 51, 69, 96–104; rescues from danger and crisis, 50–51, 73–75, 87–90, 106–16, 139, 154–57, 164; teaches proverbs, 65; teaches halakhah, 175, 177, 178, 180, 189 194; as traveler and patron of travelers, 75, 79, 86, 148, 155, 164, 177, 189; travels between earth and heaven, 46–47, 85

Elijah stories, form criticism of: chapter 4 *passim*, 136–41; generic groups, 18–19, 59–60; medieval, 146–51, 156–57, 161–62; modern, 155, 164–68; in rabbinic texts other than the Bavli, 45–46, 90, 99–100, 202*n*2; *see also* form and genre criticism

Elisha ben Abuya, *see* Aher

Elman, Yaakov, 25, 26–27, 79, 199*n*8, 201*n*44, 211*n*15

emperor, Roman, 22, 55, 57, 89, 90, 156

empire, *see* Roman empire

Enoch, 47–48, 83

Eruvin: Bavli 43a, 180

eschatology, 66; *see also* Messiah

Esther, 105, 119, 130, 185–86, 214*n*54

ethical teaching, 3, 16, 52, 142

ethnopoetics, 42

exemplum, 16, 107–8, 112, 126–27, 149, 157, 215*n*65

exile, 141, 178, 179

Ezekiel, 54, 89, 176–77

faith, 16, 143, 157–58

fallibility, 48–50, of Elijah, 3, 62, 175–76; of the angel of death, 199*n*8

fasting, 99, 101, 150, 175, 207*n*81

fate, 79, 128

Finnegan, Ruth, 20–21

Foley, John, 5–6, 29, 34–35

folk group, 7, 21

folklore studies, and rabbinic narrative, 33–42

folklore, 6–11; and aggadah, 29–32; and rabbinic society 21–22

folktales, and Elijah stories, 36–37, 146–47, 157

form and genre criticism, 11–19, 31, 43

Fraenkel, Yonah, 2–4, 8–9, 215*n*64, 217*n*5–7

Friedmann, Meir, 2